# “Baptized and Sent,” but for What?

# "Baptized and Sent," but for What?

## *Catholic Missionary Malaise in the Twenty-First Century*

MATTHEW W. I. DUNN

WIPF & STOCK · Eugene, Oregon

"BAPTIZED AND SENT," BUT FOR WHAT?
Catholic Missionary Malaise in the Twenty-First Century



Wipf & Stock
An Imprint of Wipf and Stock Publishers
199 W. 8th Ave., Suite 3
Eugene, OR 97401

www.wipfandstock.com

PAPERBACK ISBN: 978-1-6667-7506-8
HARDCOVER ISBN: 978-1-6667-7507-5
EBOOK ISBN: 978-1-6667-7508-2

VERSION NUMBER 03/20/26

# Contents

# Abbreviations

| | |
|---|---|
| *ANF* | *The Ante-Nicene Fathers* (references are to volume and page numbers) |
| *BHS* | *Biblia Hebraica Stuttgartensia* |
| CBC-PNGSI | Catholic Bishops' Conference of Papua New Guinea and the Solomon Islands |
| *CCC* | *Catechism of the Catholic Church* (references are to paragraph numbers) |
| CDF | Congregation for the Doctrine of the Faith |
| CTI | Catholic Theological Institute of Port Moresby |
| ESV | English Standard Version |
| FABC | Federation of Asian Bishops' Conferences |
| FC | The Fathers of the Church: A New Translation (references are to volume and page numbers) |
| NABRE | New American Bible, Revised Edition |
| NJB | New Jerusalem Bible |
| *NJBC* | *The New Jerome Biblical Commentary* |
| *NPNF*$^2$ | *A Select Library of the Nicene and Post-Nicene Fathers of the Christian Church*, 2nd series (references are to volume and page numbers) |
| PNG | Papua New Guinea |
| Vatican II | Second Vatican Council (1962–1965) |

# Acknowledgments

THERE ARE SEVERAL PERSONS to thank for the genesis and production of this book:

First and foremost, I must give praise and thanksgiving to God the Father through his Son, Jesus Christ (see Eph 5:20). Jesus has been my best friend throughout all of my life: I love him. I also adore and glorify the most holy and life-giving Spirit, who has led me.

Secondly, I must honor and thank Mary, Christ's immaculate and holy mother, for her prayers, guidance, and love.

Thirdly, I offer gratitude to my "namesakes" in baptism—namely, St. Matthew the Apostle and Evangelist and St. William the Abbot. I also thank my "namesake" in the mystery of chrismation: St. Ignatius Loyola. Thanks for your prayers, guys!

Also . . . thank you, Felix! (It knows who it is.)

I wish also to thank very much Brandon Zimmerman, PhD (candidate), and his wife, Rebecca, for their many kindnesses, not least of which was sharing the joy of their large family. Brandon acted as dean of studies for the Catholic Theological Institute of Port Moresby (CTI) in Papua New Guinea. He was truly a workhorse for that institution and for its students and faculty. Rebecca shepherded me in her work as head librarian of the school. If it had not been for Rebecca's having kept a blog of the family's experiences, titled *Plotinus in the Jungle*, then I would never have even contacted CTI for a job.[1] I am extremely indebted to both of them as well as to their wonderful children (the little saints, running around and climbing through the jungle)! They have since come back to the United States. God bless them! I also want to express my gratitude to Reverend Joseph Vnuk, OP, who was president of CTI at the time. I will always

1. The third-century-AD philosopher, Plotinus, is the focus of Brandon's doctoral thesis.

value greatly his decision to take a chance on my coming out to Papua New Guinea and allowing me to make a contribution, albeit small, to CTI's mission. It is safe to say that the book you are reading now would not have come to pass without the help of the aforementioned.

I would also like to thank everyone at Wipf and Stock, especially George Callihan, Hannah Starr, and the typesetter for helping me to bring my humble and meager work to fruition.

A final thanks goes out to my mother, Cynthia, who encouraged me vociferously to . . . *get the book done!*

# Note Regarding Bible Translation

UNLESS OTHERWISE INDICATED, all explicit citations of the Sacred Scriptures in English that have been given throughout this book are based on the Latin text of *Nova Vulgata Bibliorum Sacrorum Editio* (2nd ed.), promulgated by His Holiness Pope St. John Paul II. The translation of the Latin text into English is my own work, and I have tried to adhere carefully to the meaning of the Latin. I have consulted the original texts (namely, in Hebrew, Aramaic, or Greek) when and where deemed necessary, which I have tried to indicate in the footnotes. The translation is, therefore, my own, but it is done with the permission of the proper authorities at Libreria Editrice Vaticana, which is the holder of the rights to the Latin text. I am very grateful to Francesca Angeletti of the Holy See's Dicastery for Communication for helping me with this.

Please, note that I have followed the numbering of the sacred books' chapters and verses as given in the *Nova Vulgata*. This may not in some places always agree with that found in many modern translations.

A copy of the *Nova Vulgata* (2nd ed.) can be found online on the Vatican's website.

# Introduction

THIS BOOK COMES OUT of my experience of having attended a missiological symposium at a Catholic educational institution in Papua New Guinea (PNG), where I taught in 2019.

The symposium met at the behest of Pope Francis, who had convoked a special "missionary month" for October 2019 to commemorate and evaluate the one-hundredth anniversary of Pope Benedict XV's apostolic letter *Maximum Illud*. That letter's focus had been the renewal of the church's missionary efforts after the devastation of World War I. The theme of the missionary month as well as the symposium was "Baptized and Sent: The Church of Christ on Mission in the World."[1]

Answering Pope Francis's call, the Catholic Bishops' Conference of Papua New Guinea and the Solomon Islands (CBC-PNGSI) held a missiological symposium on September 24–25, 2019. (I forget exactly why it could not be held in October, but it was probably due to when everyone could get together.) It was held at the Catholic Theological Institute of Port Moresby, or CTI, a small school providing undergraduate and graduate education to both seminarians and lay candidates for the church in PNG. At the time, I served as senior lecturer in theology, Bible, and church history, during which time I both attended and participated in the symposium.

So over two warm, sunny days in September 2019—not October, but close enough—I sat in an open-air auditorium attending the symposium, taking notes, asking questions, and recording the event.[2] (I also led a small discussion group.)

1. A website was produced for the event: see http://www.october2019.va/en.html. In April 2025, while I was still writing this book, His Holiness Pope Francis fell asleep in the Lord. May God remember him in his kingdom!

2. See my YouTube channel at Dunn, "CTI Symposium."

By the end of the event, however, I had to admit that I was somewhat disturbed. For I had come hoping to hear the call for a robust reinvigoration of the church's mandate to bring Christ to those who did not yet know or experience him. On the contrary, I heard reasons why such efforts were not practicable—or even desirable—in the current scene. It was not the case with every speaker. But it was the case with enough of them that I had become concerned. Yes, baptized and sent . . . *but for what?* I was also unsure of the substitutes that were being suggested in place of traditional mission—for example, purely humanitarian and environmental concerns, which, while all well and good, seemed to me to detract from the essentially supernatural purpose of the church's mission in the world.

If such a judgment sounds harsh (at least, at this preliminary stage), the purpose of the first part of this book wherein I recount the contents of the presentations is to document how and why I arrived at such a general unease. From the beginning of his pontificate, Pope Francis has called for the church's mission of actively bringing Christ to others to become reinvigorated, to be renewed and strengthened.[3] Yet, I did not feel that some of the presentations evinced this same goal; their focus was sometimes elsewhere. If I thought that the presentations I encountered were somehow deficient in this regard, then I felt it was incumbent on me in subsequent chapters of this book to explain why I felt so strongly and to offer a constructive response.

## Benedict XV, *Maximum Illud*

In 1919, Pope Benedict XV issued the apostolic letter *Maximum Illud*, titled "On the Propagation of the Faith Throughout the World." It came out under the dark specter of the "Great War" (1914–1918), which had destroyed so much of Europe and whose effects had disrupted life throughout the rest of the world.[4] Many parts of Western Europe lay devastated, particularly those countries which had been providing candidates for the church's missions. Thus, the church's supreme mission of spreading the gospel of Christ to the world had also been severely disrupted; and it was normalcy in this area which the pope sought to recover.

3. See e.g., his apostolic exhortation, *Evangelii Gaudium*.

4. The pope avers to this event in Benedict XV, *Maximum Illud*, §41.

In the letter, the pope expresses concern over "the misfortune" of vast numbers of human beings who had still not yet even heard of or accepted the gospel. For this reason, and yearning to share with non-Christians "the divine blessings of the Redemption," he wrote *Maximum Illud*, not only to add his encouragement to Catholics' missionary efforts but also "to point out methods [missionaries] can adopt to further the fulfilment of this momentous undertaking."[5]

Addressing the superiors of missions, the pope advocates a fatherly concern for their missions and the clergy within them. Superiors are to be alert, efficient, and charitable leaders who rejoice with their charges when things go well and sympathize with them when they do not.[6] Above all, the superior's chief concern should be for the expansion of the mission to local non-Christians.[7]

The pope reminds missionaries of God's severe judgment on them if they treat his vineyard as their own private property—that is, for their own interests. Rather, the pope advocates missionary cooperation, such that the missionary should look everywhere for assistants, whether or not they belong to his own religious order or country—or, (even) whether they are male or female![8]

With farsighted practicality, the pope established that candidates for the sacred ministry must come from the local people. It is they who know their people's mentality and how to present the faith to them. Further, they have access to places a foreign-born cleric does not.[9] He recognized the essential need for training local clergy in the most excellent way so that they would no longer need to rely on foreign candidates. Moreover, they would be able to take over the administration of dioceses as well as of mission itself.[10] The church is not an alien to any country or culture. It is only right that sacred ministers should come from the local church "so that their countrymen can look to them for instruction in the law of God and leadership on the way to salvation."[11]

The pope writes prophetically against the use of the church's mission to further the territorial and worldly interests of a missionary's own

5. Benedict XV, *Maximum Illud*, §7.
6. Benedict XV, *Maximum Illud*, §9.
7. Benedict XV, *Maximum Illud*, §11.
8. Benedict XV, *Maximum Illud*, §§12–13.
9. Benedict XV, *Maximum Illud*, §14.
10. Benedict XV, *Maximum Illud*, §§15, 17.
11. Benedict XV, *Maximum Illud*, §16.

homeland at the expense of the people to whom he has been sent: "Such behaviour would infect his apostolate like a plague."[12] For Catholic missionaries are not agents of their own countries; rather, they are ambassadors of Christ.[13]

The pope asserts the paramount need for the extensive and broad training of the missionary. Oftentimes, missionaries will not have books or other resources to answer questions regarding the faith. They must themselves be able to provide answers and reasons for their beliefs in a learned manner. "It would be a shocking anomaly," he writes, "to see those entrusted with the message of truth bested by teachers of error."[14] The pope also underlines the importance and necessity of studying the local languages since, after all, the missionary has been sent to *proclaim* the gospel.[15]

The pope identifies, however, as indispensable and "of the most critical importance" the missionary's holiness of life. He declares, "Preaching by example is a far more effective procedure than vocal preaching, especially among unbelievers, who tend to be more impressed by what they see for themselves than by any arguments that can be presented to them."[16] Missionaries, then, must take Christ the Good Shepherd as their model, for they are his emissaries. Thus, the missionary "makes use of all the arts of Christian kindness to attract [non-Christians] . . . , so that he may eventually lead them into the arms of Christ, into the embrace of the Good Shepherd."[17] In the end, he reminds missionaries that it is always the work of God. It is his mission which the missionary carries out.[18]

12. Benedict XV, *Maximum Illud*, §19 (see also 18). As the Congregation for the Evangelization of Peoples and Pontifical Mission Societies explains in their guidebook to the event, *Baptized and Sent*, "The countries being evangelized were Western colonies and, therefore, colonialism often took priority over any evangelical objective, especially in cases where those who were announcing the Good News came from the nations that had colonized the very people they were evangelizing" (*Baptized and Sent*, 318).

13. Benedict XV, *Maximum Illud*, §20.

14. Benedict XV, *Maximum Illud*, §§22–23.

15. Benedict XV, *Maximum Illud*, §24.

16. Benedict XV, *Maximum Illud*, §26. In a letter to Archbishop Fernando Filoni of the Congregation for the Evangelization of Peoples, Pope Francis expressed the same sentiment, declaring that "the proclamation and the love of the Lord Jesus, spread by holiness of one's life and good works, are the sole purpose of missionary activity." Francis, "Letter to Fernando Cardinal Filoni."

17. Benedict XV, *Maximum Illud*, §28.

18. Benedict XV, *Maximum Illud*, §29.

Notably, the pope praises the work of religious sisters in the missions.[19] He also commends all Catholics to support the missions: through prayer, fostering vocations, and economic aid.[20] Finally, he lauds the activities of certain groups, like the Society for the Propagation of the Faith and the recently established (at the time) Missionary Union of the Clergy.[21] Driven together by common purpose, the pope hoped that Catholics might recover for the missions the losses which they had incurred due to the war.

Invoking the help of Mary the Queen of the Apostles, he concluded by imparting his apostolic blessing.[22]

The letter's impact for the church was highly consequential. Historian Thomas Bokenkotter describes *Maximum Illud* as "epochal" and "the charter" for the church's missionary efforts for the twentieth century.[23] The document is a *tour de force* of pastoral vigor, evincing a clear-sighted and practical missionary vision. And let there be no mistake: it is *missionary*. For Benedict XV, everything the church does, whether through direct preaching or indirect social welfare, is meant to conduct souls to Christ and his church. That is her mission.

## A Brief Note on Terminology

It needs to be noted that there is a divergence of opinion among contemporary missiologists about the usage of the terms *evangelization* and *mission*.

Many people, myself included, would tend to use them interchangeably to indicate the act of someone's proclaiming the message of Jesus Christ to nonbelievers in order to help them believe in him and accept baptism into his church—in other words, "converting" them. The words could also be understood basically in the same way as "proselytism," which has now (for some reason, of which I am not quite sure) become a "dirty word" for missiologists and some church leaders.[24]

19. Benedict XV, *Maximum Illud*, §30.

20. Benedict XV, *Maximum Illud*, §§31–36.

21. Benedict XV, *Maximum Illud*, §§37, 40.

22. Benedict XV, *Maximum Illud*, §§41–42.

23. Bokenkotter, *Concise History*, 386.

24. His Holiness Pope Francis was especially vociferous in his denunciation of "proselytism," though Pope Benedict XVI had also mentioned it at times. Neither, however, was ever quite clear about how he was using the term, or why it was necessarily a bad thing.

But for North American and European theologians, the word *evangelization* is understood inclusively. It means the church's general and overall activity by which she brings the "good news" about Jesus—the *euangelion*—to others. It is a capacious reality, including anything from her sacramental worship to social welfare programs to preaching the message of Christ. The word *mission* means specifically the act of proclaiming the "good news" about Jesus to nonbelievers in order to bring them to belief in Christ. But for theologians in South America and Asia, the meanings are in the reverse: *evangelization* means specifically the act of proclamation unto conversion and *mission* designates the broader reality of the church's total activity (which includes proclamation, but is not limited to it alone).[25]

So how do we sort this out?

In the 1991 statement *Dialogue and Proclamation*, published jointly by the Congregation for the Evangelization of Peoples and Pontifical Commission for Interreligious Dialogue, the Holy See (finally) weighed in (somewhat) on the matter. In that document, the authors recognize that what the church does—from her worship and prayer, to her presence and witness, to her commitment to human welfare, to her interreligious dialogue, to (yes) her proclamation of the gospel to nonbelievers—forms a single, albeit complex, reality. It is not just one thing; rather, it includes various components.[26] So they basically "split the difference" on the question, so to speak, by effectively combining the two terms into the phrase "evangelizing mission." The church, then, uses the phrase "evangelizing mission" to designate her overall activity in the world on behalf of the gospel. It indicates a broad reality through which she brings the "good news" to all areas of human society . . . which—yes, they acknowledge—might also include announcing the Lord Jesus to those who do not yet believe in him.[27] For the church's specific task of announcing the gospel to others in order to convert them to the faith, the document reserves the

25. See e.g., Jacob Kavunkal's discussion of the matter in "Mission or Evangelization?"

26. See Congregation for the Evangelization of Peoples and Pontifical Commission for Interreligious Dialogue, *Dialogue and Proclamation*, §2. According to Pope Francis's apostolic constitution, *Praedicate Evangelium* (2022), these curial offices have been renamed. The former is now known as the "Dicastery for Evangelization" and the latter, the "Dicastery for Interreligious Dialogue."

27. See Congregation for the Evangelization of Peoples and Pontifical Commission for Interreligious Dialogue, *Dialogue and Proclamation*, §8. And yet, the authors do still keep the word *evangelization* as a shorthand way of referring to the church's "evangelizing mission" (see §8).

word *proclamation*.[28] Of course, this begs the question of why, given its specific mandate, the congregation (now, dicastery) still bears the word *evangelization* in its title. Should it not be the "Dicastery of *Proclamation*"? Be that as it may, we can be grateful to the Holy See for some attempt at conceptual clarity. I will try to follow the lead of *Dialogue and Proclamation* throughout this book by attaching the phrase "evangelizing mission" to the church's broader mission of witness and service and *mission* to her specific mission of conversion and church planting. If I sometimes get muddled in this terminology, I apologize to the reader. Nevertheless, I hope the context will always make my meaning clear.

## The Church and "Mission" a Century After *Maximum Illud*

But where is the church's sense of "mission" in the sense of "proclamation" one hundred years later?

As mentioned above, to mark *Maximum Illud*'s centennial anniversary, Pope Francis announced a worldwide "extraordinary missionary month" for October 2019. The theme was "Baptized and Sent: The Church of Christ on Mission in the World." The pope encouraged Catholics to "rediscover the missionary dimension of [their] faith in Jesus Christ . . . graciously bestowed . . . in baptism."[29] Their relationship to God as his sons and daughters through baptism was "a treasure to be given, communicated and proclaimed."[30] Further, "God wills that all people be saved by coming to know the truth and experiencing His mercy through the ministry of the Church, the universal sacrament of salvation."[31] For Pope Benedict XV in *Maximum Illud*, the church's missionary dimension is incontrovertible. Based on Christ's charge in Mark 16:15, Catholics are called to proclaim the gospel to every creature. Pope Francis's message still seems to enunciate the same vision—namely, Catholics are called to share the gospel with others in order to bring them to belief.

But the situation "on the ground"—or, at least, at the missiological conference I experienced—can be altogether different. There was a general acceptance among the symposium's speakers that since the

28. See Congregation for the Evangelization of Peoples and Pontifical Commission for Interreligious Dialogue, *Dialogue and Proclamation*, §8.

29. Francis, "World Mission Day 2019."

30. Francis, "World Mission Day 2019."

31. Francis, "World Mission Day 2019."

Second Vatican Council (1962–1965), a "missionary malaise" had befallen the church: people simply did not want to get involved either in the church's evangelizing mission or in proclamation. But why? And most importantly, what to do about it? For me, the speakers' responses to these questions were not always clear or helpful. I felt that some presenters' views represented a retreat from the vision of Benedict XV. Rather than embracing the church's evangelizing mission as primarily and fundamentally proclamation, that particular view now seems to be seen with disfavor: as the relic of an exclusivist past which must be transcended or as a rude expression of triumphalist "ecclesiocentrism."[32] In fact, attempting to bring someone from one religion into the church is excused away or sometimes actively discouraged. Or, proclamation is presented not as the summit of evangelization but as an option among other works that Christians can do.

Yet, nature abhors a vacuum; and the church still needs some reason for being. So the focus seems to fall on the church's broader mission of social welfare and good works—that is, on humanitarian efforts and this-worldly projects for social justice, gender equality, environmentalism, and so forth. They function, if nothing else will, as substitutes for the supernatural charge to proclaim. None of these, of course, is objectionable in its own right, and, it might be argued, each is demanded by the gospel. But they can also seem to overshadow and even de-center the church from her ultimate purpose, traditionally construed as bringing the message of the gospel to all creatures (see Mark 16:15). To the extent that the church loses sight of that evangelizing mission in its truest and limited sense, it will mean the "malaise" and even death of mission. And the effect of that malaise will not be limited, for it will affect even the church's broader evangelizing mission of being present to society as seed and leaven of the kingdom of God (see Matt 13:31–33).

In this book, then, I hope to call the church back to her original supernatural end of proclaiming the gospel to those who do not yet believe. I shall also offer some correctives and cautions to some of the views I heard expressed which, I believe, are not unheard of in missiological circles.

32. However, *Dialogue and Proclamation* clearly affirms that proclamation is "the foundation, centre, and summit of evangelization." Congregation for the Evangelization of Peoples and Pontifical Commission for Interreligious Dialogue, *Dialogue and Proclamation*, §10 (citing Paul VI, *Evangelii Nuntiandi*, §27).

## Outline of the Book

Chapter 1 provides a summary of the missiological conference as I experienced it. It represents the notes I took from each speaker. It also includes the opening statements as well as the panel discussion which followed the formal presentations. It has been checked and revised based on my video recording of the event.[33] This is an important chapter for understanding my overall reaction to the symposium and concerns about the presentation of mission.

Chapter 2 looks at Christ's "great commission" in Matt 28:19–20. That commission has long been seen as the divine basis for the church's missionary activity to the nonbelieving world. But no more for some. Some now challenge the Scripture's missiological importance. I show how Matt 28:19–20 still comprises the paradigmatic statement of the essence of the church's evangelizing mission.

Chapter 3 addresses how, rather than being held up as fundamental to the church's evangelizing mission, the church's commitment to proclamation has been softened. Then, church leaders—even at the highest level—fumble about asking rhetorical questions about why "mission" is not happening among Catholics. This chapter is a kind of *cri de cœur* to the church's leadership—even at the highest level—to finally look deeply at and candidly address the crisis of faith evident here.

Chapter 4 looks at the connection between Catholics' loss of fervor for evangelizing mission and the astonishing loss of faith in some essential tenets of the Catholic religion. This is demonstrated through discussion of the uproar accompanying the Holy See's issuance of the declaration *Dominus Iesus*, which proclaimed that salvation was only to be found in Jesus Christ and through his church. The document was seen by some as a betrayal of Vatican II's doctrine; others saw it as bearing the residue of a "triumphalist exclusivism" still to be found in Vatican II's documents; and others, even at the Vatican, wanted to simply forget the document had ever happened.

Chapter 5 addresses how Christ's message of the kingdom of God is often pitted against the church—and even opposed to Christ himself! I call for a better, more tutored use of the biblical data by missiologists and theologians, while showing how the "kingdom" is also Christ's. Moreover, I discuss how the "kingdom" and the church, albeit not the same thing, are inseparable.

33. See Dunn, "CTI Symposium."

Chapter 6 challenges the false dichotomy sometimes set up between witness and proclamation. There is an overemphasis, whereby the Christian's witness of life is set up as the absolute value. Proclamation is minimized even to the point of a mute "non-witness": nothing is actually ever proclaimed at all! On the contrary, I maintain that this silent non-proclamation deprives witness of its very marrow, making it otiose.

All of these have a singular rationale: to recall again and again that if the church loses sight of her essential evangelizing mission to proclaim the gospel to those who do not believe, then "mission" itself (however understood) will become foreign to her. It will wither and die.

An epilogue follows in which I summarize the main points previously made as well as introduce some new ones.

An appendix concludes the book with the reproduction of the message sent by Archbishop Fernando Cardinal Filoni, the prefect of the Congregation for the Evangelization of Peoples, to participants in the missiological symposium held at Catholic Theological Institute.

*Nota bene:* As anyone who uses the internet knows all too well, it is a commonly encountered issue that resources on the "web," which were available when one consulted them, may become inoperative or unavailable later on. In any case, where an online resource is no longer accessible or available, I highly recommend that the reader use the excellent service called the "Wayback Machine" (https://web.archive.org), which is maintained by Internet Archive (https://archive.org/).

# I

# The Symposium

## *"Baptized and Sent"*

### Opening Statements

It was CTI's president, Joseph Vnuk, OP, who opened the symposium. The event, he observed, reminded Catholics of their missionary vocation.

He warned against an unhealthy institutionalization—that is, one which got caught up in structures while losing one's sense of mission. Vnuk painted an allegory taken from John Landis's 1980 comedy film *The Blues Brothers*. The story is simple: Two ne'er-do-wells are brought back to the Catholic orphanage in which they had been raised to be compelled by the domineering nun, who reared them, somehow to get enough money to save the failing institution. So they are sent out with that job in hand. But it is only later during a "prayer-and-praise" service at a Pentecostal church that the brothers are touched by grace and experience their reality for what it truly is: a mission from God. In Vnuk's allegorical interpretation, it reveals a dilemma for the church. It shows how the church's ability to run institutions and care for people does not necessarily or always translate into a sense of mission for her members. Why that seemed to be so was an issue that needed to be grappled with.

He was followed by Archbishop Kurian Mathew Vayalunkal, the apostolic nuncio to PNG and the Solomon Islands.[1] According to Vayalunkal, Christ's Great Commission to his disciples to go and make

1. In 2021, Vayalunkal was made papal nuncio to both Algeria and Tunisia.

disciples of all nations (see Matt 28:19–20) had now been handed over to us. As Catholics, we are sent into the world to evangelize: "to bring the good news of the gospel to all those we encounter."[2] Evangelization, then, must be at the center of all that Catholics do. (Whether he means evangelization as proclamation or in its wider sense of evangelizing mission is not especially clear.) He quoted the 2011 address of Pope Benedict XVI to the Pontifical Mission Societies, stating that all sectors of pastoral life, catechesis, and charity must be missionary in nature.[3]

Vayalunkal noted how PNG and the Solomon Islands were still missionary lands. When missionaries began coming to PNG, he said, they trusted in God and "with extraordinary resilience [they faced] innumerable difficulties."[4] But today's missionary challenges are different from when the first missionaries came. There is better accessibility. Also, due to better travel facilities and modern communications technology, "the world is on our fingertips."[5] A new order, then, is needed to reach out effectively to modern humanity.

As Pope Benedict XVI said, the purpose of the "new evangelization" is to bring all people into an encounter with the living Christ, to know him as a living reality.[6] Christians are to be as close to Jesus as those who followed him "on those dusty roads in Galilee."[7] The aim—as Pope Francis "always insists"—is not proselytism, since the church evangelizes through her witness. Instead, by their words, actions, and attitudes, Catholics proclaim their adherence to Christ: the way, the truth, and the life (see John 14:6). By thus leading others to Jesus, Vayalunkal said, "we are doing the real mission."[8]

But questions remain: Do Catholics' lives attract others to Jesus? Are they active agents of the "new evangelization"? How successfully is technology used for evangelization? Which changes need to be made to become better missionaries? Is the church reluctant to adapt?

2. Dunn, "Apostolic Nuncio," 2:37.

3. Dunn, "Apostolic Nuncio," 3:28. See Benedict XVI, "Pontifical Mission Societies." Pope Benedict fell asleep in the Lord in 2022 (RIP).

4. Dunn, "Apostolic Nuncio," 4:04.

5. Dunn, "Apostolic Nuncio," 4:45.

6. Actually, I think Vayalunkal had in mind a statement by Pope St. John Paul II: see e.g., *Ecclesia in America*, §68.

7. Dunn, "Apostolic Nuncio," 6:03.

8. Dunn, "Apostolic Nuncio," 6:17.

He concluded by reading a message from Cardinal-Archbishop Fernando Filoni, head of the Vatican's Congregation for the Evangelization of Peoples.[9] That message is reproduced in the appendix.

## Speakers and Topics

The speakers and topics were in the following order of presentation:

1. Reverend Clarence Devadass, "Changes in Mission from *Maximum Illud* to *Gaudete et Exsultate*"
2. Paolo Baleinakorodawa, "The Laity at the Forefront of the Mission"
3. Reverend Edgar Javier, SVD, "The New Evangelization: Concept, Objectives, and Strategies"
4. Reverend Andrew Moses, "The Parish in Mission"
5. Agatha Maria Ferei, "The Mission in the Era of Media and Instant Communication"

### Clarence Devadass, "Changes in Mission from *Maximum Illud* to *Gaudete et Exsultate*"

Reverend Devadass is a priest of the Archdiocese of Kuala Lumpur, Malaysia, and director of the Catholic Research Centre located there.[10]

He opened by noting his own context: in Malaysia, Christianity is a minority religion, and Christians are limited in their missionary expression. On the contrary, that is not the situation in PNG.[11] Both places were united, though, in having received Christianity from missionaries.

Pope Francis had asked for the "extraordinary missionary month" to reflect on mission. But mission, Devadass explained, was not of itself extraordinary; rather, it was part of the church's foundational nature.

9. See Dunn, "Apostolic Nuncio," 8:11. According to Pope Francis's 2022 apostolic constitution, *Praedicate Evangelium*, this Vatican office is now known as the Dicastery for Evangelization.

10. The website can be found at http://www.crc.org.my.

11. According to *The World Factbook* of the Central Intelligence Agency, Muslims make up 61.3 percent of the population of Malaysia, where Islam is also the official religion. Christians are only 9.2 percent of the population (Central Intelligence Agency, "Malaysia"). In contrast, Christians make up circa 95 percent of religious adherents in Papua New Guinea (Central Intelligence Agency, "Papua New Guinea").

The church exists for mission. Neither exists without the other. Indeed, Francis has called every baptized person a "mission," which indicated for Devadass the anthropological center of mission.[12]

For Devadass, mission was too often viewed as an activity or program to be initiated. He acknowledged the origin of the call to mission in Jesus' missionary command in Matt 28:16–20. Still, "the identification of mission," Devadass maintained, "must come from the very nature of the existence of the church," which is not so much activity as *relationality*.[13] Relationality is mission's core dimension: to bring others into a relation with Jesus Christ.

Mission, Devadass explained, is anthropologically based—that is, bound up with humanity's nature and existence. While human nature bears the mark of sin, humankind is also blessed by God. Despite the weakness of sin and its own failures, humanity carries within it God's grace, calling men and women to be transformed for God's greater glory.[14]

"Far too often," Devadass asserted, people appeal to Christ's mandate in Matt 28 as the foundation for mission—namely, "Go, therefore, make disciples of all nations; baptise them in the name of the Father and of the Son and of the Holy Spirit, and teach them to observe all the commands I gave you" (vv. 19–20a NJB).[15] Instead, Devadass thought the opening chapters of the book of Genesis (that is, chapters 1–2) were more foundational. For the creation of humankind in Genesis provides the original understanding of mission itself. Adam and Eve are given a mission of stewardship by God. That mission is not just to themselves but also to all that God has created. Thus, according to Devadass, mission is "fundamentally required by God."[16] When he created man and woman in his image and likeness, God entrusted to human beings the care of his creation. Mission rests on this relationship of man's creation by God, which, Devadass claimed, "biblical commentators would call . . .

12. "This missionary mandate touches us personally: I am a mission, always; you are a mission, always; every baptized man and woman is a mission. People in love never stand still: they are drawn out of themselves. . . . As far as God's love is concerned, no one is useless or insignificant. Each of us is a mission to the world, for each of us is the fruit of God's love" (Francis, "World Mission Day 2019"). A similar thought is expressed in Francis's apostolic exhortation, *Evangelii Gaudium*, §273.

13. Dunn, "Fr. Clarence Devadass," 14:50.

14. He said this comment came from Vatican II, but did not specify where. I have not been able to locate it.

15. Dunn, "Fr. Clarence Devadass," 16:43.

16. Dunn, "Fr. Clarence Devadass," 17:46.

the covenantal relationship."[17] It is this covenantal relationship which is the basis of mission; and it is "at the very core" of the mission to which Catholics are called.[18]

Returning to the mandate of Matt 28:19–20 above, Devadass opined that the four tasks enumerated—namely, to go, to make disciples, to baptize, and to teach—did not necessarily exist in a single continuum, Instead, "they would [could?] be four different tasks that Jesus offers . . . his disciples."[19]

What is more, he felt it was important to look at other Scriptures "which are often left isolated."[20] For example, he mentioned Mark 1:14–15, where, after his baptism, Jesus begins his own mission by proclaiming the kingdom of God. There is also Luke 4:16–30 wherein Jesus reads from the book of Isaiah about his having been sent in the Spirit of the Lord. Finally, there was John 20:21 where Jesus tells his disciples, "As the Father has sent me, I also send you." Devadass believed the last Scripture from the Gospel of John offered the key to understanding the missionary command—namely, just as God the Father had sent Jesus on mission, so Jesus passed on that mission to his followers. The mission, then, is not Christians' own, but it is Jesus' mission which they are continuing.

Next, Devadass presented some key points from church mission documents over the past century. The documents covered were:

- Pope Benedict XV's apostolic letter *Maximum Illud* (1919);
- Pope Pius XI's encyclical letter *Rerum Ecclesiae* (1926);
- Pope Ven. Pius XII's encyclical letters *Evangelii Praecones* (1951) and *Fidei Donum* (1957);
- Pope St. John XXIII's encyclical letter *Princeps Pastorum* (1959);
- The Second Vatican Council's decree *Ad Gentes* (1965);
- Pope St. Paul VI's apostolic exhortation *Evangelii Nuntiandi* (1975);
- Pope St. John Paul II's encyclical letter *Redemptoris Missio* (1990), apostolic letter *Novo Millennio Ineunte* (2001), and apostolic exhortation *Ecclesia in Oceania* (2001); and

17. Dunn, "Fr. Clarence Devadass," 18:24.
18. Dunn, "Fr. Clarence Devadass," 18:40.
19. Dunn, "Fr. Clarence Devadass," 19:18.
20. Dunn, "Fr. Clarence Devadass," 20:02.

- Pope Francis's apostolic exhortations *Evangelii Gaudium* (2013) and *Gaudete et Exsultate* (2018).[21]

Benedict XV issued *Maximum Illud* just after World War I. He recognized how the church had expanded into much of the world through the colonization efforts of the Western nations. But now many colonies were starting to seek independence. He asked how the church's mission would continue after the colonial powers left.[22] The pope's answer was to encourage the training of local, indigenous clergy, which Devadass identified as an important aspect of the document.

Then Devadass looked at the encyclicals *Rerum Ecclesiae* of Pius XI ("On Catholic Missions") and *Evangelii Praecones* of Ven. Pius XII ("On the Promotion of Catholic Missions"). These continued the call for native clergy and hierarchies in the emerging churches. In *Rerum Ecclesiae*—"and now this is something new," remarked Devadass—Pius XI acknowledged the benefit of the clergy working together with lay catechists and religious.[23] In *Evangelii Praecones*, Ven. Pius XII recognized the growing response made to *Maximum Illud*'s call to establish local clergy. As Devadass eagerly pointed out, though, the pope also counseled Catholic missionaries to respect the natural goodness, justice, and beauty of the non-Christian cultures they encountered, which the pope compared to "a thriving forest"![24] Devadass also noted the pope's recognition of the role of lay associations in helping spread the gospel.

A notable shift occurs with Pius XII's *Fidei Donum*: "On the Present Condition of the Catholic Missions, Especially in Africa." According to Devadass, whereas previous papal statements had tended to focus on

21. He acknowledged other important statements could be added but that he would only focus on these.

22. Frankly, I did not find these comments in *Maximum Illud*. Perhaps Devadass meant Pope Pius XI's *Rerum Ecclesiae* (see e.g., §22).

23. Dunn, "Fr. Clarence Devadass," 28:10. Though, Benedict XV did praise the work of religious sisters in the missions in *Maximum Illud* (see §30).

24. The complete—and remarkable—statement found in *Evangelii Praecones* deserves to be quoted in full:

> The Church from the beginning down to our own time has always followed this wise practice: let not the Gospel on being introduced into any new land destroy or extinguish whatever its people possess that is naturally good, just or beautiful. For the Church, when she calls people to a higher culture and a better way of life, under the inspiration of the Christian religion, does not act like one who recklessly cuts down and uproots a thriving forest. No, she grafts a good scion upon the wild stock that it may bear a crop of more delicious fruit. (Pius XII, *Evangelii Praecones*, §56)

the nations of the "Far East," this encyclical focused on Africa, where independence movements had also begun to arise.

Saint John XXIII's encyclical letter *Princeps Pastorum* was issued on the fortieth anniversary of *Maximum Illud*, leading Devadass to note how often *Maximum Illud* had already been celebrated over the years.[25] Some of the same themes emerge: the church's overall concern for mission, the continued development of native hierarchies, and the recognition of lay participation. Devadass emphasized how the focus here was on the "emerging" and "young" churches.[26] Notably, the pope further commended the study of missionary theory.[27] He highlighted the need for clerical holiness and encouraged the establishment of cultural centers and schools. Although one might think it was a new idea, Devadass observed that already in *Princeps Pastorum* the church was talking about the need to adopt modern techniques in spreading the faith.

Next, Devadass turned to Vatican II's decree, "On the Missionary Activity of the Church," or *Ad Gentes*. He pointed to *Ad Gentes* §3: "The Lord preached that one time . . . [and] what was wrought in Him for the saving of the human race, must be spread abroad and published to the ends of the earth." He saw in this text a close relationship with the biblical texts mentioned above: "What Jesus did is what we are called to do and . . . continue."[28] And we are to do this until Jesus comes again. The decree, notes Devadass, describes missionary activity as an epiphany (see §9), which, he adds, is "the manifesting of God's presence in the world, how God works in the history of salvation."[29] Devadass also cited *Ad Gentes* §1: "In the present state of affairs, out of which there is arising a new situation for mankind, the Church, being the salt of the earth and the light of the world . . . is more urgently called upon to save and renew every creature, that all things may be restored in Christ and all men may constitute one family in Him and one people of God." The council acknowledged that the missionary landscape had changed, according to

25. As the Congregation for the Evangelization of Peoples and Pontifical Mission Societies explain in their guidebook for the event, *Baptized and Sent*, St. John XXIII's encyclical is an "essential" companion to *Maximum Illud* (*Baptized and Sent*, 321).

26. Dunn, "Fr. Clarence Devadass," 32:30.

27. *Maximum Illud* also mandated the study of missiology at the Urbanian University (see §23).

28. Dunn, "Fr. Clarence Devadass," 34:31.

29. Dunn, "Fr. Clarence Devadass," 35:05.

Devadass. Moreover, he thinks that this statement more than any other in the document defines the church's missionary nature.

In the apostolic exhortation *Evangelii Nuntiandi* ("On Evangelization in the Modern World"), Devadass observed how Pope St. Paul VI identified Jesus as the author of mission: Christians are his agents. All Christians, the pope states, are called to mission—not just professionals. Devadass praised the exhortation for its practical vision and "down-to-earth" view of evangelization.[30] He also praised its presentation of novel ways of thinking, for example, its affirmation that the church's witness came *before* preaching. Albeit now taken for granted, the pope's statement was a novel idea at the time. The church's personal witness to Christ takes priority over proclamation, which Devadass considered an important point.

Devadass then turned to Pope St. John Paul II. In *Redemptoris Missio* ("On the Permanent Validity of the Church's Missionary Mandate"), the pope reasserted the urgency of missionary evangelization. Saint John Paul II made, however, a unique contribution, Devadass said, by discussing the Holy Spirit's role in mission, naming him its "principal agent."[31] Religious freedom is underlined. Still, the encyclical recalls Christians' duty to the missionary task. Devadass lauded the encyclical's statement that the church *proposes* but never *imposes*: "I think that's quite a nice caption for us to remember, especially when we are in mission."[32] Devadass remarked on how the idea of Christian witness had become progressively more and more pronounced in the church's missionary documents. *Redemptoris Missio* is no exception: the pope declares that living a Christian life is the first and irreplaceable form of mission.[33] Overall, Devadass believed this encyclical opened "a new pathway" for understanding the church's interaction with the other religions.

As the church entered the new millennium, St. John Paul II provided a new direction. In *Novo Millennio Ineunte*, the pope recalled

30. Dunn, "Fr. Clarence Devadass," 37:35.

31. The late pope's contribution in this regard is summarized in Fredericks, "Catholic Church," 233–38.

32. Dunn, "Fr. Clarence Devadass," 40:32. "On her part, the Church addresses people with full respect for their freedom. Her mission does not restrict freedom but rather promotes it. *The Church proposes; she imposes nothing.* She respects individuals and cultures, and she honors the sanctuary of conscience. To those who for various reasons oppose missionary activity, the Church repeats: *Open the doors to Christ!*" (John Paul II, *Redemptoris Missio*, §39; emphasis original).

33. See John Paul II, *Redemptoris Missio*, §42.

Christ's command to Simon Peter to put out into the deep waters (see Luke 5:1–11). For Devadass, this recalled every Christian's call to follow Jesus and take part in his mission. Notably, the pope invited Catholics to discern how the light of Christ's face could shine in the new millennium, as well as what it might be asking of the church.

Devadass opined that St. John Paul II's *Ecclesia in Oceania* would probably be the closest to the hearts of his listeners in PNG and the Solomon Islands. Again, the call goes out for the church to find new and appropriate ways to present to the people of Oceania the "good news" of Jesus Christ as Lord and Savior, which Devadass hoped would be a fruit of the present symposium. There were admittedly challenges (for example, traditional religions, cultures, secularization, social media, etc.), which would necessitate finding creative responses. Again, the proclamation of the truth comes not just in words but also in action. Devadass referred to *Ecclesia in Oceania* §26: "The Church regards the social apostolate as an integral part of her evangelizing mission to speak a word of hope to the world; and her commitment in this regard is seen in her contribution to human development, her promotion of human rights, the defence of human life and dignity, social justice and protection of the environment." There is, Devadass said, an "interplay" and "convergence" between the church's traditional understanding of the practice of mission as proclaiming the gospel and her sense of social mission.[34]

In *Evangelii Gaudium*, Pope Francis envisions a "missionary option" for the church.[35] According to Devadass, any theologian trained since the 1970s would recognize this language as connected to the poor. Francis, then, has done something "revolutionary" by applying it to the church's missionary activity.[36] Several times Francis asks Catholics to be "missionary disciples."[37] No matter their education or standing, all the baptized are called to be part of the church's evangelizing mission. It is not just for professionals—"for people who attend symposiums"—but it also belongs to every one of the faithful.[38] Then, Devadass wanted to look at Francis's apostolic exhortation on holiness, *Gaudete et Exsultate* ("On the Call to Holiness in Today's World"). Rather than being a "personal, salvific event," holiness requires one to bear witness to others. So,

34. Dunn, "Fr. Clarence Devadass," 46:19.

35. See Francis, *Evangelii Gaudium*, §27.

36. Dunn, "Fr. Clarence Devadass," 47:43.

37. See e.g., Francis, *Evangelii Gaudium*, §§24, 40, 50, 120, 173.

38. Dunn, "Fr. Clarence Devadass," 48:19.

observed Devadass, even holiness is conceived by the pope according to its missionary dimension.[39] If holiness makes one more like Jesus, then it follows that one would also appropriate his mission.

What are the key takeaways from these documents?

In all the documents discussed, Devadass sees the *missio ad gentes*—that is, the church's need to go forth in proclamation—as a constant theme. Whereas the spread of the faith had previously been tied to the state and the spread of colonial empires, that was no longer the case with the new age of independence and nonsectarian governments. The church's mission needed to develop and grow internally. After Vatican II, according to Devadass, "the language seems a little bit softer."[40] Strictly speaking, proclamation is not excluded, but the concept of witnessing starts to be acknowledged and emphasized after the council.

The church's view of mission is both Christ-centered and Spirit-centered. The author of mission is Jesus himself. But later documents elucidate how the Holy Spirit is the one who sends people forth, who "authorizes" them for mission.[41]

The importance of the establishment of the local church slowly becomes a priority. The universal church began to recognize the need for a transition from colonialism to independence and from foreign missionaries to local clergy. The documents provide concrete proposals and directions in those areas for seminaries, priestly formation, methods, and (even) lay missionaries.

Contextualization is acknowledged and accepted. While many of the documents above responded to both universal and particular concerns, Devadass notes that there seems to be a contemporary interest for the church to address more particular issues, like family life (*Amoris Laetitia*), the environment (*Laudato Si'*), and youth (*Christus Vivit*). So for Devadass, the church already seems to be setting out her mission for the future.

Dialogue among ourselves, but also with other religions and communities, is another important idea. As Pope St. John Paul II makes very clear, one opens himself to the other and to God through dialogue.

There are also the ideas of human liberation and accompaniment. Devadass reminded his audience that the former was affirmed as an integral part of the church's mission in *Ecclesia in Oceania*, while the latter

39. Dunn, "Fr. Clarence Devadass," 48:38.

40. Dunn, "Fr. Clarence Devadass," 50:54.

41. Dunn, "Fr. Clarence Devadass," 51:45.

comes from the vocabulary of Pope Francis, who calls on Christians to walk with others without judgment.

Finally, Devadass saw a sense of "eco-consciousness" and concern for the care of humanity's common home, the planet.[42] The ecological crisis has become the common responsibility of the world and part of the church's mission for peace and the whole of creation. The message of *Laudato Si'* is offered not only to the church but also to the whole world, and comprises part of the church's transforming mission.

Devadass sketched five "paradigm movements" regarding the church and mission:

1. From the church existing as a foreign entity to being recognized as a local one
2. From a clergy-led and clergy-centered mission to lay involvement
3. From seeing non-Christians as subjects of conversion to seeing them as companions and pilgrims in the world
4. From viewing cultures negatively as incompatible with the gospel to seeing them positively as complementary and acceptable places for the gospel to take root
5. From an ecclesiocentric, church-centered vision that is concerned with expanding the church to a "regnocentric," kingdom-centered vision which places the church more broadly within the kingdom of God[43]

Devadass suggested Pope Francis called the "extraordinary missionary month" because the church was becoming self-referential, self-seeking, and self-preserving. It is then that she needs to be reminded to go out. Devadass thought there were signs that the church might have become introverted and introspective and needed to hear that call to move out. His proposal was for the church to start seeing herself "as a communion with other communities": as a participator, a dialoguing partner, and a prophetess.[44]

He asked his audience to look at how they wanted to *be* church: "Mission must not be reduced to some activity; it must be the DNA of the Christian identity. In other words, it must be *who we are* and not what

42. Dunn, "Fr. Clarence Devadass," 55:30.

43. Dunn, "Fr. Clarence Devadass," 56:03.

44. Dunn, "Fr. Clarence Devadass," 1:01:46.

we do."[45] He told the story of a Malaysian woman—"a really young active youth"—who told him how insecure she felt because, during the extraordinary missionary year, even though she was very active, she felt that she had not *done* anything.[46] On the contrary, each one of us will have to find his or her mission in his or her own existence, which comes from having been created in God's image and likeness. Mission, then, should be what we are and what the church is. He hoped the event would bring Catholics back to the basics of the faith so that their relationship with God would find its meaning and sense.

### *Question Period*

For the "question period," Dr. Brandon Zimmerman, CTI's dean of studies and resident philosopher, requested a more precise definition of *mission*.[47]

In reply, Devadass explained that *mission* is part of the human person. It is relational: humans were not created for themselves alone, but to go out to others. This is the basis of mission. The church, therefore, does not exist for her own existence, but to go out to others. In the Bible's creation accounts, God gives a mission to human beings, for example, to care for the environment. Nevertheless, in the end Devadass hesitated at confining himself to any single idea of *mission*, for it could be defined in many ways.

I asked Devadass to comment on the declaration *Dominus Iesus* of the Congregation for the Doctrine of the Faith. For instance, I wanted his opinion on its assertion that religious conversion was still the primary thrust of the church's evangelizing mission.[48]

*Dominus Iesus*, Devadass remarked, was a document "highly talked about, debated, critically looked at."[49] None of documents he discussed diminished the need for proclamation. Returning to "that passage we are

45. Dunn, "Fr. Clarence Devadass," 1:02:36; emphasis added.

46. Dunn, "Fr. Clarence Devadass," 1:03:04.

47. He is also working on his PhD, teaching philosophy, acting as the CBC-PNGSI's ecumenical representative, and raising five—now, six—wonderful children! His invaluable wife, Rebecca, works as head librarian.

48. See my article: Dunn, "CDF's Declaration." According to Pope Francis's 2022 apostolic constitution, *Praedicate Evangelium*, this Vatican office is now known as the Dicastery for the Doctrine of the Faith.

49. Dunn, "Fr. Clarence Devadass," 1:10:07.

all comfortable with," the essence of Matt 28:16–20 is that God sends forth his disciples: Go forth (first) . . . *then* make disciples, baptize, and teach! The passage represents "four distinctive, distinct actions that Jesus gives to his disciples."[50] Although proclamation is not diminished, it is important to see one's context. Devadass related,

> If I were to take *Dominus Iesus* literally . . . I wouldn't be standing here before you speaking. Probably, I would be behind bars, because there are laws in Malaysia that prevent me from proselytizing, from sharing the Faith explicitly. Even giving out a brochure to a Muslim in Malaysia—I could end up in jail.[51]

Context, then, makes one think about what *proclamation* means. Traditionally, it is has been seen as talking. Yet, Devadass recalled the saying (perhaps) of St. Francis of Assisi: "Proclaim the gospel—if necessary, use words!"[52] Context is important for defining what proclamation means. When presented with the opportunity, Christians need to proclaim Jesus, but they also need to be witnesses of the gospel.

## Paolo Baleinakorodawa, "The Laity at the Forefront of the Mission"

Baleinakorodawa is the co-founder and director of Transcend Oceania, a peace-and-justice nongovernmental organization.[53] He has a master of arts in conflict transformation (2004) from Eastern Mennonite University in the United States. He has been a peace-building specialist and consultant across the Pacific.

He felt humbled, honored, and privileged to speak on a central part of his faith: the layperson's mission to be the visible expression of Christ's invisible love, especially to the lost, the neglected, the poor—also, to those in unjust, violent situations that call for the enlightenment of the gospel.

Baleinakorodawa described himself as a "basic layperson" trying to understand God in his life. He asked his audience, therefore, to eschew

50. Dunn, "Fr. Clarence Devadass," 1:10:54.

51. Dunn, "Fr. Clarence Devadass," 1:11:18.

52. Dunn, "Fr. Clarence Devadass," 1:12:00. Devadass was correct to say "perhaps," since the Franciscan origin of the statement is doubtful. See my comments below.

53. Transcend Oceania seeks to advance sustainable peace and development through the practice of justice and nonviolent action. Its website can be found at http://www.transcendoceania.org.

asking him any theological or philosophical questions. Rather: "Ask me practical questions about how mission is done!"[54]

Baleinakorodawa grew up in rural Fiji. His father was a local Catholic catechist; his mother, a convert from Methodism. His parish was made up of many scattered communities located "in a geographically challenged location" of Fiji, ranging from coastal lowlands to rugged mountains.[55] Priests would typically visit only for Easter and Christmas. His father was a catechist, though; Baleinakorodawa would accompany him on long walks to the villages to perform and serve at "para-liturgies" for the people.

He then went to teacher's college and became a teacher.

After teacher's college, he applied and was accepted to the lay missioner program of the Missionary Society of St. Columban. The orientation introduced him to many of the church's teachings on mission and the role of the laity in Christ's own mission. Those formation months helped ground him in the faith and explain the "how" of doing mission.

At the end of formation, Baleinakorodawa was told he would be sent to the Philippines. He had many questions. A Filipino priest gave a talk to his group during which the priest asked, What if, upon arriving to a mission territory, one already found Jesus present there among the people? Baleinakorodawa struggled with that question. He realized mission was not only about bringing Christ to others through one's life—more so than through what one says or preaches—but it was also about finding Christ in others and in the situation one found oneself. He brought with him the gift of being a teacher, which he used to both share and learn about Christ in the Philippines.

For three years, he lived in a squatters' settlement near a parish in Manila. He was part of a team of laypeople ministering to inmates at a prison four hours away. The incarcerated were male and female—from as young as twelve-years-old! Many times, he felt he could do nothing for these prisoners except "be present" as a hopeful sign for the prisoners. He learned that "mission" was also about presence: being with people; lending a listening ear and heart; valuing them in times of challenges, difficulties, and hopelessness. He offered catechism classes to all who wanted them, "focus[ing] more on Christ's way of life and what he did to save the world, rather than the specifics of the Catholic faith."[56] Discussion sometimes

54. Dunn, "Mr. Paolo Baleinakorodawa," 9:25.

55. Dunn, "Mr. Paolo Baleinakorodawa," 10:27.

56. Dunn, "Mr. Paolo Baleinakorodawa," 15:52.

led to why the prisoners were there, how prison impacted them, or how their actions hurt people. The group gave pastoral care and counseling on the impact that the inmates' actions had had on themselves and the community. The process included helping the prisoners think about how to make things right not only for themselves but also for their victims and the community. This "restorative approach" resulted in mediations and dialogue between offenders and victims, leading to some form of reconciliation.[57] His group also established, albeit informally, a program in literacy and arithmetic.[58] Finally, the group ministered to "death-row" prisoners. "Imagine," Baleinakorodawa said, "the feeling you have when you know you are numbered for execution!" This work contained "the most difficult moments of my life," for he felt powerless to change the prisoners' choices or the consequences. Instead, all he could really do was visit, assuring them of Jesus' love for them.[59]

Back in Fiji, Baleinakorodawa decided to do "reverse-mission" work. He used his experience to help establish small "lay, local, intercultural, mission-oriented groups" using Bible reading and reflection as tools for discerning and implementing mission activities.[60] Meeting each week for prayer and Bible sharing (usually on the gospel reading from Sunday Mass), the members decided on a "cross-boundary, cross-culture" activity to be done which exemplified that week's reading.[61] At the next meeting, they reflected on their experiences.

He also participated in teams that went into remote areas of Fiji that were hardly visited by priests, so as to facilitate programs for the community. A priest would accompany the team—but only to act in a sacramental and theological-advisory role. Moreover, Baleinakorodawa

57. Dunn, "Mr. Paolo Baleinakorodawa," 19:01.

58. Baleinakorodawa told the story of "Solomon," an accused murderer. Illiterate, at his court sessions he needed to place his thumb on an ink pad to sign the court documents. But after attending the literacy program, Baleinakorodawa described how proud Solomon was when he was finally able to ask the court for a pen so as to sign the papers himself. Mission, Baleinakorodawa said, was also about ensuring that a person's dignity and rights were respected and promoted.

59. Dunn, "Mr. Paolo Baleinakorodawa," 19:48 He also mentioned participating in demonstrations protesting against the use of the death penalty.

60. Dunn, "Mr. Paolo Baleinakorodawa," 20:53. They were using the "Seven Steps Gospel Sharing" method developed by the Lumko Institute of the Southern African Catholic Bishops' Conference; see Lumko Institute, "SACBC." See also Office of Laity and Family, "Seven Steps Method."

61. Dunn, "Mr. Paolo Baleinakorodawa," 21:38.

was involved with teams sent out to promote the awareness of mission as well as vocations.

Next, Baleinakorodawa wanted to discuss how he experienced mission in his parish.

He had chaired the parish pastoral council at Our Lady of Fatima Church, Suva, which is one of the largest parishes in Fiji. During his tenure, the council visited parish members to listen to their needs. They realized "a major gap" in catechesis: whereas some faith instruction was given prior to the sacraments of baptism and confirmation, almost nothing was given during the several years between those sacraments.[62] Since religious education was not a priority in the schools, many years of instruction were being lost. So Baleinakorodawa and his group started offering catechesis to the people after Sunday Mass, designing their content according to the liturgical-year cycle.

The pastoral council members also sensed their meetings had become more like business meetings, leading to a lessening of the "faith-based" dimension of their role.[63] Thus, the meetings were reformatted as an opportunity for the faith formation of the parish's lay leadership, for example, by studying and discussing church documents.

Baleinakorodawa asked several questions: Why are so few laypeople involved in mission? Do they just not understand? Or, do they see mission as the job of the clergy? "We need to find out why," he suggested.[64] He also wondered how missionary desire could be instilled and sustained in laypeople. How can laypeople be prepared for mission in a world of injustice, violence, and greed?

## *Question Period*

The Most Reverend Francesco Panfilo, SDB, archbishop of Rabaul (East New Britain Province),[65] used Baleinakorodawa's question time to ask both Reverend Devadass, who had already spoken, and Baleinakorodawa for some comments.

He noted how he had first been sent as a missionary to the Philippines. When he was ordained a priest in 1974, people were already

62. Dunn, "Mr. Paolo Baleinakorodawa," 23:52.
63. Dunn, "Mr. Paolo Baleinakorodawa," 25:25.
64. Dunn, "Mr. Paolo Baleinakorodawa," 28:18.
65. Panfilo retired in 2020.

questioning church mission. If God is present among non-Christians, some asked, why was the church sending out missionaries? The attitude was, on the contrary, "Remove your sandals, because God is already present!"[66] Yet Jesus' command to go, announce, and witness is very clear. But one cannot deny that there has been "a very serious crisis" in this area. He asked Devadass for comment.

Panfilo continued that it was true the Lord was already present wherever the missionary went. Still, Panfilo noted that the feast day of Bl. John Mazzucconi would be celebrated the next day. Mazzucconi was a missionary who had been martyred on Woodlark Island, PNG.[67] The archbishop paraphrased the observation of one of Mazzucconi's companions, Carlo Salerio, who said of his experiences on Woodlark Island, "God was there before us—but also the devil!"[68] Panfilo asked Baleinakorodawa if he had experienced the presence of the devil on his missionary journeys.

Devadass answered first: he stated that Christ's missionary command remained, although Devadass admitted that he struggled with the "how" of it.[69] The missionary command changes according to different places and eras—and the current landscape has changed tremendously. The missionary documents Devadass discussed came out at a time when (some feel) the church made herself the center of the world and tended towards self-preservation and self-protection. Rather than being the center of everything, the missionary month reminded the church to go out of her comfort zone. Devadass felt Catholics were "in a rut": they had become comfortable with what they had and did not want to think creatively about what needed to be done.[70] The challenge of mission changes and evolves from period to period. Christ's mandate has not been taken

66. Dunn, "Mr. Paolo Baleinakorodawa," 44:48.

67. Blessed John-Baptist Mazzucconi (1826–1855) was a priest and charter member of the Pontifical Institute for Foreign Missions (PIME). Sent to Oceania in 1852, he spent a couple years evangelizing the islands off PNG's southeastern coast (Milne Bay Province). Having had no success, he returned to Australia. Having returned to the area, though, the ship he was on was attacked by local islanders, who hacked him to death. He was beatified in 1984. See Rabenstein, "Mazzucconi"; also, Wiltgen, *Founding*, 248–51.

68. Dunn, "Mr. Paolo Baleinakorodawa," 46:45. I could not find this exact quote that the archbishop refers to. In a letter, however, Salerio does describe Woodlark Island as being "under the control of seven demons" ("Letter to Giuseppe Marinoni, Dec. 4, 1853," in Wiltgen, *Founding*, 224)!

69. Dunn, "Mr. Paolo Baleinakorodawa," 47:50.

70. Dunn, "Mr. Paolo Baleinakorodawa," 50:00.

away, for Catholics must move away from themselves and reach out. How? "In different forms."[71] Still, discussions needed to continue on how to make it a reality.

Baleinakorodawa replied he was not sure what Panfilo meant by "devil." For him, the "devil" represented societal injustice, which was encountered every day. The "devil," then, would be a normal, everyday encounter.[72]

Bishop Rolando Santos of Alotau-Sideia (Milne Bay Province) observed how missionaries had been in some countries in Asia for a long time but with few results. The symposium was meant to revive the church's awareness of and commitment to her mission. Pope St. John Paul II, he said, lamented in *Redemptoris Missio* that Catholics were not following Christ's mandate to proclaim.[73] Sometimes, Catholics hesitate even to *mention* Jesus Christ. If mission means encountering Jesus, as Pope Francis says, how could it occur without even mentioning him? Yet, Pope Francis says evangelization requires boldness and courage.[74] Sometimes, Santos believed, the problem in mission stemmed from missionaries and their concept of mission.

Devadass responded: evangelization and mission have gone through different phases. Evangelization—by which, I believe, he meant proclamation—can still happen, even if not in the construct as historically understood by the church. He reminded his audience there were *two* patrons of mission, who demonstrate two different types: St. Francis Xavier, who went out, and St. Thérèse of Lisieux, who never left her convent. So evangelization has many different ways in how it is done. Furthermore, Devadass reminded his audience that Catholics are a minority in Malaysia, where evangelizing Muslims is illegal. Some people, though, are still open to accepting Jesus. Then, there is the resurgence of Hinduism and Buddhism against Christianity's perceived threat: "We are constantly battling this challenge and trying to find some equilibrium in how we coexist with each other in a country that is multicultural, multiethnic."[75] So, he said, Malaysians have had to define in their own way what it means to evangelize and be on mission. He mentioned the difficulty of foreign

71. Dunn, "Mr. Paolo Baleinakorodawa," 51:22.

72. Dunn, "Mr. Paolo Baleinakorodawa," 51:56.

73. He gave no reference. Perhaps, he meant John Paul II, *Redemptoris Missio*, §36.

74. Again, no references were given. I expect he could have meant statements found in Francis's *Evangelii Gaudium* (see e.g., §§259, 264).

75. Dunn, "Mr. Paolo Baleinakorodawa," 1:05:16.

missionary groups, which come to Malaysia to preach door-to-door. Since many Malaysians do not distinguish among the Christian denominations, they see all Christians as creating tension. So new ways have to be found.

Devadass himself advocated witness and dialogue as ways to embrace people. He noted proudly that, despite limitations, the church in his area received several hundreds of people each year at the Easter Vigil:

> Every year in West Malaysia—the peninsula of Malaysia—we have about eight hundred people every year who are received into the Catholic Church at Easter Vigil—eight hundred people—despite the challenges and difficulties of not being able to say . . . : "Jesus is your savior. Come, join us!"[76]

While the path of witness and dialogue might not work specifically for PNG, it is "a way that works for us."[77] Some people might come to belief in Jesus yet might not be able to fully practice, for example, due to family issues which must be resolved. The forms of evangelization, then, must be deconstructed and reconstructed. Still, given that many people do join, he said, "Something must be working."[78] God must be revealing himself in the church's members.

The Malaysian church has chosen to be a "bridge-builder," especially through interreligious dialogue and ecumenism in which she has been "a catalyst" and "the prime mover." But with the government now providing public services, the church has lost her "public face." So she has needed to find new ways to evangelize, which are also "bearing fruit."[79]

He concluded, "We are not dispensed from proclaiming Jesus—but, [it is a question of] how do we do it. We are still proclaiming—maybe not as explicit as those of you would like us to do—but that causes itself a barrier, [it] puts a wall for us. So, we find new ways in how [to do the evangelizing mission]. . . . Thank God we have all these adult conversions that happen. So, I believe that God is working . . . amongst us."[80]

76. Dunn, "Mr. Paolo Baleinakorodawa," 1:06:27.
77. Dunn, "Mr. Paolo Baleinakorodawa," 1:06:52.
78. Dunn, "Mr. Paolo Baleinakorodawa," 1:07:45.
79. Dunn, "Mr. Paolo Baleinakorodawa," 1:08:20.
80. Dunn, "Mr. Paolo Baleinakorodawa," 1:09:18.

## Edgar Javier, SVD, "The New Evangelization: Concept, Objectives, and Strategies"

Reverend Javier is a Divine Word Missionary (SVD) with a doctor of missiology from Rome's Gregorian University. He was editor of the journal *Missio Inter Gentes*. Currently, he is director of the Divine Word Institute of Mission Studies in Tagaytay City, the Philippines.[81] Some of his "best years," he said, were spent travelling around the Pacific, especially living in Samoa.[82]

Javier admitted everyone was struggling with the "how" of evangelization. Saint Teresa of Calcutta said, however, no matter where one was, he or she should do something beautiful for God every day. For example, he related how a confrere in Macau evangelized through playing and teaching guitar. Later, the children would come back, asking for baptism: "That little thing, that little gesture, was very powerful in making them decide to join the Catholic Church."[83]

Javier began by acknowledging humankind's new socio-anthropological positioning—that is, *who* people are now and *where* they are now. Globalization is now an irreversible reality. Like it or not, all are members of the "global village." What are the consequences for evangelization?

First, the "market economy" dominates, setting a price on everything. "You smile," he said, "[and] there is a price." Instead, Javier advocated "a conversion of mind" to realize that everyone, even the rich, are "poor," for each person is lacking in something.[84]

Second, the church needs to be a place of dialogue. (Though, he did not elaborate further; see below.)

Moreover, technology controls human beings' existence. People have become less *homo sapiens* than "techno sapiens": they are programmed by technology.[85] Javier noticed this as an educator: "The 'culture of research' is going down and the 'culture of copy-and-paste' is going up more and more."[86] The result leads to students who are full of information but who have little knowledge. So the church needs to understand what this is all about.

81. The group's website can be found at http://dwims.ph.

82. Dunn, "Fr. Edgar Javier," 2:28 (see also 4:01).

83. Dunn, "Fr. Edgar Javier," 5:55.

84. Dunn, "Fr. Edgar Javier," 9:51.

85. Dunn, "Fr. Edgar Javier," 11:46.

86. Dunn, "Fr. Edgar Javier," 12:07.

The church needs to be intercultural. The church is in the "post-paschal" era of salvation—namely, Jesus' death and resurrection, even Pentecost, have already occurred and passed. Now, the church needs to be guided and challenged by the Holy Spirit to go outside "the gate" of the church, outside "the gate" of Christianity, to the "other."[87] The "other" means those of different races, sexes, religions, and so forth. Catholics are not sent to convert them, however, for the church is not God and should not play his role. Mission and conversion are *God's* privilege; Catholics are only his "hands" and "feet."[88] The church goes out to extend God's love by affirming each person's significance and worth.

As Francis—"my favorite pope"—writes in *Evangelii Gaudium*, the church goes out to see God in the faces of the migrant, the refugee, and the suffering.[89] Albeit not a new phenomenon, migration happens now at an enormous rate ("mega-migration").[90] People go out seeking a better fortune. This pursuit of money, which is the root of all evil (see 1 Tim 6:10), in turn disrupts family life. Then, there is "mega-urbanization": people moving from the countryside into cities. "We would like to transform Asia and Africa into one immense city," Javier remarked.[91] Nevertheless, as St. John Paul II counseled, the church must respond by going out not just into the wilderness but also into the cities where many of the marginalized also live.[92]

Finally, he spoke about "mega-mediatization"—that is, people are less thinkers and more "techno sapiens."[93] For instance, he has seen babies who cannot even walk yet who are playing with gadgets. Technology has both advantages and disadvantages.

For Javier, Christ's missionary mandate remains. But how should it be done in today's new context? He finds that people do not want to talk about the new context: globalization, secularization, postmodernism, interculturality, religious pluralism, ecological destruction. Rather, they are "more at home with things that pertain to the Catholic faith or the

87. Dunn, "Fr. Edgar Javier," 13:45. The reference is to Heb 13:12–13.

88. Dunn, "Fr. Edgar Javier," 15:00.

89. Dunn, "Fr. Edgar Javier," 15:17. No specific section of *Evangelii Gaudium* was given, but I think that he possibly means §§209–16.

90. Dunn, "Fr. Edgar Javier," 16:02.

91. Dunn, "Fr. Edgar Javier," 17:17.

92. The reference might be to John Paul II, *Redemptoris Missio*, §37.

93. Dunn, "Fr. Edgar Javier," 18:15.

teachings of the church."[94] Javier affirmed his fidelity: "I am faithful to the church."[95] But missionaries must talk about Jesus Christ and his teachings. Christianity is a religion of the gospel—not of church teachings.

The content of the church's mission remains—namely, God is love, which he wants to extend to the world through Christians. Jesus is the model *par excellence* of mission, and the Holy Spirit is its "supreme" agent. It is the Spirit who does mission *to* Christians; they do not do it *for* him.

Pope St. John XXIII advocated reading the signs of the times.[96] Mission does not occur in a vacuum, so the church must be up-to-date in her dialogue with the world. Javier proposed several ways to reimagine what the missionary should be:

- The missionary is a "bridge." Just by being from another place, missionaries mediate culture, spirituality, religion, and so forth from one group to another.[97]
- He or she is a "listener/learner." As Javier himself learned, there is so much to learn from other religions, cultures, and spiritualities. The missionary should create a "home away from home"—that is, the missionary ought to create a space in his or her life for the other culture in order to listen to and learn from it, to be able to participate in it.[98] The missionary should not think he or she already knows everything. Otherwise, there would be no room for the Holy Spirit to teach him or her anything. Through experience, Javier said that he learned a lot because he listened a lot.
- The missionary is a "healer/reconciler." Javier attributed much of the world's "brokenness" to migration, which has destroyed family life.[99] Such destruction became evident to him from his ministry in the Philippines to victims of incest. The abuse had occurred because the parents were absent due to work obligations. Moreover, drug dealers prey on the children of migrant workers. Modern development has not fulfilled its promise to make life more comfortable; rather, it has destroyed the earth and societies. Humanity is crying.

94. Dunn, "Fr. Edgar Javier," 20:23.

95. Dunn, "Fr. Edgar Javier," 20:34.

96. The reference is to Pope St. John XXIII's apostolic constitution *Humanae Salutis*, by which he announced the convocation of the Second Vatican Council.

97. Dunn, "Fr. Edgar Javier," 24:00.

98. Dunn, "Fr. Edgar Javier," 25:52.

99. Dunn, "Fr. Edgar Javier," 31:08.

There is a tremendous amount of brokenness in society and in the created world.

- Missionaries must be "caretakers of God's household."[100] They must be environmentalists. They must care for the earth as their "mother," or as God's temple, or as humanity's common home.[101] They must love the earth, for to destroy it is to destroy the *oikos* (Greek, "house") that God has made for humanity and, hence, to destroy humanity itself.
- The missionary is a "mystic." Missionaries must be "men and women of silence," for silence is "the language of God."[102] He related how he brought God to each part of his day, for instance, before leaving for school, saying, "Okay, God, let's go to university!" Or, before class: "Okay, God, teach my students through me!" It is not the extraordinary mysticism of the saints, like John of the Cross or Teresa of Avila, but the mysticism of one's ordinary relationship with God.[103]

Javier then spoke a bit about the skills and habits that need to be developed. For example, he opened by talking about the cultural sensitivity that must be shown by the missionary when going out. The Philippines is a nation of many diverse cultures. Some cultures represent "spicy," some represent "sweet," some represent "salty." But put them all together, and "[it is] very nice!"[104]

Mission is very challenging. But it can be a beautiful challenge if one has a paradigm shift by realizing that God is the missionary and that the missionary himself or herself is only his instrument. He is a "missionary God";[105] the missionary's job is to share his love with all people.

The church needs to be a place of dialogue and friendship. Through dialogue and friendship, missionaries discover the true, good, and beautiful in other peoples and cultures. Whatever is good reflects the *Summum Bonum*, which is God. All cultures, he believed, have traces of God in them, called the *vestigia Dei* or *mirabilia Dei*. All cultures and religions have truth. They also make "truth claims." To the extent that their claims

100. Dunn, "Fr. Edgar Javier," 35:22.

101. Dunn, "Fr. Edgar Javier," 35:54.

102. Dunn, "Fr. Edgar Javier," 36:56 (see also 38:13).

103. Dunn, "Fr. Edgar Javier," 38:44.

104. Dunn, "Fr. Edgar Javier," 40:07.

105. Dunn, "Fr. Edgar Javier," 41:52.

are in fact true, they reflect the "eternal wisdom."[106] Further, missionaries must love the beautiful. Javier referenced Pope Benedict XVI's statement during his 2010 visit to Malta in which he encouraged Catholics to follow the way of beauty.[107] The missionary, then, Javier said, should love what is beautiful in other cultures and religions because God is beautiful.

Basing himself on *Evangelii Gaudium*, Javier proposed two models for mission: a "missiology of attraction" and a "missiology of beauty and silence."[108]

Jesus had a magnetic personality. Crowds followed him; people wanted to hear him. Javier averred, "He was a very attractive person with a very attractive message."[109] Jesus told people God loved them and had prepared a "kingdom" for them. This message also made the early Christian communities attractive because they loved one another and shared with each other.

Previously, the church emphasized God's justice, but now she emphasizes God's beauty.[110] All cultures and religions have beautiful things in them, which can be used to build a better world. Christians and non-Christians can work together "to build God's global kingdom here on earth."[111] Building God's kingdom is *not* the church's monopoly; it includes all people of good will, both Christian and not. Instead of trying to convert non-Christians, Catholics must respect their chosen religion. On the contrary, conversion comes from God's grace; it is his work.

When Javier was a student of missiology, his aim was to go to the missions to convert, but he later changed his mind. Why? He saw a different reality. His view of mission was "ecclesiocentric" and "exclusivist." But then, he went to the Gregorian University and came to see a bigger reality. That experience led him to become "inclusivistic" and (later)

106. Dunn, "Fr. Edgar Javier," 42:30.

107. See Benedict XVI, "Visit to the Grotto."

108. Dunn, "Fr. Edgar Javier," 45:39. Pope Francis does indeed speak about missionary attraction and "the way of beauty" in *Evangelii Gaudium* (see e.g., §§14, 34, 167–68, 265). I could not find, however, anywhere in *Evangelii Gaudium* where he called for the *silent* proclamation of the gospel. See my comments about this below.

109. Dunn, "Fr. Edgar Javier," 46:05.

110. I am not entirely clear what Javier means by the church's emphasis on "justice." Perhaps, Javier means that religions were previously judged by how much or how little they authentically gave God his due of worship. Obviously, then, the true religion of Catholicism would have been placed at the highest level of that spectrum.

111. Dunn, "Fr. Edgar Javier," 47:55.

"pluralistic."[112] He declared, "You cannot deny that God is a very generous God. He has revealed himself through many religious traditions. Ultimately, the definitive revelation of God will be Christianity. He has revealed himself in many ways known to him alone."[113] Today's challenge is to be converted to the "others" because they show us God's face, "in their culture, in their religion, in everything that they have."[114]

Javier agreed with Devadass that non-Christians are co-pilgrims with Catholics—"a very beautiful metaphor."[115] Thus, Christians and non-Christians are all marching towards God's kingdom, where he has prepared many mansions.

### *Question Period*

During the question period, James Wau, an SVD seminarian at CTI, asked Javier how *mission* and *evangelization* were being used.

Javier responded that *mission* was generic while *evangelization* was particular. Anything the Christian does is mission, but evangelization means bringing the gospel to non-Christians. This use of *evangelization* goes back to the Bible and was used by Pope St. Paul VI for the *missio ad gentes*.

## Andrew Moses, "The Parish in Mission"

Reverend Moses is a priest of Daru-Kiunga Diocese (Western Province) in PNG.[116]

112. Dunn, "Fr. Edgar Javier," 49:07. As British theologian Gavin D'Costa explains, *exclusivism* holds "that only one single revelation is true or one single religion is true and all other[s] . . . are false." Salvation, then, is obtained only in that true revelation or religion; all others are not saved. *Pluralism* "hold[s] . . . all the major religions have true revelations in part, while no single revelation or religion can claim final and definitive truth." All religions are, then, more or less true and, hence, more or less valid as salvific pathways. In this way, humanity's many religions are each shown genuine, proper respect. Tracing a middle way is *inclusivism*. It "claim[s] that one revelation or religion . . . is the only one true and definitive one, but that truth and . . . salvation can be found in various fragmentary and incomplete forms within other religions" (D'Costa, "Pluralist View," 223–24).

113. Dunn, "Fr. Edgar Javier," 49:54.

114. Dunn, "Fr. Edgar Javier," 50:30.

115. Dunn, "Fr. Edgar Javier," 50:55.

116. It is PNG's largest province, which is accessible only by boat or plane.

While acknowledging all the clergy, religious, and missionaries present, he wanted particularly to thank the laypeople for being "the backbone" of parish mission: "You are there, and the parish is alive."[117]

Moses's talk focused on how to apply missiological theory "at the base level"—that is, to the parish.[118] Papua New Guinea has nineteen different dioceses, placed in different parts of the country, each within its own context. The question: How do we visualize the process of mission at the parish level, while applying Pope Francis's vision? The pope has set the theme of mission in the world by Christ's church as a current matter involving all the church's elements. Parishes are called to become places of holiness and spiritual creativity so as to realize again the missionary call: the faith is present; mission has been done. But Christians realize once again the missionary dynamism and the task of reinvigorating the gospel. For Moses, "to be baptized is to be on a mission."[119] Before his own mission, Jesus was baptized by John and commissioned. Through their own baptism, Catholics are given a mission as well, though it is really Jesus' mission.

He reminded his listeners that mission is directed at *subjects* and not *objects*, for Jesus came for humanity and not for buildings. Baptism is the common denominator: before he was ordained a priest—before he was anything—Moses was a baptized person.

What have been the fruits of the church's missions? As Christ mentions in the parable of the sower (see Matt 13:1–9), the result of the "fruit" depends very much on the richness of the "soil." How has the church made the soil rich for mission work, especially at the parish level? For "the parish . . . is the heart of other levels of church administration."[120] First, he outlined, there is the universal church, the pope and the cardinals, which promotes and teaches doctrine at that level. Second, there is the diocese with the bishop, who carries out his pastoral plans with his priests. Then, there is the basic level, the parish, which is the priest and the laypeople together.

Pope Francis says in *Evangelii Gaudium* that parishes are "the church living in the midst of . . . Her sons and daughters."[121] The parish is

117. Dunn, "Fr. Andrew Moses," 3:16.

118. Dunn, "Fr. Andrew Moses," 4:11.

119. Dunn, "Fr. Andrew Moses," 8:22.

120. Dunn, "Fr. Andrew Moses," 12:49.

121. Dunn, "Fr. Andrew Moses," 13:53. See Francis, *Evangelii Gaudium*, §28. Actually, Francis himself is just quoting from Pope St. John Paul II's apostolic exhortation

where people are baptized and nourished, where they have been raised, and the place from which they are sent out "to serve goodness."[122] It is where families and communities are. It is where the Sacred Scriptures are proclaimed and welcomed into hearts, where they are lived out and witnessed to. The parish is where Catholics live out the virtues of faith, hope, and love. It is where they experience God's compassionate love and whence they spread his message of peace, joy, and forgiveness. It is where they live their lives as disciples of Jesus. "Basically," said Moses, "the parish is where all the baptized are; and that is where you do most of the mission."[123] What was the parish's primary mission? To provide worship, teaching, and pastoral care.

Moses noted the important ecclesiological shift of Vatican II, which deepened the understanding of the church and of mission. Previously, *church* meant the parish priest, and *missionary* meant those men and women who belonged to religious communities. It was a more clerical understanding involving a few people. It was rather the priest who preached the sermon, cared for the sick, dispensed the sacraments, and gave pastoral and moral advice. At the parish level, it was "a paternalistic type of ministry where 'Father' knows everything."[124] There was no space for collaborative ministry. But now parish ministry is more representative: there are pastoral teams at various levels, who assist in doing the jobs above. He attributes this shift to Vatican II's recognition of the church as the "people of God."[125] Moses recalled St. Paul's teaching in 1 Cor 12 that there were different gifts, ministries, and works in the church, but the same God. All are part of the body of Christ who, working together with their diverse gifts, make the church alive today. Ministry is not a specific action, explained Moses, but it is how one lives with others through presence and relationality. It is a call of the Holy Spirit to live the gospel life in communion with each other.

Parish renewal relies on the church becoming less heavily institutional and clerical, focusing instead on personal communion. Jesus called his followers to a communion of love. So all church levels should exist to foster communion with God and among members. While the *idea* of "communion" is expounded in church theology, it is poorly worked out

*Christifideles Laici* (see §26).

122. Dunn, "Fr. Andrew Moses," 15:10.

123. Dunn, "Fr. Andrew Moses," 16:22.

124. Dunn, "Fr. Andrew Moses," 19:03.

125. See Vatican II's dogmatic constitution, *Lumen Gentium* (§§9–17).

in practice. Moses asked what could be done concretely so that members of the church could be instruments of building communion at the parish level. Relying on the previous authoritarian and clerical stance seemed to Moses like "we are trying in our parishes to put new wine into the old bottles."[126] On the contrary, everything that is done at the parish level must be done to create and promote communion. For him, the relational, person-to-person aspect of ministry is most important. The end result of mission in the parish is to build mutual and lively relationships with God and among each other. Moses declared, "If we agree that the quality of mission work in the parish will be in proportion to the dearth of communion, then the first order of business must be renewing the structures of the parish to make spiritual communion possible."[127] Communion-building is, then, a "priority."[128]

In promoting communion as a spiritual value of the church, Moses asks, What do we see? First, there must be a sense of belonging in the church's mission among the common people. Second, he recommended creating and participating in "basic ecclesial communities."[129] Moses sees a lot of "movement" at this level since people want to be a part of the church.[130] Also, there is the need to create a feeling of ownership of the church through people taking part. At the parish level, space is created for people to participate in the church, like in rosary groups.[131] Moses also highlighted the value of making sure that the roles are defined so that people know what they can contribute.

Moses identified several key challenges to mission in PNG:

126. Dunn, "Fr. Andrew Moses," 23:50.

127. Dunn, "Fr. Andrew Moses," 25:40.

128. Dunn, "Fr. Andrew Moses," 26:00.

129. "Basic ecclesial communities" (BECs) are small communities that operate at a level beneath the parish structure. They are intended to deepen the participants' human and Christian relationships. As Catholic groups, they still require the service of priests and must be linked to the bishop (see e.g., FABC, "Asian Colloquium," §40). Pope Francis praises BECs as "a source of enrichment . . . raised up by the Spirit for evangelizing different areas and sectors" (*Evangelii Gaudium*, §29). Though he cautions their members not to disengage from parish life.

130. Dunn, "Fr. Andrew Moses," 32:09.

131. Moses related how in his parish he noticed that men were not joining the Legion of Mary or rosary groups due to a feeling of a lack of inclusion. (In other words, the majority of the members were female.) So they started the Chaplet of the Divine Mercy as a group for the men. Ultimately, it is about creating space for people so that they feel like they have something to do.

- It is right that there is ongoing renewal, but, observed Moses, globalization has its repercussions: "The time is changing, values are changing, systems are changing."[132] As Catholics are called to renew mission work, they are nonetheless challenged by the characteristics of the time.
- There is a lack of infrastructure. There is a parish in the north of his diocese (namely, St. Paul's) that can only be accessed via airplane. But if the plane is broken or has no fuel, then it is a five-day trek to get there. The parishes in his diocese are scattered, so it is hard to reach all the people.
- There are many Christians in the parishes who are influenced by materialism and consumerism, who do not want to satisfy their desires spiritually. This materialism has led to new forms of paganism. Then, there is the "money culture": people want remuneration; otherwise, they will not do anything for the parish. Moses noted that there is a leadership crisis in the country in this regard, and "that is affecting us also."[133]
- There is moral decay: "People do not see . . . the right from wrong; everything they do is good."[134] Since everybody takes drugs, the assumption is that it is all right. Moses sees a lot of social issues which affect the parish: alcoholism, prostitution, corruption, domestic violence, and so forth. He recommended the need to reach out in order to teach what is good and bad.
- There is doctrinal confusion. Catholics are confused by the number of Christian sects and movements in the country, some of which teach false teachings. "When our people are not grounded in faith," he said, "when they cannot defend their faith, we are losing a lot of people."[135] The question then becomes how to help Catholics know and defend their faith.
- Moses noted the shortage of priests. The Eucharist is the center of the church. So he praised the "communion ministry" of laypeople, which aided priests (who could not be in all places) in making the

132. Dunn, "Fr. Andrew Moses," 39:40.
133. Dunn, "Fr. Andrew Moses," 42:30.
134. Dunn, "Fr. Andrew Moses," 44:20.
135. Dunn, "Fr. Andrew Moses," 46:10.

Blessed Sacrament available. This is another way that the relationship can come.

- Still, he worried that "faith is not consistent."[136] Whereas adult converts are expected to go through the Rite of Christian Initiation of Adults (RCIA)[137] and receive baptism in full consciousness, he finds that, in the case of children, there is a discontinuity and a gap in their catechetical formation: "People are not progressing forward to the faith."[138] Pastors, therefore, need to be concerned for the continued formation of their people. If they do not do that, then they will lose people.
- There can be a lack of skills for pastoral planning so that there can be a lack of a systematic view towards pastoral work: "It is 'pick-and-choose.' The formation approach is not there. There are no goals, no aim, [no] vision in pastoral planning. In other words, we have a parish without mission."[139]

While continuing Jesus' mission, Catholics are faced with the times' challenges. One has to be aware of those challenges so that one's pastoral work is more focused and addresses the contemporary needs of the people. Moses repeated the point mentioned before that it was "very, very important" for Catholics to read the signs of the times.[140] Furthermore, Moses reminded his hearers that the church "exists for the world."[141] Responding to the challenges posed to the church by the modern world ought to be reflected in dioceses' and parishes' pastoral plans and programs, while keeping in mind the church's aim to renew the world. Pastoral ministry must succeed in helping the church give a clear response to the world.

Moses finished his talk with "a few indicators":[142]

He advocated for placing new wine into new wineskins. The church needs to be renewed in her mission, spirituality, processes, methods, programs, and so forth in order to address the challenge of suffering

136. Dunn, "Fr. Andrew Moses," 48:01.

137. Now called (more properly) the "Order" of Christian Initiation of Adults, or OCIA.

138. Dunn, "Fr. Andrew Moses," 48:47.

139. Dunn, "Fr. Andrew Moses," 49:48.

140. Dunn, "Fr. Andrew Moses," 50:40.

141. Dunn, "Fr. Andrew Moses," 50:56.

142. Dunn, "Fr. Andrew Moses," 51:34.

humanity today. She needs to be the beginning and seed of the kingdom of God.[143] To that end, Moses recommended a "diagnostic approach" to mission work.[144] The church must first know the root of a problem in order to prescribe an appropriate solution. This is "very vital," for one needs to see the problem and why it is happening.[145] For example, "many Catholics are running to the other churches."[146] Why is that happening? Or, why are priests and religious leaving their communities? There must be a clear approach as well as programs at various levels so that one can find out what is really happening and, then, choose the best effort for addressing it. After that, services can be provided.

Moses recognized the paradigm shift from individual spirituality to communal spirituality. While not denying the importance of personal spirituality, he noted how there is now an emphasis on the communion of members: "We journey together; we have a mission together."[147] The idea of "moving forward together as one people" makes us realize the concept of the church as a communion.[148] Catholics' mission is to grow in holiness together as a people. Baptism raises Christians to a special dignity so that they are all brothers and sisters of Jesus, their Lord and Savior. Because of their sharing in the divine life, they are also inheritors of the kingdom and, in a deep and spiritual way, come into communion with the Trinity. Moses insisted that the proper vision of mission was not to unite humanity or build missions—no—but "to bring people together so that they could live an experience of love, of care, of forgiveness."[149] Today, Catholics are the body of Christ. But he linked modern mission to the church of the early Christians, who shared their spiritual and material goods "all for the goal of this communion."[150] Our mission today is to promote, share, and build this type of communion.

He concluded with a call for all-inclusive pastoral planning at all levels. He also called for parishes to become "dynamic and living extensions of communities."[151] Communion should be promoted at every level of

143. As per Vatican II, *Lumen Gentium*, §5.
144. Dunn, "Fr. Andrew Moses," 52:20.
145. Dunn, "Fr. Andrew Moses," 52:40.
146. Dunn, "Fr. Andrew Moses," 53:13.
147. Dunn, "Fr. Andrew Moses," 55:11.
148. Dunn, "Fr. Andrew Moses," 55:21.
149. Dunn, "Fr. Andrew Moses," 56:48.
150. Dunn, "Fr. Andrew Moses," 57:08.
151. Dunn, "Fr. Andrew Moses," 57:32.

parish life, suggesting (again) "basic ecclesial communities" as a unique way for doing this. He called for Christians to become holy together. The Niceno-Constantinopolitan Creed says that Catholics believe in a "holy" church. So the church is not just a manner of acting but also of "be-ing." Holiness equals wholeness. When Catholics become holy together, the whole community benefits.[152]

## Agatha Maria Ferei, "The Mission in the Era of Media and Instant Communication"

Ferei is director of Caritas Fiji, which acts as the social arm of the Catholic Church in that country.[153]

Though she did not have a missionary background, Ferei wanted to speak from the perspective of the different roles she had, most importantly, that of a mother.

Ferei focused especially on the media. "The world of media," she observed, "is one that is worrying, that is changing; it has influences that are good as well as those that are negative."[154]

She took as her guiding thought the following statement from Eucharistic Prayer IV of the Mass: "You [that is, God] formed man in your own image and entrusted the whole world to his care, so that in serving you alone, the Creator, he might have dominion over all creatures."[155] Mission is one's journey in this world as a Catholic. Catholics need to be Christlike towards others, to see Christ in others, "from the little child, to creation, to other people in our journey together."[156]

Ferei asked what kind of messages the church was putting out in terms of reminding social communicators of the church's mission in this era of instant communication. For Christians are likened to a city that

152. Dunn, "Fr. Andrew Moses," 59:02.

153. The group's website can be found at https://caritasfiji.org. Ferei's tenure ended in 2022.

154. Dunn, "Mrs. Agatha Ferei," 11:58.

155. Dunn, "Mrs. Agatha Ferei," 12:34. See "The Order of Mass," in Catholic Church, *Roman Missal*, 657 (§117). Please note: In her talk, Ferei actually cites the text of the eucharistic prayer according to its previous—outdated and, frankly, dreadful—English translation. I have substituted the current English translation that went into effect in 2010.

156. Dunn, "Mrs. Agatha Ferei," 13:00.

sits upon a hill, or to lamps that are lit and set upon a lampstand.[157] She cited (without explicitly referencing it in her talk) Pope St. John Paul II's message for the twenty-sixth World Communications Day (1992) in which he declared that the church must use the modern means of social communication to amplify the volume of her voice.[158] Yet, we are still at the point of just beginning to understand how the modern situation of instant communication could be used for this. Christ told his followers to shout the "good news" from the housetops—and today, how many housetops were fixed with satellite dishes! Christians must make sure that the message of the word of God is firm, that Jesus and the faith are proclaimed, when using this form of communication, for it is an opportunity to deepen Christians' dialogue with the world around them. Ferei said, "We are in the 'digital age,' the 'electronic age,' the 'dot-com era.' And it is important for us to use this culture to explain our beliefs, the way we are thinking [or] what we are thinking about, and to explain our beliefs to the world around us, [to] believers and nonbelievers."[159]

Nevertheless, the "media world" has its own values with which it tries to influence public opinion.[160] The church has to learn how to use the media to get her own values out there to the public in order to create "a parallel curriculum."[161] She quoted (without explicitly referencing it) Pope St. John Paul II's message for the twenty-fourth World Communications Day (1990) in which he affirmed that, by ordinary service to family and community, a person could see his own work as a continuation of God's work—that is, as his or her personal contribution to the historical fulfillment of God's plan.[162] Ferei approved of this: "As we commit to any task, big or small, and we are faithful to it, that is the extension . . . of our mission and proclamation of Christ; and also it is part of this whole divine plan of the Father."[163]

What is the present context, she asked. Ferei spoke about Sophia, whom Ferei called a "media baby."[164] Sophia was only three years old, yet she had already been flooded with media images. Before she could

157. See Matt 5:14–15. See also Mark 4:21 and Luke 8:16, 11:33.

158. See John Paul II, "26th World Communications Day."

159. Dunn, "Mrs. Agatha Ferei," 18:20.

160. Dunn, "Mrs. Agatha Ferei," 18:50.

161. Dunn, "Mrs. Agatha Ferei," 19:01.

162. See John Paul II, "24th World Communications Day."

163. Dunn, "Mrs. Agatha Ferei," 20:00.

164. Dunn, "Mrs. Agatha Ferei," 20:41.

even speak her native language, she could recognize the trademarks of McDonald's, Samsung, Nike, and so forth. Ferei related the following anecdote:

> One day, Sophia was talking with her "auntie." She told Auntie about a girl in her school, "Jennifer," who was very smart:
> "Jennifer likes to use big words," said Sophia.
> Auntie asked her what kind of big words.
> "The password and the 'F-word'!" Sofia replied.
> Auntie asked, "What is the password?"
> Sophia replied seriously, "If I tell you, then we'll both be in *big* trouble!"[165]

Then there was Paul. Paul asked his mother whether they were rich or not. "Of course, we are!" replied his mother. "We are rich in love and peace and happiness and family and friends." But Paul did not accept this answer because it was not what he had been told being "rich" meant.[166]

Family, religious communities, and peer groups are still influential, Ferei noted, albeit not as much. More influence comes from mass media, communication technologies, and globalization. She advocated the need to connect with this generation: to hold their hands and communicate with them as human beings.

Ferei listed some of the realities faced:

- The media presented "unparalleled curricular packages."[167] The media, she outlined, offered built-in role models, that in turn emphasized fast-paced entertainment. Their focus is consumeristic and pleasure-seeking according to an unsustainable lifestyle. There is a complete disregard of the spiritual.
- Further, the mainstream media is controlled by external forces that control the space, the time, the money spent, and so forth. Whether those external forces are certain people or governments or businesses, it is still only a few who are in control.
- Advertisers run thirty-second ads in which their message has to be tightly packed and concise. Ferei suggested that Christians need to rethink how they could run a parallel curriculum to this.

165. Dunn, "Mrs. Agatha Ferei," 21:50; emphasis added.
166. Dunn, "Mrs. Agatha Ferei," 22:37.
167. Dunn, "Mrs. Agatha Ferei," 25:55.

- The media exposes youths to harmful or misleading messages, like violence and death. Values are turned into products: "Freedom [is] a feminine napkin. Trust [is] a contraceptive. Hope [is] a cigarette. Joy [is] bathroom tissue. Honesty [is] perfume."[168] The media tells one what he or she should get out of something.
- Culture has become wholly consumeristic: anything is for sale; everything can be bought. It propagates the message that *people are to be used* and *things are to be loved.* It stresses the individualistic and orients people only to the "Now." Thus, people are moved away from the experience of community and any connection with the past or future. This consumeristic, market culture creates artificial and superficial needs. In Fiji, for instance, some people do not have enough money for food—but they have cell phones!
- The market culture offers a whole new orientation of values related to products and having them. So children just want . . . and want . . . and want—without realizing how much things cost. Rather than family values, there is now the influence of "media-mediated values," like "instancy" and the market.[169] This consumeristic "market" culture, she asserted, does not care about a person's well-being; rather, its focus is on whether someone has bought its product or not. It reframes values in relation to products and their purchase: without its product, the person will not be happy.
- Ferei further remarked how ads were filled with young people: youthfulness was definitely stressed. While not disparaging youthful energy, she nevertheless wondered if it came at the expense of the age and wisdom of the elders. Yet, one needed to "walk" with the youth in discerning truth from distortion, sensationalism, and "fake news."[170]

There was little critical assessment of these realities, she claimed. As long as consumers were happy, there was little questioning of where a product came from, how it was made, or where it would go. A lot of times people do not question the people or the labor behind the brands which they buy, but Ferei counseled that "they need to."[171]

168. Dunn, "Mrs. Agatha Ferei," 28:13.
169. Dunn, "Mrs. Agatha Ferei," 31:25.
170. Dunn, "Mrs. Agatha Ferei," 34:24.
171. Dunn, "Mrs. Agatha Ferei," 36:04.

For Ferei, Christians must connect with Jesus in order to speak and act out against these trends. This can begin in the home through the lack of wastefulness, concern for the environment, and so forth. She cited Pope St. John Paul II's observation: "So often freedom is presented as a relentless search for pleasure or new experiences. . . . True freedom could never condemn the individual . . . to an insatiable quest for novelty. In the light of truth, authentic freedom is experienced as a definitive response to God's 'yes' to humanity, calling us to choose, not indiscriminately but deliberately, all that is good, true, and beautiful."[172]

Ferei advised connecting these principles and lessons to our own children. She recommended speaking to people in their own language and context. The young needed to have "spaces to talk," to feel like they were part of the learning and decision-making processes.[173] One thing Ferei encouraged was the practice of "family meetings" in order to promote the togetherness and connectivity of human persons, as well as to allow the opportunity for people to speak for themselves. People need to be given the space to speak so that they can go out into the world and speak.

## The Panel Discussion

A panel discussion was held focusing on the topic "Justice to Creation Is Justice to Mankind." It included (alphabetically):

- Reverend John Glynn, Diocese of Kavieng;
- Paul Harricknen, president of the Catholic Professionals' Society of PNG;
- Annemarie Mondu, development secretary for Caritas of CBC-PNGSI;
- Donatus Nahak, refugee resettlement officer, Caritas of CBC-PNGSI;
- Catherine Nongkas, principal of John Bosco Technological Institute, Port Moresby; and
- John Cardinal Ribat, MSC, archbishop of Port Moresby.[174]

172. Dunn, "Mrs. Agatha Ferei," 36:37. Actually, the statement comes from Benedict XVI, "41st World Communications Day."

173. Dunn, "Mrs. Agatha Ferei," 38:00.

174. There was also a "Bernard" on the panel from the CBC-PNGSI. He spoke on migrants and refugees. Unfortunately, his name was not printed in the schedule. Also,

The panel identified the following issues as new areas of concern for church mission:

- "Climate change"
- The environment
- Poverty
- Migration
- Gender equality

Reverend John Glynn is a priest of the Diocese of Kavieng (New Ireland Province). Glynn addressed the matter of the urban poor. They cannot provide the leadership they need, for the structures of traditional Papua New Guinean society are not there in the city.

He noted how many Papua New Guineans were functionally illiterate. A 2011 report on literacy in five of PNG's twenty-two provinces revealed that 85 percent of the populace was functionally illiterate in English. That was so, despite the fact that 70 percent of the respondents claimed to have been able to read and write in the national language.[175]

There was also a report from Save the Children Australia, which maintained that 40 percent (*sic*) of children in the Pacific region received violent discipline in the home.[176] Children experienced exceptionally high levels of physical, emotional, and sexual violence. He claimed that over 25 percent of parents and caregivers in PNG admitted to using

given the echoey nature of the open-air hall, I could not get his name or hear much of what he said.

175. See Asia South Pacific Association for Basic and Adult Education and Papua New Guinea Education Advocacy Network, *PNG Education Experience Survey*.

176. Here and following, he was referencing the report from Save the Children Australia in Suthanthiraraj, *Unseen, Unsafe*. With all due respect to Reverend Glynn's memory, the actual number is a lot higher. In fact, according to the report he mentions, between 70 to 87 percent of children in the Pacific region, aged one to fourteen years, was reported as having been given "violent discipline" within the month before (pp. 9–10; see also p. 2 of the report for the group's definition of "violent discipline" [also p. 40n3]). As for PNG, the report states,

> In Papua New Guinea alone, an estimated 2.8 million children—equivalent to over 75% of the child population—experience violent discipline in the home. In two provinces surveyed by Save the Children, 70% of children aged 6 to 8 years reported feeling "scared and in pain" in their community. Sexual violence is also exceptionally high, with Médecins Sans Frontières (MSF) reporting that children were the victims in over 50% of the sexual violence cases referred to their clinics. (Suthanthiraraj, *Unseen, Unsafe*, 4)

physical punishment "over and over again, as long as they could."[177] Seventy percent of children surveyed reported being scared or in pain in their communities.[178]

Whereas leadership is provided within ethnic communities, that leadership does not cut across ethnic groups. There are people whom Glynn called "shepherds" who fill the void (but are not real leaders). Due to the lack of leadership, people often fall back on their perceived notion of how their ancestors would have always responded in particular situations, for example, during tribal or clan fights. In such cases, it is hard to determine who the leader is on either side . . . or even who started the fight. Rather, everybody just joins in because it is (they believe) how they have behaved over thousands of years.

There is little access to services for the urban poor. The "operating principle" for access to services, said Glynn, was, "If you want my services, you must meet my requirements."[179] So, for example, one must find money for the school uniforms and materials. When a family cannot meet those requirements, then it is *the child* who is punished and, thus, disadvantaged.

Glynn observed that the urban poor do not get married; rather, they form "partnerships." He talked about the situation of groups of children whose "family" consisted of a single mother and several different fathers.[180] They spend their time squatting and fighting and stealing from each other. The level of emotional distress for these children, growing up in "these highly dysfunctional situations," must be "really terrific," he said.[181]

Yet, Glynn remarked that there was the presence of so many "saints" among "our people" in the urban poor. These are people, for example, who pick up and "adopt" the feral children wandering about and make them a part of their family.[182]

Glynn noted the Catholic Church's lack of presence and effort among the people living in the settlements. The only group offering religious services in the slums were the Seventh-day Adventists.

177. Dunn, "Panel Discussion," 37:29. I admit that I could not find that specific statistic in the report.

178. Dunn, "Panel Discussion," 38:24.

179. Dunn, "Panel Discussion," 40:40.

180. Dunn, "Panel Discussion," 41:25.

181. Dunn, "Panel Discussion," 42:15.

182. Dunn, "Panel Discussion," 42:25.

He then went on to describe his own group, the Foundation for Women and Children at Risk (WeCARe).[183] It is a charity group offering financial and logistics support to community "carers," who in turn assist vulnerable women and children in their community. The group has only one requirement for anyone seeking support: the inquirer must accept responsibility for his or her own problems. Then the question is, How does "WeCARe" meet the inquirer's needs?

Finally, Glynn addressed how the church could maintain a presence among the urban poor. For they do not go to school because the schools are too far away—but they do not go to church, either.

Paul Harricknen is president of the Catholic Professionals' Society of PNG. Harricknen noted that his group was approved by the bishops' conference in 2014. Calling themselves "*Catholic* professionals" gives them an extra responsibility in ethics and morals and how members conduct themselves.

The church has become focused on the laity to be sent out to re-evangelize, which is a big task for them: "We feel the burden; and we feel the responsibility."[184] Granting that laypeople were called to evangelize, Harricknen observed that they felt "constrained" by a lack of formation, resources, and training.[185] These were offered to seminarians and clergy—but hardly at all to the laity. Laypeople, he said, were also unsure about their place and role in the church's mission, with many believing the missionary call consisted only in helping out the priest in the parish. Pope Francis talks about clericalism—and Harricknen is inclined to believe it is true! Yet, he reminded, it was *the laity* who were supposed to be the ones sent out to bring the gospel into the world.

Harricknen recommended that Catholics not just have a Bible but also *read* and *live* it! How do we get that message into the mind of the layperson?

Another issue is having access to church documents, especially for those who cannot read or write. Laypeople should also own and read the *Catechism of the Catholic Church*.

Catholic laity, Harricknen further observed, stayed within the comfort of their parish; they did not go out to talk to non-Catholics. So when his society wanted to present a seminar on Pope Francis's encyclical letter on the environment, *Laudato Si'*, instead of holding it in a "church

183. The group's website can be found at http://wecarepng.org.pg.

184. Dunn, "Panel Discussion," 1:01:30.

185. Dunn, "Panel Discussion," 1:01:40.

environment" (no pun intended), his group specifically chose a nonsectarian venue so as "to bring the teaching out into the world."[186] For him, it was "a first step" to engage the secular institutions and to have influence on their negotiations and policies.[187]

"Those who can pray, pray!"—but Harricknen called on Catholics who work in the world to engage with the world so that they could share and help those in the world see "a bigger source" to it.[188]

Donatus Nahak is the refugee resettlement officer for Caritas of CBC-PNGSI.[189] He asked how the church could teach the message of salvation in these times of difficulties.

He asked the audience how many had read *Laudato Si'* on the environment. Only some raised their hand: "Less than twenty people in this room," he observed ruefully.[190] Nahak encouraged all present—"as a good Catholic"—to read it so that they would understand what "the gospel of salvation is, [which is] to save the planet."[191]

In reading it, he realized that "many times we, as Christians, fail to take good care of our environment."[192] Nahak agreed with Pope Francis's remark in *Laudato Si'* that the Genesis creation stories (for example, Gen 1:28) were used to warrant the unbridled exploitation of the earth.[193] We use this privilege of having been created as "a higher creature," Nahak added, to take charge of everything given to us by God: "We harvest what

186. Dunn, "Panel Discussion," 1:05:10.

187. Dunn, "Panel Discussion," 1:05:53.

188. Dunn, "Panel Discussion," 1:06:20.

189. See https://www.caritas.org.pg.

190. Dunn, "Panel Discussion," 24:24.

191. Dunn, "Panel Discussion," 24:34. To my discredit, I was not yet able to raise my hand at the time. I have since rectified the situation. In October 2023, Pope Francis issued an apostolic exhortation, *Laudate Deum* ("On the Climate Crisis"), which he intended as a supplement to the encyclical.

192. Dunn, "Panel Discussion," 25:00.

193. The pope writes,

> We are not God. The earth was here before us and it has been given to us. This allows us to respond to the charge that Judaeo-Christian thinking, on the basis of the Genesis account which grants man "dominion" over the earth (see Gen 1:28), has encouraged the unbridled exploitation of nature by painting him as domineering and destructive by nature. This is not a correct interpretation of the Bible as understood by the Church. Although it is true that we Christians have at times incorrectly interpreted the Scriptures, nowadays we must forcefully reject the notion that our being created in God's image and given dominion over the earth justifies absolute domination over other creatures. (Francis, *Laudato Si'*, §67)

we want, because we can; we own the land, because we can—without consideration to our neighbors and the sustainability of our program or how our neighbor will face the consequences of our actions."[194]

Where is our mission in these very challenging times, he asked. What could Catholics do to inform, educate, and respond to others' needs? What could they do, as Christians, to stop or prevent the carbon emission output into the air? Nahak noted the attitude called "pass[ing] the buck," since what might happen tomorrow is not affecting people today.[195] For example, he mentioned the American president (namely, Donald Trump) who refused to invest since climate change was not a problem affecting too many people yet. Nahak was further saddened by the logging companies that were allowed to enter PNG "and do business like crazy."[196] Yet, these forests keep us alive: they provide oxygen; they are a home to species not found anywhere else.

Nahak described how a few years ago Caritas formed a partnership with the Seventh-day Adventist communities of PNG and Australia. These groups realized that the church and other Christian denominations were always responding *after* natural disasters: "After the mess is done, we go in and respond to the people's needs."[197] He related how people in PNG viewed these natural disasters as God's curse on them or as the fault of other tribes. These are, he said, simple and uneducated people, who have a lack of information. They do not understand that the oceans are warming due to carbon emissions or that they are rising due to ice melting in the Arctic. In short, they did not understand humankind's own role in creating these disasters through climate change or global warming. So it is difficult, while distributing supplies, to try to communicate that the disaster is not a curse from God; rather, it is on account of natural phenomena or "our own doing."[198] They asked how they could bring peace during this time of the gospel of salvation. So they proposed a framework to address the difficult issues of climate change and natural disasters from a biblical viewpoint when one was out in the field. The result was a series of Bible studies called "A Theology of Disaster Resilience in a Changing Climate," explaining the situation and showing the many things that Christians could do to address it.

194. Dunn, "Panel Discussion," 26:05.

195. Dunn, "Panel Discussion," 27:23.

196. Dunn, "Panel Discussion," 28:17.

197. Dunn, "Panel Discussion," 28:42.

198. Dunn, "Panel Discussion," 30:34.

For there are many things that one can do to serve God. In confronting the climate crisis, Nahak asked, "What is my role: . . . As a leader? . . . As a student? . . . As an indigenous [person] living here in this country? . . . As a 'visiting person' in this country? . . . As a teacher?"[199] Christians must ask what is their mission to save this planet so that everyone, made in God's image, can enjoy our common home, "this beautiful garden of Eden."[200]

Catherine Nongkas is the principal of John Bosco Technological Institute, East Boroko, Port Moresby.[201]

She noted the scene of Greta Thunberg, "a climate activist," addressing the UN.[202] It was a moment to hear the prophetic voice of the young generation and see its horror at adults' inaction in regards to the environment. Youths are demonstrating in the streets for their own future: to tell their own leaders their opinions of what kind of world, those youths believe, they are leaving for them.

Nongkas contributed to the environmental theme, describing how the region along PNG's coast where she grew up had been changed and degraded. The beaches' coconut trees had been washed away so there was no shade to walk; the sea was full of garbage. She asked, "Where am I in all this?"[203] Nongkas was brought up to be rational and proficient, to think before acting: "I am not saying that this is wrong. . . . But my continual struggle today is to bring my mind and my heart together to operate in a holistic manner."[204] Nongkas credited her illiterate mother, who could predict the weather just by looking at trees' leaves, with teaching her "environmental literacy."[205] Nature is a great teacher. Thus, she learned to read the signs of the times from the environment.

Nongkas encouraged her students at Don Bosco to become better informed of their context, of their place in society, and of their responsibilities to their own and their children's futures. Finally, she wanted to prepare them to advocate for the care of our common home, the earth.

John Cardinal Ribat is the archbishop of the Archdiocese of Port Moresby. He spoke about the government's proposal for experimental

199. Dunn, "Panel Discussion," 32:15.

200. Dunn, "Panel Discussion," 32:43.

201. See their website at https://www.dbti.ac.pg.

202. Dunn, "Panel Discussion," 5:28.

203. Dunn, "Panel Discussion," 7:59.

204. Dunn, "Panel Discussion," 9:02.

205. Dunn, "Panel Discussion," 10:03.

"deep-seabed mining" (DSM) off the coast in PNG's Bismarck Sea. The project was called "Solwara 1." It was to have been conducted by the Canadian company Nautilus.[206] He was concerned about the proposal's environmental and cultural impacts. He asked the government what they could tell him regarding deep-sea mining and its effect on the environment, sea creatures, green life, and so forth. He got no response but was eventually told the government did not know. The video footage he saw of the actual mining process (wherein rocks were dug up out of the seafloor, their minerals extracted, and the residue deposited back into the ocean) particularly disturbed him. He related the locals' fear that they would not be able to fish either during or after the mining contract. Ribat himself feared the larger environmental impact of the process and was not convinced of its safety. He felt the need for a strong response against the practice.

## Closing Remarks

Bishop Rochus Tatamai, MSC, of the Diocese of Kavieng closed the symposium.[207] As Tatamai reflected on the interactions during the symposium, he felt a sense of joy. Nevertheless, he expressed disappointment that so few laypeople from the Port Moresby archdiocese were able to come to the symposium since the theme was about them. He observed that there was still a long way to go ahead.

Tatamai felt "personally challenged" as a bishop. He realized that the homilies presented on Sundays were insufficient for the people: "They are not enough."[208] He continued, "Many times as priests and bishops, we talk over the heads of our people. We presume that they know what we are talking about, including our religious[!]. But for many times they do not even comprehend because there are so many 'missing links' in their listening."[209]

206. Dunn, "Panel Discussion," 48:00 and following. For a website about the "Solwara 1" project, see Mineral Policy Institute, "DSM in PNG." The site is hosted by the Mineral Policy Institute (http://www.mpi.org.au), a voluntary, civic organization which seeks to help communities affected by mining projects as well as to bring about mining industry reform.

Within a month of the symposium, the Canadian company developing the project went bankrupt (see Stutt, "Nautilus Minerals"). Unfortunately, the PNG government held a substantial stake in the company, and was expected to lose about $24 million.

207. In 2020, Tatamai was appointed the archbishop of Rabaul (East New Britain Province).

208. Dunn, "Bp. Rochus Tatamai," 5:17.

209. Dunn, "Bp. Rochus Tatamai," 5:45.

He repeated the call for the formation of catechists: though they are expected to perform more, they are not given the needed formation.

He related how he started offering presentations after Sunday Mass: "I say . . . 'If you want to hear something, you can stay back; if you want to go home, then don't worry—it's okay.' And to my surprise, everybody stayed!" After he finished, the people said, "Some more!"—so he talked for another hour![210] He announced he would give another talk the next day: "In case you are still interested tomorrow, at six o'clock tomorrow, I will be here. If nobody comes, I'll pray the Rosary and I'll go back to my house."[211] The next day, he found people already waiting for him forty-five minutes early! So he started holding a second session. This experience showed him that although his people had gone through school and some had even graduated from university—they were "technically professionals"—they nevertheless had a "kindergarten faith."[212] They had the faith given to them by the catechists when they were young, but it had not been developed. They had not had the Scriptures explained to them or had the proper accompaniment in the faith.

Tatamai criticized his fellow countrymen for relying too much on outsiders, like missionaries, to make the effort to spread the faith to their own countrymen. He called on the church's clergy "to be more realistic about the people they are serving and the issues they are finding."[213] The issues of the PNG church needed to become clearer. He hoped people would realize the connection between the faith and sacraments, and the lives that they were living. He gave the example of Catholic women who would come up to receive Christ, the "bread of life," in Holy Communion, while yet practicing contraception. This made them "dead," when their bodies should be life-giving. "You cannot live a life of contradictions," he counseled.[214] He likened the colonialists and their missionaries who came to PNG to "big tsunamis which hit our shores."[215] It is now the task of Papua New Guineans themselves to go to the shore and pick up what is valuable from what they brought. Nevertheless, Christ is the "first missionary," and he "set the tone for us."[216] To be baptized means to be sent.

210. Dunn, "Bp. Rochus Tatamai," 6:24.
211. Dunn, "Bp. Rochus Tatamai," 7:10.
212. Dunn, "Bp. Rochus Tatamai," 8:00.
213. Dunn, "Bp. Rochus Tatamai," 11:00.
214. Dunn, "Bp. Rochus Tatamai," 13:28.
215. Dunn, "Bp. Rochus Tatamai," 14:31.
216. Dunn, "Bp. Rochus Tatamai," 15:30.

# 2

# Still on Christ's Mountain

## *Matthew 28:19–20*[1]

At the very end of the Gospel According to Matthew (ch. 28), the risen Christ appears to his eleven disciples atop a mountain in Galilee (v. 16). They fall down in worship before him (v. 17). He tells them that he has been given all cosmic power—that is, all authority both in heaven and on earth (v. 18)—and sets before them the following charge:

> Go therefore and make disciples of all nations, baptizing them in the name of the Father and of the Son and of the Holy Spirit, teaching them to observe all that I have commanded you. (Matt 28:19–20a ESV)[2]

Then, Jesus promises his disciples that he will be present to them until the end of time (v. 20b).

Few would deny the importance of this episode in Matthew's Gospel. Indeed, German theologian Otto Michel famously claimed that this final pericope of Matthew's Gospel was the key to understanding the whole Gospel![3] Many interpreters see this final pericope as a synthesis of the gospel's entire message. The evangelist intended that this final pericope

1. A version of this chapter was previously published in *The Fellowship of Catholic Scholars Quarterly*. Used with permission.

2. The *Nova Vulgata* preserves the alternate reading found in the Old Latin (i.e., Vetus Latina or Itala) tradition, which goes a little bit differently: "[Jesus says to them:] 'Going therefore teach all nations [*docete omnes gentes*], baptizing them in the name of the Father and of the Son and of the Holy Spirit, teaching them to observe everything, whatever I have commanded you.'"

3. Michel, "Abschluß des Matthäusevangeliums," 125.

should cast its shadow over the rest of the gospel, thus making crystal clear everything that preceded it. As South African missiologist David Bosch writes, "There can be little doubt that the entire gospel was written from the theological vantage point of this final pericope. Scholars today are agreed upon the pivotal character of these verses, which are to be regarded as the key to understanding the entire book. In a way they sum up everything Matthew wrote in his gospel. All the threads woven in to the entire fabric of the gospel, from chapter 1 onward, draw together here."[4]

Few would also deny the indelible influence that this statement of Jesus has had on Christian self-understanding, especially in the modern era. It has been called the "Great Commission,"[5] which has acted as the seal of approval for Christian missionary efforts. It has impelled and continues to impel masses of Christians to go out among the nations: to make disciples, to baptize, and to teach them Christ's commands.

But as noted in the talk by Reverend Clarence Devadass above, appreciation for the evangelical and missiological pedigrees of this statement has waned. On the one hand, it is viewed as tainted by the Christian West's ruthless expansionism across the world's other cultures and ethnic groups. On the other, it has been colored by an exclusivist reading, which sees the religious "other" as merely the object of conversion to Christianity. For example, Indian biblical scholar Joseph Pathrapankal observes, "Though this text refers to the authority, which the risen Jesus has been given, it was spontaneous on the part of the church and its missionaries to presume that this same authority was given to them also to do all what they wanted with the proclamation of the Gospel and the conversion of the people. Since there was no one to challenge and question this usurpation of authority, it got established through the centuries, and that, too, with the assistance of the colonial powers."[6] He readily admits, however, that Matt 28 is not the only text: there was also Paul's emphasis on preaching the gospel to the unevangelized (e.g., in Rom 10). "With such ready-made biblical texts as the basis of a theology and its praxis," he writes, "missionaries of all sorts went around the world baptizing

4. Bosch, "Scope of Mission," 20.

5. Though when this phrase first came to be used and who used it is not known. Scholar David F. Wright makes a valiant attempt to track down its origins (see Wright, "Great Commission," 153–57). However, the most he can say after his investigations is that the expression had come to be conventionally used sometime around 1870—but from whom he could not say ("Great Commission," 155).

6. Pathrapankal, "Christian Evangelization," 31.

millions and making them Disciples of Christ, thereby assuring them eternal salvation."[7]

Of course, there are in each culture all sorts of elements which cause one to question or even criticize the validity of the Great Commission.

For Westerners, like Europeans, it may be the recognition of the injustice of their country's imperial or colonial legacy. For they recognize that Christianity often came along with their soldiers and mercantilists and was imposed on, rather than offered to, foreign peoples—typically, without the latters' permission or consent. Hence, Westerners—and rightfully so—want to make amends for the past. There is a guiltful sensitivity about trying to get people to change their native religions to a "Western" one, as Christianity is perceived to be.

For Easterners, like in India, it may be their pleasure at the coexistence of so many different religious paths in their cultures. By changing (read: converting) people from those different paths, they fear losing the enrichment which these non-Christian religions bring not just to them but also to the world. Always lurking, however, is remembrance of the West's imperial and colonial past and the fear of being controlled by some outside power, usually situated somewhere in the Western world (Rome, the Southern Baptist Convention USA, and so forth). These concerns are not unwarranted; they are based on actual experience. There is a legitimate place for eisegetically bringing one's own concerns to the biblical text, of questioning its possible use for oppression and injustice. The problem can be that one reads injustices *ex post facto* into the text, which proper exegesis reveals are not there.

Is Matt 28:19–20 still a serviceable Scripture for mission? Should it be reread more irenically, apart from any conversionary tactics? Or on the contrary, should it simply be dust-binned? I will argue that Matt 28:19–20 is still a suitable statement for Christian evangelizing mission—indeed, a paradigmatic one. But it must be understood properly in order to show how a truly Christian mission to the world ought to be done.

7. Pathrapankal, "Christian Evangelization," 31. Other texts were also added to the mission command, like those affirming Jesus' unique mediatorship of salvation (see 1 Tim 2:5, Acts 4:12).

## Reception History of Matt 28:19–20

Christianity has always been a "missionary" religion. The point is so obvious as to hardly require any justification.[8] The New Testament testifies everywhere to Christians' instinct to spread the message about Jesus. From their earliest days, Christians felt compelled to actively communicate God's "message of reconciliation" in Jesus Christ (see 2 Cor 5:19), first, to the world of their Jewish brethren and, then, to the gentiles.[9] Indeed, the earliest evidence we have for Christianity per se is a group of writings composed by an itinerant Jewish-Christian preacher for his converts. He is known to us as "Paul of Tarsus." He was a missionary: he travelled throughout the Eastern Mediterranean, proclaiming the Christian message and making converts to the faith. In fact, the bulk of (what would become) the Christian Scriptures, the New Testament, comprises Paul's writings to his communities of converts, both from Judaism and from paganism. Matthew 28:19–20, which was composed much later than Paul's writings—perhaps by twenty years—obviously sits within this preexistent missionary matrix. It derives, then, from the earliest contextual stance of the "Jesus Movement."

But this only makes Matt 28 evidence for Christianity's early missionary stance. It does not necessarily make Matt 28 *the* text for Christian mission. How did that come about?

Swiss New Testament scholar Ulrich Luz points out the paradox that the passage, which is so missionary in character and intent, seems itself to have had little to no missiological relevance for the early church. He writes, "The ancient church scarcely ever appealed to [it] for its own universal missionary task."[10] Instead, early Christian exegesis on Matt 28:19–20 was primarily focused on addressing theological or practical matters, like belief in the Trinity or whether or not babies should be baptized. Yet, as can be inferred from Luz's statement, the proclamation of the gospel to nonbelievers was clearly already happening—no matter which particular Scripture might have been in the back of a missionary's mind.

8. See e.g., Latourette, *Expansion of Christianity*.

9. One could point immediately to the "sending out" stories in the Gospels of Matthew (10:5–15), Mark (6:7–13), and Luke (9:1–6 and 10:1–12), as well as to the Acts of the Apostles.

10. Luz, *Matthew 21–28*, 626.

Moreover, to the extent that early Christians did view Christ as having given a missionary command in Matt 28, it was mostly seen as having been addressed solely or primarily to the blessed apostles. It was not viewed as a universal call for all Christians. Once the apostles had gone forth into the world and sealed their testimony with their own blood (in most cases), people believed that Christ's charge had for the most part been fulfilled. After their deaths, it was thought that Christ's missionary charge had naturally been transferred to their successors, the bishops.[11] So it is not surprising that, even during the Christian West's territorial expansion into the nonbelieving world in the late Middle Ages, Matt 28 still did not function as a major scriptural proof for the church's understanding of her evangelizing mission.[12] I should add here that this is not to say that there were no Scriptures at all that factored in the church's impulse to spread the faith. There was Mark 16:15 ("And [Jesus] said to [the apostles]: 'Going into the whole world preach the gospel to every creature'"). There was also Paul's comment in 10:14–15 of the Letter to the Romans ("How therefore will they call on the one in whom they have not believed? Or how will they believe in him, whom they have not heard? Yet, how shall they hear without one preaching? Indeed, how shall they preach if they neither are sent?"). It was just that Matt 28:19–20 itself was not the major text for mission yet.

Luz identifies the Protestant Reformation, specifically the Anabaptist movement, as the source of the text's subsequent importance. Anabaptists saw the text as applicable to their own times: as a command addressed directly to them. Since the Anabaptists rejected hierarchy of any sort, they believed that Christ's command had become the required object of all Christians—not just of popes or bishops.[13] As South African scholar David Bosch notes, the Anabaptists' interpretive tradition gained support among the Lutheran Pietists, though not without some opposition from the Lutheran "orthodox" establishment. For Luther (as well as the other Reformers) had followed the traditional exegesis, which thought that only the apostles had been given the command in Matt 28—which they had fulfilled. The missionary command was, then, no longer binding on Christians.[14] As Harry R. Boer, Dutch-American scholar and pastor, writes,

11. Luz, *Matthew 21–28*, 626.

12. Luz, *Matthew 21–28*, 626.

13. Luz, *Matthew 21–28*, 626–27.

14. See e.g., Bosch, *Transforming Mission*, 239–61, especially at 252–54 (see also

> In the conception of the Reformers and of the majority of seventeenth-century theologians the Great Commission was binding only on the apostles. When they died Christ's command died with them. It does not extend to the Church which the apostles founded. . . . The Church . . . has no mandate to preach the gospel and found churches in distant parts. The authority of each minister or bishop is limited to the congregation or area over which he has been placed.[15]

It was not until 1792, however, when William Carey, a British Baptist, published the book *An Enquiry into the Obligations of Christians, to Use Means for the Conversion of the Heathens* that the Scripture entered fully into Christians' missionary consciousness.[16] In that book, Carey appealed to Matt 28:19 as a general call for all Christians to spread the gospel. It is from that book by Carey that the text of Matt 28:19–20 begins to receive its conspicuous status as the Scripture *par excellence* for Christian missionary activity.[17] As Luz summarizes, "For Carey [Matt] 28:19a is the central text of missions. . . . Through Carey [it] became '*the* mission command' that influenced the church and evangelical missionary societies of the nineteenth and twentieth centuries that grew out of the revival movements."[18]

---

Bosch, "Structure of Mission," 218).

15. Boer, *Pentecost and Missions*, 18. Indeed, he adds, "material from the writings of the Reformers and of leaders in the post-Reformation Church setting forth this view is so abundant that even a cursory survey would lead us much too far afield" (*Pentecost and Missions*, 18).

16. Luz, *Matthew 21–28*, 627. Carey's complete work can be read online (see Carey, *Enquiry*).

17. Luz, *Matthew 21–28*, 627.

18. Luz, *Matthew 21–28*, 627; emphasis original. David Bosch, however, argues that Carey's work has been misread. According to him, Carey merely wanted to show that Christ's command in Matt 28:19 applied to all Christians. In other words, it was the work of everyone: both lay and cleric, man and woman. Carey was not arguing in his book that the text was the biblical foundation per se for Christian missionary activity (see Bosch, "Scope of Mission," 19–20). Bosch may be right: Carey only ever cites Matt 28:19 at the very beginning of his book (and even then in piecemeal fashion, and not completely); it never appears again in the whole work. This is hardly to be expected if Carey's specific purpose was to establish the text's normative importance. On the contrary, the biblical text that seems to figure most prominently for Carey is Rom 10:12–15, which is reproduced in full on the book's title page. However, in my opinion, Bosch may be cutting too fine a distinction here. For what does it matter if Carey were just intending to use Matt 28:19 to challenge the opinion that Christ's charge only belonged to religious leaders or specialists, and not to every Christian? It still assumed that the text of Matt 28:19 itself constituted a command by Christ to bring the gospel

Some might think that Luz's summary of the reception history of Matt 28:19–20 tends to delegitimize or diminish the text's missionary significance. But he or she would be wrong. For even if the missionary overtone of the passage has been made patent only in the last five centuries, Luz nevertheless thinks that such a modern interpretation corresponds accurately to Matthew's view of discipleship. It fits in with the passage's overall trajectory. He writes,

> With its special position at the end of the Gospel it is clear that Jesus's mission command for the church has a fundamental significance. Matthew actually thinks that the church is basically and fundamentally a missionary church, and he conceives of its mission concretely as a "going" to all nations. That today many Christians and churches can no longer read this text uncritically as the Magna Carta of their missionary proclamation has reasons external to the biblical text. I am thinking here in particular of our modern understanding of the relationship between missions, colonialism, and the export of Western civilization and of the more intensive contacts with non-Christian religions. However, these insights should not keep us from recognizing clearly what the text says.[19]

Luz's description of the reception history of Matt 28:19–20 is surely helpful, showing that the history of Christians' interpretation of the Bible is never purely static. Later interpretations—even much later ones—can sometimes draw out or realize the implications of a scriptural passage. So the Anabaptist contribution was to cause Christians, both Protestant and Catholic, to rediscover the Matthean community's original self-understanding as a community of missionary disciples.

The influence of that rediscovery has been widespread. Matthew 28:19–20 came to be seen as the "go-to" proof text for Christianity's evangelizing mission, especially among Protestant missionaries, who hammered away at its significance for their own missionary efforts. Such has been the influence of Protestants' rediscovery of the text as a missionary statement, that even the Catholic Church, which has always had a missionary enterprise, has also begun to rely on Matt 28:19–20 as the ideal and exclusive scriptural rationale for her evangelizing mission.[20] Indeed,

to the unevangelized.

19. Luz, *Matthew 21–28*, 628.

20. See e.g., *CCC*, §849, which posits Matt 28:19–20 as the standard for missionary activity.

the text's (now) venerable status in Catholic missiology is confirmed throughout the documents of the Second Vatican Council:

- According to the Dogmatic Constitution on the Church, Matt 28:16–20 contains Christ's "solemn mandate . . . to proclaim the saving truth . . . to the very ends of the earth."[21]
- The Dogmatic Constitution on Divine Revelation states that, in Matt 28, Jesus "commissioned the Apostles to preach to all men [the] Gospel which is the source of all saving truth and moral teaching."[22]
- The Decree on the Missionary Activity of the Church says that the passage embodies Christ's "express command" that the apostles spread the faith and bring all men and women to salvation in him.[23]
- The Decree on Ecumenism maintains that Matt 28 provides the basis for establishing the church, through which the tasks of teaching, ruling, and sanctifying continue.[24]
- The Declaration on Religious Liberty states that Matt 28 imposes "the duty" of spreading among all men the "one true religion [which] subsists in the Catholic and Apostolic Church."[25]

The Catholic Church has come to receive Matt 28:19–20 as the quintessence of her missionary understanding. It is for the church's evangelizing mission what an axiom is to scientific inquiry: a statement of reality which requires no further justification.[26]

## Exegetical Considerations

What follows is not a thoroughgoing exegesis of Matt 28:19–20. Instead, I want to highlight certain ways in which I believe that the text has been interpreted according to a certain pluralist *Tendenz* that minimizes or rejects its missionary import.[27]

21. Vatican II, *Lumen Gentium*, §17 (see also §§8, 20, and 24).
22. Vatican II, *Dei Verbum*, §7.
23. Vatican II, *Ad Gentes*, §5.
24. Vatican II, *Unitatis Redintegratio*, §2.
25. Vatican II, *Dignitatis Humanae*, §1.
26. See Lackie, *Chambers Dictionary*, s.v. "Axiom," 89.
27. For a thorough understanding, one can consult the standard biblical commentaries. But for an excellent, brief summation of the issues one may consult Freeman, "Great Commission."

The whole pericope of Matt 28:16–20 is of great fascination to scholars.[28] Indeed, according to missiologist David Bosch in *Transforming Mission*, the entire gospel points to these final verses. All the threads woven into the fabric of Matthew's story, from the first chapter onwards, draw together here.[29]

Jesus, exalted above heaven and earth by his death and resurrection, approaches the eleven disciples, who represent all his followers, on a mountain in Galilee. There, he passes on to them definitively the mission that he had received from God his Father (see Matt 20:28; see also 10:40).

The content of the passage has already been quoted in English above. In the original Greek, it reads,

> *Poreuthentes* oun *mathēteusate* panta ta ethnē, *baptizontes* autous eis to onoma tou patros kai tou huiou kai tou hagiou pneumatos, *didaskontes* autous tērein panta hosa eneteilamēn hymin. (Matt 28:19–20a; emphasis added)[30]

The Greek text is obviously important since it is the *Grundlage* for any translation. Four verbs are presented in the commission:

- Go (*Poreuthentes*)
- Make disciples (*mathēteusate*)
- Baptize (*baptizontes*)
- Teach (*didaskontes*)

Some Bible translations, like the New Jerusalem Bible or the New Community Bible, translate the passage as a series of commands each in its own right: "Go! . . . Make disciples! . . . Baptize! . . . Teach!" This is important to note since one can sometimes hear in missiological circles, as in Devadass's talk above, that by having these four imperatives the text of Matt 28:19–20 can be read as proposing a spectrum of activity. Christ's disciples are meant to go out into the world, yes—but not exclusively to

28. As New Testament scholar John P. Meier observes, "There are certain great pericopes in the Bible which constantly engender discussion and research, while apparently never admitting of definite solutions. Matt 28:16–20 seems to be such a pericope" (Meier, "Two Disputed Questions," 407). Meier fell asleep in the Lord in 2022. May Christ remember his priesthood in his kingdom!

29. Bosch, *Transforming Mission*, 56–57. Douglas R. A. Hare states, "The importance of this passage to a proper understanding of the First Gospel can hardly be exaggerated" (Hare, *Matthew*, 331).

30. Transliterated from Nestle and Nestle, *Novum Testamentum Graece*.

make disciples or impose baptism. Rather, Jesus presents a list of options, any of which one might choose to do or not do. This view, however, is untenable exegetically because only the second verb, "make disciples" (*mathēteusate*), is given in the imperative mood. Jesus commands, "Make disciples!" The other verbs are participles: going, baptizing, teaching.

The verb *mathēteuō* is notable. Its immediate meaning in Greek is "to disciple." Thus, the passage reads literally, "Disciple all the nations!" Its usage is almost exclusively Matthean (see Matt 13:52, 27:57, 28:19). The only other place that it appears is in Luke's Acts of the Apostles (see 14:21). Whenever used, it means the active sense of making someone into a disciple of Jesus and his kingdom.[31] As David Bosch observes, it is the reality of Jesus' cosmic power that leads into the "solemn challenge" of verses 19–20. For "if Jesus is indeed Lord of all, this reality just has to be proclaimed. Nobody who knows of this can remain silent about it. He or she can do only one thing—help others also to acknowledge Jesus' lordship."[32] It is, then, something that Christ's followers are to do actively, just as they were "discipled" unto Jesus. The verb "to make disciples" is central to the passage and essential to Jesus' meaning. His charge is first and foremost to make disciples. How that might occur is explicated by the other verbs. As Bosch states,

> There can be little doubt that the imperative, "Make disciples!," is the principal verb in the entire passage. The two modal participles, "baptizing" and "teaching," are clearly subordinated to "make disciples," they describe the *form* the disciple-making is to take, but are not independent actions, each with its own "weight." . . . The two subsequent participles, "baptizing" and "teaching," further qualify and explicate the main verb, "make disciples." They are not independent activities. . . . The followers of Jesus make disciples of others, and this they do *by baptizing them* in the name of the Father, the Son and the Holy Spirit, and *by teaching them* all that Jesus has commanded.[33]

This point is supported by the history of Christian hermeneutics. The Western church, following St. Jerome (d. AD 420), has traditionally

31. See Bosch, *Transforming Mission*, 73.

32. Bosch, *Transforming Mission*, 78 (see also 74).

33. Bosch, "Scope of Mission," 21, 24; emphasis original. See also Bosch, *Transforming Mission*, 73. As R. T. France explains, "The sentence structure is of a main verb in the imperative, 'make disciples,' followed by two uncoordinated participles, 'baptizing' and 'teaching,' which spell out the process of making disciples" (France, *Gospel of Matthew*, 1115). See also Luz, *Matthew 21–28*, 625.

viewed Christ's statement as an outline of the different levels of catechetical pedagogy.[34] As Jerome writes in his commentary on Matthew's Gospel,

> *"Go therefore, teach all nations, baptizing them in the name of the Father, and of the Son, and of the Holy Spirit."* First they teach all nations, then they dip in water those who have been taught. For it is not possible that the body receives the sacrament of Baptism unless the soul first receives the truth of the faith. . . .
>
> *"Teaching them to observe all things whatsoever I have commanded you."* The sequence is extraordinary. He has commanded the apostles first to teach all nations, then to dip them in the sacrament of faith, and after faith and baptism they are to instruct them in the things that must be observed.[35]

Of course, it should be pointed out immediately that Jerome follows the Latin Vulgate tradition above by translating *mathēteusate panta ta ethnē* as "teach all nations." Nevertheless, since we know the Greek basis for his text, the effect of his exegesis is the same: both baptizing and teaching Christ's commands are subordinately related to and flow out of Jesus' essential directive to "disciple" the nations of the world. So Jesus does not lay out a continuum of options for his disciples or a spectrum of choices that they might make. Instead, he clearly indicates the pattern which Christian mission ought to take—namely, to make people his followers through baptism and catechesis. Christ's words are not intended as a disjunctive list of possible tasks; they are an interrelated sequence. If any continuum exists, its centripetal point is always the command "Make disciples!" It alone explains the purpose for the apostles' going out into the world. Matthew 28 also gives the reason for that going, which is to baptize and teach. In this way, Matt 28:19–20 becomes the focal statement of Matthew's whole Gospel.

We do need to remember, though, the caution of David Bosch regarding the peril of basing the entirety of the New Testament's theology of missionary activity on any one scriptural text.[36] The point is countenanced by Pope St. John Paul II in his encyclical letter *Redemptoris Missio*. He recognizes that each evangelist concludes his Gospel with a "missionary mandate."[37] That fact alone should say something about

34. Luz, *Matthew 21–28*, 625.

35. Jerome, *Commentary on Matthew* 4.28.19–20 (Scheck, FC 117:327); italics in original.

36. See Bosch, "Scope of Mission," 20.

37. See John Paul II, *Redemptoris Missio*, §22. In addition to Matthew's mandate,

the vital importance which the early Christian community placed on its missionary nature: the church was sent forth to make disciples for Christ! This point is made by American biblical scholar Raymond E. Brown, when he writes, "Matthew, Luke, John [ch. 20], and the Marcan Appendix [that is, 16:9–20] all follow a basic pattern in describing this appearance of Jesus to the Twelve [apostles]. When the disciples are gathered together . . . Jesus appears and is recognized. . . . He then gives them a solemn missionary command. This appearance does far more than assure the disciples of Jesus' victory over death; it commissions them to preach, to baptize, to forgive sins—in short to carry to men the news of Jesus and the salvation wrought by him."[38] So, as the pope points out above, a mandatory commissioning is not per se a unique feature of Matthew's Gospel. It occurs in the other three canonical Gospels as well. Further, he notes how each Gospel has its own distinct emphasis: for Mark, it is proclamation to bring others to faith in Christ; for Matthew, it is the formation of the church and process of teaching; for Luke, it is witness to the resurrection to lead people out of sin and into God's mercy and love.[39]

Given that these common elements are found, in what way can I argue that Matt 28 is still paradigmatic?

While it is true that each Gospel contains a scene at the end where the risen Christ sends out his followers as his witnesses to the world, for none, except Matthew, is that scene intended to be necessarily the defining feature, the distinguishing characteristic, of that particular Gospel.

---

which is outlined above, there are also the following:

- "And [Jesus] said to them: 'Going into the whole world preach the gospel to every creature'" (Mark 16:15).
- "And [Jesus] said to them, 'Thus it is written, for the Christ to suffer and to rise again from the dead on the third day. And penance unto the remission of sins is to be preached in his name unto all nations, beginning at Jerusalem. You are witnesses of these things'" (Luke 24:46–48; see also Acts 1:8).
- "[Jesus] said therefore to them again: 'Peace be to you! As the Father has sent me, I also send you'" (John 20:21).

38. Brown, *Gospel According to John (XIII–XXI)*, 973.

39. See John Paul II, *Redemptoris Missio*, §22. Yet, each Gospel, while having its own distinct emphasis, shares common elements: First, there is "the universal dimension of the task entrusted to the apostles, who are sent to 'all nations' (Matt 28:19); 'into all the world and . . . to the whole creation' (Mark 16:15); to 'all nations' (Luke 24:47); 'to the end of the earth' (Acts 1:8)." Second, there is Christ's assurance to the apostles that they will not be alone in their task; they will receive the strength and means necessary from Jesus and his Spirit to carry out their mission (see John Paul II, *Redemptoris Missio*, §22).

On the contrary, Matthew intends precisely that in Matt 28. As Craig S. Keener describes, "Matthew's Gospel closes with what Christians have often called the 'Great Commission.' This commission is no afterthought to Matthew's Gospel; rather, it summarizes much of the heart of his message."[40] He goes on to say, "The Great Commission is not an idea tacked inelegantly to the end of Matthew's Gospel, as if Matthew had nowhere else to put it."[41] Matthew's statement itself is intended to transform the entirety of the Gospel's preceding chapters into *a missionary charter*.[42] The evangelist's purpose is to bring home directly to each disciple, in a way that is not as readily apparent in the other Gospels, how he or she has been committed by Jesus himself to the missionary enterprise, which is to make disciples of nonbelievers, bring them to baptism, and teach them the commands of Christ. Aside from Matthew, none of the mandates in the other Gospels seems to have been so constructed with such an acute missionary vision.

Devadass proposes John 20:21 as perhaps a better text for mission, although he is vague as to why. He does have some support for this view in St. John Paul II's *Redemptoris Missio*. The pope writes that only John 20:21 embodies an explicit mandate for mission, where Jesus says, "As the Father has sent me, I also send you." I would note, however, that Jesus' statement "Going therefore" in Matt 28:19 seems to me to at least approximate a mandate, since it indicates Christ's wish that the apostles ought not to remain on the mountain. The Johannine mission, states the pope, is to allow people to share in the communion of love existing between God the Father and his Son, who has been sent into the world (see John 5:20, 15:9). Hence, Pope St. John Paul II calls John 20:21 "a very important missionary text," for "it makes us understand that we are missionaries above all because of *what we are* as a Church whose innermost life is unity in love, even before we become missionaries *in word or deed*."[43] Who am I to

40. Keener, "Matthew's Missiology," 3.

41. Keener, "Matthew's Missiology," 19–20.

42. As David Bosch observes, Matthew's Gospel "is essentially a missionary text" outlining how his community should understand its calling and mission (Bosch, *Transforming Mission*, 57–59).

43. John Paul II, *Redemptoris Missio*, §23; emphasis original. American Scripture scholar Raymond E. Brown outlines,

> Throughout the account of Jesus' ministry John has avoided designating the disciples as apostles (those sent) and he has not described an occasion on which they were sent out. . . . But in vs. 21 John joins the common Gospel tradition that the risen Jesus constituted apostles by entrusting

disagree with a sainted pope? And I shall not. I shall let his view remain against my own as a reminder that while I believe Matt 28:19–20 to be a paradigmatic statement for evangelizing mission, I recognize that it does not embody the complete vision of evangelizing mission. Other missionary texts should not be neglected since they express insights which can be enriching and (even) corrective. For example, a Johannine vision of mission as participating in the communion of love between God and his Son could act as a corrective for those who might interpret the Matthean paradigm in an aggressive, intolerant manner.

As South African missiologist David Bosch asserts, the Gospel According to Matthew is basically a missionary text.[44] Matthew articulates a vision for his community as "identity-in-mission." His Gospel is permeated with the idea of mission, both to Jews and gentiles, such that he has designed his Gospel in order to culminate in the "Great Commission" of Matt 28:19–20.[45] This can be seen from the fact that "virtually every word of this commission reaches back to the story of Jesus as told in earlier passages of the gospel: the fact that the meeting took place on a mountain in Galilee; the disciples' wavering between worship and doubt; the references to Jesus' authority, to making disciples, and teaching, and expressions such as 'go,' 'therefore,' 'observe,' 'command,' 'I [am] with you,' and 'the close of the age.'"[46] Matthew 28:16–20, particularly verses 19–20, does not just act as a recapitulation of the entire Gospel, but it also functions as its key to understanding. In other words, Matt 28:19–20 is not to be understood apart from the twenty-seven chapters which have preceded it. Those twenty-seven chapters, however, do not make full sense without Christ's concluding commission to the eleven apostles. So as Craig S. Keener writes, "This commission is no afterthought to Matthew's Gospel; rather, it summarizes much of the heart of his message."[47]

---

> a salvific mission to those to whom he appeared. The special Johannine contribution to the theology of this mission is that the Father's sending of the Son serves both as the model and the ground for the Son's sending of the disciples. Their mission is to continue the Son's mission. . . . Similarly the disciples must show forth the presence of Jesus so that whoever sees the disciples is seeing Jesus who sent them. . . . This becomes possible only through the gift of the Holy Spirit (vs. 22), whom the Father sends in Jesus' name . . . and whom Jesus himself sends. (Brown, *Gospel According to John [XIII–XXI]*, 1036)

44. Bosch, *Transforming Mission*, 57.

45. Bosch, *Transforming Mission*, 80.

46. Bosch, *Transforming Mission*, 80. See also Bosch, "Scope of Mission," 20–21.

47. Keener, "Matthew's Missiology," 3.

Early audiences would have heard the whole Gospel read to them; and having heard it read from beginning to end, they would have recognized chapter 28 as a fitting conclusion that weaved together themes from the whole. Thus, Keener continues, "we must read [Matt 28] in light of the entire Gospel it is intended to climax."[48]

It is understandable, then, that Jesus' final words—"And behold I am with you all days, even to the completion of the age" (Matt 28:20)—should mark off an *inclusio* with the beginning of Matthew's Gospel. For these words hearken back to Matthew's citation in 1:22–23 of the prophecy regarding Jesus' birth: "Yet all this was done, that it should be fulfilled, what was said by the Lord through the prophet saying: '*Behold, a virgin shall carry in her womb and bear a son, and they shall call his name Emmanuel*,' which is interpreted *With us is God*" (italics in original; see Isa 7:14). But whereas Jesus' presence as Emmanuel is focused mainly on the people of Israel, Matthew changes its meaning to include all of his disciples, whoever or wherever or whenever they may be. The presence of Christ is also permanent and everlasting. He is continuously present to his community, even forever into the future. Hence, there is no ascension into heaven or pouring out of the Spirit or mention of a parousia in Matthew's Gospel.[49] Still, as David Bosch observes, "Jesus' abiding presence is . . . intimately linked to his followers' engagement in mission. It is as they make disciples, baptize them, and teach them, that Jesus remains with those followers. . . . The clause 'I am with you always' is, however, not logically subordinated to the 'go . . . and make disciples.' It is, rather, the other way round—because Jesus continues to be present with his disciples, they go out in mission."[50] Espousing the return of Christ was unnecessary, given that he was already and forever present with his community: "It was precisely because of such bold fusion of the awareness of the present lordship of Christ with his empowering his followers to make disciples of all nations that the delay of the parousia did not cause a catastrophe in the early church."[51] On the contrary, the Matthean community's involvement in mission was an integral part of its expectation of the return of the risen Jesus: "a kind of 'proleptic parousia.'"[52]

48. Keener, "Matthew's Missiology," 3.

49. Bosch, *Transforming Mission*, 77 (see also 80).

50. Bosch, *Transforming Mission*, 78.

51. Bosch, *Transforming Mission*, 80.

52. Bosch, *Transforming Mission*, 80. See also Meier, *Vision of Matthew*, 37–38, 212, 215n270, 218.

## Paradigmatic Usage of Matt 28:19–20 for Evangelizing Mission

More than just a summation of Matthew's Gospel, the pericope demonstrates what kind of Gospel it is and what kind of community Matthew envisions. The Matthean community has been sent out to bring others to belief in Jesus and to baptize them into his church. As Ulrich Luz states, "With its special position at the end of the Gospel it is clear that Jesus' mission command for the Church has a fundamental significance. Matthew actually thinks that the Church is basically and fundamentally a missionary church, and he conceives of its mission concretely as a 'going' to all nations."[53] For American biblical scholar John L. McKenzie, Matt 28:16–20 is an essential statement of the Matthean community's reason for being, which is missionary: "The apostolic commission is couched in terms of the experience of the early church. Brief as it is, it is an unusually clear presentation of what the apostolic Church understood itself to be. The Church acts in virtue of the commission that Jesus has received—a commission that is without limit. By his authority [the church] may make disciples of all nations."[54] Donald Senior observes, "Many commentators have labeled this concluding segment of Matthew's Gospel a synthesis of the evangelist's entire message. From our perspective it should not be forgotten that this final synthesis is a *mission* charge, highlighting the dynamic thrust of the entire Gospel."[55] For the passage outlines the *how* of the church's extension of Christ's mission to all peoples. The church is called to do it just as Jesus himself had done it throughout the previous chapters of Matthew's Gospel—that is, in acts of *agapē* and healing and by reconciling the outcast and the marginalized. These are the "kingdom values" which Jesus sent the apostles out to proclaim as well as enact in Matthew chapter 10, and which they were to teach to the disciples whom they would make for him: "Going, preach [Greek, *kēryssete*] saying, 'The kingdom of heaven has drawn near.' Heal sick persons, raise dead men, cleanse lepers, cast out demons; freely you have received, freely give" (vv. 7–8). Matthew 28:19–20 presents the expectation of a missionary enterprise to the whole world, but how it expects that enterprise to go is not made explicit. Rather, one must read Matthew's whole Gospel first to understand what discipleship looks like in order to understand what mission

53. Luz, *Matthew 21–28*, 628.

54. McKenzie, "Gospel According to Matthew," art. 43, §206.

55. Senior and Stuhlmueller, *Biblical Foundations for Mission*, 251; emphasis original.

should look like. David Bosch describes the essence of that mission as to make disciples, baptize, and teach.[56] Discipleship is of prime importance for the author of Matthew's Gospel. He himself actively inserts the word into the traditional material that he has received (see e.g., Matt 8:32 and parr.). When not using the actual word, he frequently alludes to the idea with the verb, *akolouthō* ("follow").[57] Yet, as David Bosch describes, by the time Matthew (whoever he was) wrote his Gospel, the word "disciple" (*mathētēs*) had already acquired among Christians a predominantly ecclesiological meaning. "It is," Bosch writes, "against this background that we have to understand Matthew's use of the verb *mathēteusate* in 28:19."[58] For during the time of Jesus' ministry, Matthew normally prefers to use the word *kēryssō*—"to proclaim or preach"—whose practice is also often linked specifically by the evangelist with the coming of the kingdom of heaven, or God (see e.g., Matt 4:23, 9:35, 24:14, and 26:13). However, in Matt 28 when the glorified Christ, risen from the dead, appears before his eleven apostles, "proclamation" is replaced by the evangelist with "discipling." As Bosch observes, "The substitution dramatically signals the new situation which obtains for Matthew and his community: When the Master still walked this earth, proclaiming the kingdom or the gospel were appropriate terms [*sic*]; now he is himself the Kingdom and the Gospel." Discipleship, then, means entering Jesus' community, the church.[59]

Yet, these injunctions ought not to be misunderstood in any coercive or aggressive manner, as may have happened in the past and may still be a temptation in the present. For David Bosch points out that the "Great Commission" must not be divorced from the "Great Commandment" of love of God and of neighbor (see Matt 22:37–40):

> For Matthew . . . being a disciple means living out the teachings of Jesus, which the evangelist has recorded in great detail in his gospel. It is unthinkable to divorce the Christian life of love and justice from being a disciple. Discipleship involves a commitment to God's reign, to justice and love, and to obedience to the entire will of God. Mission is not narrowed down to an activity of making individuals new creatures, of providing

56. Bosch, *Transforming Mission*, 66. I would add "go" as a fourth aspect, since one would hardly have expected the apostles to have remained there on the mountain forever!

57. Bosch, "Structure of Mission," 232.

58. Bosch, "Structure of Mission," 232.

59. Bosch, "Structure of Mission," 232. Bosch seems to be relying here on the thought of Ernst Lohmeyer (see Lohmeyer, *Evangelium des Matthäus*, 418n2).

> them with "blessed assurance" so that, come what may, they will be "eternally saved." Mission involves, from the beginning and as matter of course, making new believers sensitive to the needs of others, opening their eyes and hearts to recognize injustice, suffering, oppression, and the plight of those who have fallen by the wayside.[60]

So Christians will not just be judged by how they have fulfilled Jesus' Great Commission—or not—but also by how they have fulfilled the Sermon on the Mount and all of the ethico-moral teachings of Christ—or not—in the execution of his will.

Indian biblical scholar George Soares-Prabhu blames the "christological concentration [of] the mission command" for ignoring the motivations of the missionaries and the welfare of the people—"the nations"—to whom the missionaries were sent. He worries about the sometime "aggrandisement of the missioner" at the expense of the missionized.[61] On the contrary, if anything, the Christocentrism of Matthew's text ought to direct the missioner's attention to the One who is really in charge and for whose purpose he or she has been sent out. It should recall the one who is always in control of mission. It should remind any missioner of the demeanor of Jesus, who came as a "ransom" (see Matt 20:28), who welcomed the gentile (see 8:5–13), who neither stepped on a bruised plant nor extinguished a smoldering candle (see 12:20). The focus, then, should lie on the example of Christ as it is actually communicated in Matthew's Gospel. The point is spelled out admirably by Pope Benedict XV in *Maximum Illud*: "Like his model, the Lord Jesus, the good missionary burns with charity, and he numbers even the most abandoned unbelievers among God's children, redeemed like everyone else with the ransom of the divine blood. . . . His bearing toward them is neither scornful nor fastidious; his treatment of them is neither harsh nor rough. Instead, he makes use of all the arts of Christian kindness to attract them to himself, so that he may eventually lead them into the arms of Christ, into the embrace of the Good Shepherd."[62] To the extent that missionary activity ignores its norm and model, who is Christ, then Soares-Prabhu should be rightly concerned—but, perhaps, not because Matt 28 is too Christocentric but because its actualization has not been Christocentric enough!

60. Bosch, *Transforming Mission*, 81.

61. Soares-Prabhu, "Two Mission Commands," 281–82.

62. Benedict XV, *Maximum Illud*, §28.

What has been has been. Nothing can now be done to effectively transform the historical exchanges—admittedly, not always positive—that happened centuries ago between Christian missionaries and nonbelieving peoples. The past is behind us forever. And we realize with great frustration and disappointment that other people have made decisions and given interpretations—sometimes, very wrong ones—that we, who are living now, cannot possibly change. Nevertheless, we should follow the caution that we not just presume the bad faith of previous generations, as if they had not been sincerely trying to do what they believed in conscience was the will of Christ in how to spread his gospel. Their methods would almost surely not work now, and perhaps they should have not worked ever. But in some ways, they did work. And whole populations did accept Jesus Christ as their Savior and (more importantly) have chosen to continue to accept him as such. What we can do—*what we should and must do*—no less than former Christians is: *repent*! We should identify and learn from previous mistakes, failures, and misunderstandings, and commit ourselves not to repeat them. Jesus is always and in every way the "canon" for our discernment of how to actuate his missional mandate . . . which has not changed. Matthew 28:19–20 *remains*. Against Soares-Prabhu's view, I believe that it is not a lessened Christocentrism but a more focused and vigorous one, that allows for a reading of Jesus' command that is faithful to its meaning while nevertheless attending well to how we treat others who do not believe. There should be a constant self-examination of the church's evangelizing mission in the light of the Christ: of his deeds and his message. I think that there is no doubt that, in Matt 28:19–20, Christians are given the mission by Jesus to make nonbelievers into believers of him. That is what he wants. In this way, the "kingdom of heaven" that he was sent to preach can break out ever more fully into the world. Otherwise, it remains enclosed, sectarian.

Concerns, especially among Asians, that the West still maintains a colonialist-imperialist posture towards their people are real. They see this posture exhibited, for example, in attempts by missionaries (usually, from the West) to convert their people to the Christian religion, which is the equivalent, to them, of also trying to impose Western civilization. These perceptions of the continuation of the West's previous colonizing efforts and subjugation of peoples are, as I just affirmed, real. Yet, it should be recalled that Matt 28:19–20 did not come to prominence as a "missionary" text among colonizers or subjugators. Rather, its full and true missionary import was intuited by a small, marginal group of "radical" Protestant

Christians, who were not engaged in any colonialist or imperialist enterprise to speak of.

Nevertheless, unmasking hidden agendas is important—*on both sides!* I would venture to say that, more often than is (perhaps) admitted, the discomfort with Matt 28:19–20 felt by some Asian missiologists has more to do with their espousal of a "pluralist" soteriology than with any actual, personal experience of the "colonialist" misuse of the text. The fact that many of these critics are Western educated and often rely on the assumptions of Western (liberal) ideologies only makes their critiques for me all the more ironic. In short, theologians and missiologists need to be careful here. They themselves come carrying their own baggage—some of it quite heavy—which they do not always fully lay out or admit to in their handling of Matt 28:19–20.

Yet, the standard for the church's evangelizing mission is not any one culture, society, or civilization. It is not an ideology. It is a Man, who met his disciples up on a mountain in order to confer on them the mandate to go out and make disciples of those who do not yet believe in him.

# 3

# The Lessening of Missionary Fervor

REVEREND CLARENCE DEVADASS NOTED in his talk how the missionary mandate of proclamation and conversion remains, but its significance has been lessened. While *missio ad gentes* was a constant theme throughout the documents that he surveyed during his talk, since Vatican II, the language has become "a little bit softer."[1] Proclamation is still not excluded. But the importance of the witness of a Christian life is acknowledged more. Devadass did not say how he personally viewed such a development.

I do not think that Devadass's views are unique to him. Nor do I think that they represent his own eccentricity. I think that what he states is the common judgment found among many contemporary missiologists. To stress proclamation of the message of Jesus to and conversion of nonbelievers is today an outlier position in the current missiological scene.

Of course, when pressed, Catholic missiological experts will still "tip the hat" to Christ's command to evangelize the nations. And how could they not? For that charge is recalled, explicitly and urgently, in the words of Christ himself, as well as in the rest of the New Testament.[2] It was understood as such by the church fathers from the earliest times. The author of *The Letter to the Corinthians* (ca. AD 96) declares, "The Apostles received the Gospel for us from the Lord Jesus Christ; Jesus Christ

1. Dunn, "Fr. Clarence Devadass," 50:54.

2. See e.g., Matt 28:19–20; Mark 16:15–18; Luke 24:46–48a; Acts 1:8; 10:42; 26:12–18; 1 Cor 1:17; 9:14, 16.

was sent from God. Christ, therefore, is from God and the Apostles are from Christ. . . . Receiving their orders, therefore, and being filled with confidence because of the Resurrection of the Lord Jesus Christ, and confirmed in the word of God, with full assurance of the Holy Spirit, they went forth preaching the Gospel of the Kingdom of God that was about to come."[3] Furthermore, it is found in statements of the church's magisterium, even at the highest level of authority, like the ecumenical council of Vatican II—to which I will now turn.

## Vatican II and Evangelizing Mission

The Second Vatican Council is especially relevant to this matter. This is so because it was a decided exercise of the universal episcopate's teaching authority in communion with the bishop of Rome.[4] Moreover, it addressed precisely in many places, like no other ecumenical council had ever done before, the church's fundamental relationship with those who do not believe in the message about Christ that she proclaims or who do not adhere fully to her faith or belong fully to her structure.

The Second Vatican Council issued several types of documents—namely, constitutions, decrees, and declarations.[5] The standard categori-

3. *1 Clement* 42.1–3 (Glimm, FC 1:42). It is often titled *1 Clement* because it has been traditionally attributed to the early "pope," Clement of Rome (see Holmes, *Apostolic Fathers*, 25).

4. See Dulles, *Magisterium*, 67–68.

5. Presumably, each document's title was meant to indicate the degree of teaching authority that it embodied. As theologian Francis Sullivan writes, "The Second Vatican Council issued two 'dogmatic constitutions,' one 'pastoral constitution,' one 'constitution,' nine 'decrees,' and three 'declarations.' There is no doubt about the intention of the council to indicate different levels of authority by these different titles" (Sullivan, *Creative Fidelity*, 21 [see also 46, 162–74]). Unfortunately—and this is extremely frustrating—in his whole book, which addresses specifically the matter of how to evaluate the magisterial status of church statements, Sullivan himself *never once* addresses how to assess the levels of teaching authority that might be attached to Vatican II's various documents.

As far as I know, the Catholic Church has never in her history clarified what specific level of authority should be attached to the various statements that she officially issues (or, "promulgates") at her councils. Yet that precise question did come up among the bishops during Vatican II. The General Secretariat of the Council replied that such a matter should be determined either (1) by the bishops' *explicit avowal of the level of authority* that they intended or (2) by *the overall context of solemnity* with which they chose to teach something. The reply was placed in a "notificatio" that was added to the end of each of the council's dogmatic constitutions, *Lumen Gentium* and *Dei Verbum*. I must admit that I personally do not find this reply to be very satisfying.

zation of the authoritative, magisterial force of Vatican II's documents—at least, as I learned it many years ago—runs as follows:

- First, the constitutions
- Then, the decrees
- Finally, the declarations[6]

This categorization makes sense to me. It would seem reasonable to assume that the church's solemn statements about what "constitutes" her necessary and established belief would be expected to be taken more seriously than any other kind. A "constitution," then, would seem to have more magisterial weight than a statement that was simply meant to "decree" changes in the application or practice of the church's doctrine—or, for that matter, to barely "declare" on a novel (and possibly, controverted) issue what the church currently thinks.[7]

---

For a brief summation of the documents' status from a canon lawyer's point of view, see Morrisey, "Papal and Curial Pronouncements," 111–12.

6. The council also produced "messages"—but these are difficult to categorize. Indeed, the council's first official *actum* was to issue a "Message to Humanity" (see Abbott and Gallagher, *Documents of Vatican II*, 1–7). Near the end of the council, the bishops sent out even more "messages" to various groups throughout the world: rulers, women, workers, youth, and so forth. They are reproduced in Abbott and Gallagher, *Documents of Vatican II* (see 728–37). As far as I know, this is the only collection of Vatican II documents in English to include them. I cannot recall at any time, however, when I have encountered someone citing Vatican II's "messages" with any kind of magisterial authority—if they are mentioned at all. Though perhaps I have spoken too soon: while doing research for this book, I happened across an article by church historian Alberto Melloni in *The Oxford Handbook of Vatican II*, in which he decries the "expung[ing]" of the messages from the official corpus of Vatican II documents (see Melloni, "Expunged and Forgotten Texts," 136–39). Be that as it may, my assumption is that their magisterial value must nevertheless be quite low.

7. Interestingly, although I learned this ordering many decades ago (somewhere, from someone), it was only recently that I stumbled upon a confirmatory source for it—namely, Bishop Marcos McGrath of the Diocese of Santiago de Veraguas, Panama. While at a "presser" held during the council by the American bishops, Bishop McGrath explained the situation to quizzical reporters. His comments are summarized thusly:

> The binding force of the various designations for council documents . . . must be established by reference to the thinking of the present council, not by invoking documents of past councils [said the bishop]. At the Council of Trent in the 16th century the most important documents were decrees, he said, and at the First Vatican Council in the 19th century the two documents issued were both constitutions.
>
> The practice in the present council has been to designate *those documents the Fathers consider most important as constitutions. Decrees are of lesser importance* with reference to the supreme teaching authority of the

Furthermore, it does seem to have become the settled opinion among the church's leadership that the council's four "constitutions" comprise its most magisterially significant documents and, hence, stand at the highest level of the exercise of its teaching authority. This was the view enunciated by the bishops who attended the 1985 Extraordinary Synod in Rome. In the Synod's *Final Report*, it stated that Vatican II's constitutions were "the interpretative key" for all the other statements issued by the council.[8]

In brief, what do these statements of the highest magisterial authority tell us about the church's evangelizing mission?

Let us begin with the council's Dogmatic Constitution on the Church (1964). As with the apostles before them, it states the bishops have been sent by Christ himself to go out to all nations, proclaiming his "good news" to non-Christians. They do this so that all men and women might be saved by accepting the gospel message, by being baptized, and by living the demands of the Christian life.[9] The church is impelled to go out on her mission of fully establishing the church in order to bring about the realization of God's plan. She proclaims to the world the message that God has made Jesus Christ the source of salvation for all men: "By the proclamation of the Gospel [the church] prepares her hearers to receive and profess the faith. She gives them the dispositions necessary for baptism, snatches them from the slavery of error and of idols and incorporates them in Christ so that through charity they may grow up into full maturity in Christ."[10] Her mission is not singularly negative though—that is, to take people away from religious error. It also comprises the positive aspect of recovering whatever is good in human beings and their lifestyles, of raising up of these goods to an even higher supernatural status, of turning them fully to the happiness of men, and of releasing them from the influence of any evil.[11]

---

> Church, *and so finally are declarations.* (Anderson, *Council Daybook*, 262; emphasis added)

I am extremely grateful to Christian Washburn's article (Washburn, "Theological Priority," 116n39) for having finally put the matter to rest for me!

8. 1985 Extraordinary Synod, *Final Report*, §1.5. Another somewhat different translation can be found in *New York Times*, "Text of Final Report."

9. Vatican II, *Lumen Gentium*, §24.

10. Vatican II, *Lumen Gentium*, §17.

11. Vatican II, *Lumen Gentium*, §17.

The council's Dogmatic Constitution on Divine Revelation (1965) maintains that God reveals himself to human beings in order to save them. In other words, God desires to bring all people into an everlasting relationship of love and happiness with him. In order to pass on the knowledge of his salvific revelation, God enters into direct relationship with humanity by sending his Son, Jesus, in whom God's revelation to humankind is fulfilled and completed. Yet, this relationship needs to be known, needs to be experienced. So Jesus sends out his followers to tell all men and women about what God has done in him. This is the "good news" which they bring: "the source of all saving truth and moral teaching."[12]

The Pastoral Constitution on the Church in the Modern World (1965) reiterates that it is the church's universal mission to proclaim the gospel and bestow God's grace. By doing these things, she ensures peace among men as well as their brotherly cooperation through her role of imparting the knowledge of God's spiritual and natural laws.[13] Moreover, the church exists to shed on the whole world the brightness of the "good news" of Christ and "to unify under one Spirit" all people of whichever country, color, or society.[14]

In the Constitution on the Sacred Liturgy (1963), the bishops of Vatican II acknowledge that no one can come to the worship of God without having first been called to faith in and conversion to him. But how can human beings come to God unless someone is sent to them to preach the word about Christ (see Rom 10:14–15)? "Therefore," the bishops continue, "the Church announces the good tidings of salvation to those who do not believe, so that all men may know the true God and Jesus Christ Whom He has sent, and may be converted from their ways, doing penance."[15]

So what can we glean from these references?

First, Christians have been sent out into the world to proclaim the message about Jesus. They need to tell others what God has effectuated for all peoples by having sent his Son as the messiah of the Jews. God's salvation, effected through Jesus' sacrificial death and glorious resurrection, is linked to the eternal destiny of every man and woman. Mankind has come from God, and humanity seeks him in its religions. In Christ,

12. Vatican II, *Dei Verbum*, §7.

13. Vatican II, *Gaudium et Spes*, §89.

14. Vatican II, *Gaudium et Spes*, §92.

15. Vatican II, *Sacrosanctum Concilium*, §9 (see also §6).

however, God shows humankind how to find the fullness of life and to return to him.

Second, the church is the extension of Christ's saving presence among humanity, existing solely and by design to achieve this will of God—namely, that all men and women be saved in his Son, whom the author of the First Letter to Timothy declares to be the only mediator of salvation (see 1 Tim 2:3–6a). It is this reality which establishes the church's own special and unique status in regards to the salvific will of God. Jesus, the one and only Savior, has chosen to offer his salvation to Israel and to the world through his one and only body, the church (see Eph 1:22–23)—which is even called by the Sacred Scriptures his "wife" (Rev 21:9).[16]

Third, Christian mission by its definition cannot be—or, at least, it should not be—self-centered or self-referential. Christians have not been sent out into the world to establish another particular social group with its own interests. Granted, as with any social group, there is the process of "routinizing" the charisma of its founder so that it might be preserved and extended for the benefit not only of the group's members but also of others. This involves the group's self-perpetuation as well as its own preservation. I do not think anyone needs to apologize for these aspects. Indeed, they are necessary for any group . . . unless that group wants eventually to become extinct! Yet, the church is not merely establishing herself among men and women but the presence of her Lord, Jesus Christ. The church exists to tell the world that God's saving will has been accomplished in his Son. It is God's plan that has been realized in Jesus: the "king" has sent the ultimate agent of his rule (see Matt 6:10a, Mark 1:15)! Moreover, the church's members have been charged by that One, Jesus, who has the right and the power to give such a command, to cooperate actively in bringing about God's rule among men. The church, then, is not just a social witness before the world of what God has done in his Son. Her role is not simply to state baldly the event and, then, play no further role. Her role, on the contrary, is to actively bring about the reign of the "king" through his Son, Jesus.

16. See e.g., John Paul II, *Redemptoris Missio*, §18. See also CDF, *Dominus Iesus*, §§16–22. In §21 of that document, the CDF warns, "It is clear that it would be contrary to the faith to consider the Church as one way of salvation alongside those constituted by the other religions, seen as complementary to the Church or substantially equivalent to her."

## What Is Jesus' Vision of His Followers' Mission?

How this should be done was spelled out by the Lord Jesus when he sent his followers out on various "mission trips."

For example, in Matthew's Gospel, chapter 10, Jesus sends the twelve apostles throughout Palestine in order to extend the influence of his own activity: "These Twelve Jesus sent, instructing them, and saying: . . . 'Going, preach saying, "The kingdom of heaven has drawn near." Heal sick persons, raise dead men, cleanse lepers, cast out demons; freely you have received, freely give'" (Matt 5a, 7–8).[17] They are given several commands by the Master: Go! . . . Proclaim! . . . Heal! . . . Raise the dead! . . . Cleanse! . . . Exorcise! . . . Give! (see vv. 6–8). In other words, they are to go out and preach Christ's message, to do his works, and to give unto others as he has given of himself to them.

Yet, each of these imperatives reveals something of the blemishes that his disciples will find in the nonbelieving world's condition.

For why does Christ tell his followers to "go," if the spiritual condition of nonbelievers is satisfactory to begin with? What is the point? Why should they be disturbed? Why is Jesus so keen on proclamation?

"And [Jesus] said to [the apostles]: 'Going into the whole world preach the gospel to every creature'" (Mark 16:15). What message do his followers have to announce to others that is lacking in the religious beliefs of non-Christians? Why is it necessary that knowledge of Jesus' presence be made explicit to others? Is he not already present among them? Or why do others need to know about *him* in particular: What does Jesus supply to nonbelievers that their own gods or spirits or religious figures do not?

Heal, raise, and cleanse, Jesus commands. But the act of healing or cleansing implies a defect. Does this not suggest that, without Jesus, the religious aspirations of non-Christians are unfulfilled and unsafe? Does it not also imply that the spiritual state of those who do not follow Jesus is, in some way, unhealthy and impure? Moreover, only Jesus himself holds a power over death that no other religious figure has. And, it is through his followers, the church, that he chooses to give life to humanity in a way that no other (human) religion ever could.

17. It is not altogether clear from the Gospels about how many times Jesus might have done this. The Gospel According to Luke records two sendings: one sending of the twelve apostles (see 9:1–6, 10) and another sending of a larger group of his disciples (see 10:1–12, 17–20). The Gospel of Mark, however, only records one sending of Christ's disciples on mission—and it is only the Twelve who are sent (see 6:6b–13, 30).

Cast out demons! Jesus prepares his followers for the expectation that they will encounter a world that is in the thrall of his spiritual enemies. These evil forces, which can include human beings, do not just seek to resist and block the proclamation of the "good news" of God's kingdom by Jesus; they also array themselves specifically against Jesus himself:

> And you shall be hateful to everyone for the sake of my name. (Mark 13:13a; see also Matt 10:22 and Luke 21:17)

And:

> Blessed shall you be, when men will hate you and when they will separate you and reproach you and cast out your name as evil for the sake of the Son of Man. Rejoice on that day and jump around, for behold your reward is great in heaven; for according to these things did their fathers to the prophets. (Luke 6:22)

And:

> If the world hates you, know that it has had hatred for me before you. If you had been of the world, the world would love what is its own; that you truly are not of the world, but I have chosen you from the world, therefore the world hates you. Remember the word, which I said to you: The slave is not greater than his master. If they have persecuted me, they will also persecute you. . . . But all these things they will do to you for the sake of my name, because they do not know him, who has sent me. (John 15:18–21)[18]

Notice that it is *Jesus specifically* who is opposed. Hardly anywhere does Jesus tell his followers that they will be hated and persecuted on account of their proclamation of the kingdom of God.[19] Rather, they will be hated and persecuted on account of *whom* they follow—that is, for the Messenger and not for the message.

How often does one hear the non-Christian world rail against Christians for opening schools? Or taking care of the poor and hungry?

18. As can be seen from the above quotations, the existence of humanity's hate-filled opposition to Jesus himself is attested at almost all levels of the gospel tradition (i.e., in Mark, the "Q" source, and John).

19. Though Jesus does say that "the one who will lose his life on account of me and the gospel, he shall save it" (Mark 8:35). Yet, he seems to be equating himself with the message. He also says that "the kingdom" suffers violence and is violently taken (see Matt 11:12; also Luke 16:16); and mention is made of those who are persecuted "for the sake of justice" (see Matt 5:10).

Or opening hospitals to treat the sick and dying? Or advocating for social outcasts? Few seem to oppose such things—even if it does seem at times that Christians are imposing their own moral beliefs on non-Christian societies. Yet, opposition hardly emerges. For example, opening a school for girls in India is acceptable, although it breaks long-standing, cultural taboos against educating females and their proper place in society. Bringing medicine into tribal societies in the Amazon is seen as completely appropriate, although it challenges their reliance on traditional methods, which often involve the use of shamans. Donatus Nahak described during the panel discussion how he was involved in giving "Bible studies" to native peoples throughout PNG where natural disasters had occurred. These studies were meant to disabuse them of their religious worldview, which saw adverse natural events as the result of having displeased God or of another tribe's having cursed them. But Nahak and his fellow Christians were trying to convince them that, on the contrary, the disasters were happening as a result of human-caused "climate change." And who could really disagree with such activities since the logic is so clear and the social benefits are so obvious?

But do *not* bring up Jesus!

In that case, a line has been crossed. It is then a matter of a "triumphalist" Christianity seeking to impose its "exclusivist" claims about its "constitutive" Savior on others. It is not the ethics of Jesus that draws men's ire; it is his status. The world can accept Jesus of Nazareth as just another holy man, but it will not tolerate him as the "Son of the most high God" (Mark 5:7).[20]

The bishops of Vatican II recognized that it might be possible to find the presence of grace, truth, and holiness in the religious quests of nonbelievers. However, they did not ignore the fact that, when going out

20. I am reminded here of the famous statement made by C. S. Lewis:

> I am trying here to prevent anyone saying the really foolish thing that people often say about [Jesus]: "I'm ready to accept Jesus as a great moral teacher, but I don't accept His claim to be God." That is the one thing we must not say. A man who was merely a man and said the sort of things Jesus said would not be a great moral teacher. He would either be a lunatic—on a level with the man who says he is a poached egg—or else he would be the Devil of Hell. You must make your choice. Either this man was, and is, the Son of God: or else a madman or something worse. You can shut Him up for a fool, you can spit at Him and kill Him as a demon; or you can fall at His feet and call Him Lord and God. But let us not come with any patronising nonsense about His being a great human teacher. He has not left that open to us. He did not intend to. (Lewis, *Mere Christianity*, 43)

into the world, the church enters into a direct struggle with evil: "By the proclamation of the Gospel [the church] prepares her hearers to receive and profess the faith. She . . . snatches them from the slavery of error and of idols [*a servitute erroris eripit*]. Through her work, whatever good is in the minds and hearts of men, whatever good lies latent in the religious practices and cultures of diverse peoples, is not only saved from destruction but is also cleansed, raised up and perfected unto the glory of God, the confusion of the devil [*daemonis*] and the happiness of man."[21] According to one of St. Paul's accounts of his vision of Jesus on the road to Damascus, the Lord sent him forth to open the eyes of the gentiles "that they may be converted from darkness to light and from the power of Satan to God, that they may accept forgiveness of sins and a destiny among those made holy through faith, which is in me" (Acts 26:18). Indeed, as soon as anyone approaches the church in order to be "illuminated" through the sacrament of baptism, the church begins the process of engaging with the hostile forces of evil that oppose that person's decision. From olden times, in the liturgies of both East and West, one sees various rites of exorcism pronounced over those seeking to join the Christian religion. These occur both during their preparation for baptism and during the baptismal rite itself. For example, the ancient church order, *The Apostolic Tradition*, requires that as candidates approach the day of their baptism, the bishop ought to lay his hands on them in exorcism every day![22] After a time of instruction (*katēchēsis*), those who have been chosen for the sacrament of baptism—the "elect"—are scrutinized on several occasions regarding aspects of the faith. Each time, the sacred minister pronounces a minor exorcism over the individuals seeking baptism. Through this series of exorcisms, the church adjures the devil and all other evil forces in the name of Jesus to flee from the baptismal candidate, who has already been chosen for Christ. In the modern liturgy of the Roman church, during the elect's Third Scrutiny given on the Fifth Sunday of Lent, the sacred minister prays,

> Father,
> source of all life,
> in giving life to the living you seek out the image of your glory

21. Vatican II, *Lumen Gentium*, §17 (see Tanner, *Decrees*, 2:862). The English translation that the Vatican reproduces on its website is based on an earlier one which, as can be seen above, sometimes deviates from the official Latin text.

22. Hippolytus, *Apostolic Tradition* 20. See Bradshaw et al., *Apostolic Tradition*, 104 (that is, according to the Coptic and Arabic recensions of the document).

and in raising the dead you reveal your unbounded power.
Rescue these elect from the tyranny of death,
for they long for new life through baptism.
Free them from the slavery of Satan,
the source of sin and death,
who seeks to corrupt the world you created
and saw to be good.
Place them under the reign of your beloved Son,
that they may share in the power of his resurrection
and give witness to your glory before all.[23]

In certain places where false worship is common, the local bishop may require the sacred minister to include a previous exorcism whenever admitting a non-Christian into the group of those being instructed in the faith. After blowing on the face of the candidate, the sacred minister declares,

By the breath of your mouth, O Lord,
drive away the spirits of evil.
Command them to depart.
For your kingdom has come among us.[24]

The witness of the East, both Orthodox and Catholic, confirms these practices. The Eastern liturgies contain several exorcisms during the

23. Catholic Church, *Christian Initiation of Adults*, 107 (§175, option B). This comes from the Roman liturgy revised after Vatican II. The older Roman liturgy features several exorcistic rituals in its baptismal rite, wherein the church's sacred minister pulls no punches in deprecating the forces of evil. For example, he says,

> I cast thee out, unclean Spirit [*sic*]. . . . Depart and vanish from this servant . . . of God. . . . For it is He Who commands thee, thou doomed and accursed one, He Whose feet trod the waves, Who reached out His saving hand to Peter when [Peter] began to sink.
>
> Wherefore, accursed demon, admit thy doom, and pay honor to the true and living God, pay honor to Jesus Christ, His son and to the Holy Spirit, and keep far from this servant . . . of God. For Jesus Christ . . . has graciously called him . . . to His holy grace and blessing, and to the fountain of baptism. And this sign of the holy Cross which we trace on his brow . . . , do thou, accursed demon, never dare to violate. (Weller, *Sacraments and Processions*, 93, 95 [§21])

At another point, the sacred minister commands, "Get thee gone, unclean spirit, and pay honor to the living and true God. Depart, thou unclean spirit, and give place to Jesus Christ, His Son. Get thee afar back, unclean spirit, and make way for the Holy Spirit, the Consoler" (Weller, *Sacraments and Processions*, 113 [§37]).

24. Catholic Church, *Christian Initiation of Adults*, 33 (§71).

baptismal liturgy. In the First Exorcism over the baptizand, the bishop or priest declares,

> The Lord forbiddeth thee, O devil, He that came into the world and made His abode among men, that He might cast down thy tyranny and deliver men. . . . I forbid thee by God, Who hath revealed the Tree of Life. . . . Be forbidden! For I forbid thee by Him that walketh upon the waves of the sea . . . and Who forbiddeth the storms of the winds; Whose glance dries up the deeps, and Whose interdict makes the mountains melt away. For it is He Himself that now forbiddeth thee through us. Be afraid, begone, and depart from this creature, and return not again. . . . Begone, and depart from the sealed, newly-elect soldier of Christ our God! For I forbid thee by Him that rideth upon the wings of the winds, Who maketh His Angels spirits, and His Ministers a flaming fire. Begone, and depart from this creature, with all thy powers and thine angels.[25]

And so we see in the church's own prayer her clear belief that she is locked in battle with the forces of evil and darkness, fighting for and redeeming the soul of the nonbeliever from the devil.

But we also need to hear the testimony of the church fathers. In his lectures that he gave sometime in the mid-fourth century to those preparing for baptism, St. Cyril of Jerusalem states the value and purpose of these exorcisms:

> Let your feet hasten to the catechisings; receive with earnestness the exorcisms: whether thou be breathed upon or exorcised, the act is to you salvation. Suppose you have gold unwrought and alloyed, mixed with various substances, copper, and tin, and iron, and lead: we seek to have the gold alone; can gold be purified from the foreign substances without fire? Even so without exorcisms the soul cannot be purified. . . . As those who are skilled in the goldsmith's craft throw in their breath upon the fire through certain delicate instruments, and blowing up the gold which is hidden in the crucible stir the flame which surrounds it . . . even so when the exorcists inspire terror by the Spirit of God, and set the soul, as it were, on fire in the crucible of the body, the hostile demon flees away, and there abide salvation and the hope of eternal life, and the soul henceforth is cleansed from its sins and has salvation.[26]

25. Saint Tikhon's Monastery, *Holy Mysteries*, 20.
26. Cyril of Jerusalem, *Catechetical Lectures*, procatechesis 9 (Gifford, *NPNF*$^2$ 7:3).

One need not accept the traditional view that evil spirits actually inhabit the souls of the unbaptized, as if they were already from birth demon-possessed. Yet, having chosen to follow the promptings of the evil one, rather than those of the good God, the first humans perverted human nature's likeness (*similitudo*) to God and willed to place themselves in some fashion under the control of the devil. Adam and Eve chose for themselves and for us to have Satan as their master. The church, in the name of God's Christ, wrests this control back. As blessed Augustine writes, "That is the reason . . . even little children are breathed upon and exorcized, so that the hostile power of the devil who deceived mankind in order to gain possession of men may be driven out of them. It is not, then, a creature of God that is breathed upon and exorcised in infants, but him under whose sway all are who are born with sin, for he is the prince of sinners."[27] It is with reason, then, that the bishops of Vatican II claimed that by bringing Jesus to the nonbelieving nations, the church aids Christ in liberating God's hidden presence among humans from the contagion of evil. Through the church, Jesus overthrows the control (*imperium*) of the devil and causes bewilderment among the evil spirits.[28]

Finally, Jesus commands his followers in Matt 10 to "give." Why would Jesus say to give, if others already have? What benefit does he intend?

Each of Christ's statements in Matt 10 implies some kind of lack: the lack of his presence, the lack of knowledge of his message, the lack of completeness or virtue, the lack of freedom. Whether these "lacks" are partial or complete is not specified. Presumably, not everyone whom Jesus encountered was without the presence or knowledge of God or his kingdom. Not everyone he encountered lacked virtue or righteousness or goodness. On the contrary, to the scribe, Jesus declares, "You are not far from the kingdom of God" (Mark 12:34). Even Jesus marvels at the faith of non-Jews, like the Roman centurion: "Amen I say to you, with none have I found such faith in Israel!" (Matt 8:10; see also Luke 7:9). And the Gospels record that it is another Roman soldier, likely a pagan, who recognizes Jesus' exalted status: "Truly this man was Son of God" (Mark 15:39 // Matt 27:54). What is clear to me is that it is Jesus alone, Jesus uniquely, who has the power to completely and fully remedy whatever is lacking in humanity's condition. The scribe recognized *Jesus* as the true

27. Augustine, *Creed* 1.2 (Liguori, FC 27:291).

28. See Vatican II, *Ad Gentes*, §9.

teacher of the kingdom of God; the pagan centurion had faith *in him and his authority*; the heathen soldier at the cross proclaimed *his exalted status*. It was Jesus whom they were ultimately needing and honoring.

## The Loss of Fervor in the Church's Evangelizing Mission

Getting back to Devadass's original comment above, I would ask, If Christ's missionary mandate has been lessened or softened, then . . . by whom?

Certainly not by the church.

For instance, consider the homily of Pope St. Paul VI at the ordination of Louis Vangeke, PNG's first native bishop. The pope declares,

> The missionary mandate, "Go, therefore, and make disciples of all nations" (Matth. 28: 19), is always relevant. Throughout the centuries Jesus Christ repeats to all classes of the baptized His missionary command: "As the Father sent me, so am I sending you" (Io. 20: 21). Our missionary duty finds its origin in this order. It finds its source in the merciful love of the Father for all mankind, without distinction of persons. . . . God chose to rely on men to be the bearers of his Gospel, the stewards of his grace, and the builders of his Kingdom. Who can claim that this is no concern of his? Since there is a variety of conditions of life, and, consequently, different ways of giving a response, every member of the Church is reached by this call which is directed to each and every one. The whole Church is missionary, for Her missionary activity, as the recent Council so forcibly reminded us, is an essential part of Her vocation. To forget it or to carry it out carelessly would be, on our part, a betrayal of our Master. We are dealing with a fundamental impulse, a duty of the first order, one which we must all accept, without leaving any room for doubt or limitation.[29]

The pope is clear: the church everywhere exists to convert people to Christ. The essence of that conversionary mission is not "proselytism," often understood as coercing or fooling someone into belief. Rather, it is the manifestation and sharing of God's mercy and love with the world. All Christians are called to this mission, albeit according to each one's

29. Paul VI, "Bishop Born in New Guinea." (PNG was still an administered territory of Australia at the time.)

state of life. Not everyone can be a missionary, going to foreign lands to preach and labor. Moreover, not everyone can even proclaim his or her faith in Christ openly in some places due to the surrounding culture or society. Circumstance certainly comes into play, whether one were to live under an anti-religious regime, like in North Korea, or in a nation like Devadass's Malaysia, where the Christian message is suppressed. Yet each one is called in his or her own way to find a place for proclamation. The call is not softened; it remains a first-order principle of the church's life.

That homily was given in 1970. Five years later there came St. Paul VI's apostolic exhortation *Evangelii Nuntiandi* (1975). That the exhortation should have needed to have been written at all, and came to be written in the way that it was, should have alerted the church's leadership that there was a serious disturbance among Catholics regarding the church's traditional understanding of her evangelizing mission. Only a decade after Vatican II, something was seriously wrong.

Although ultimately coming from the pope, the document was supposed to have been the work of the 1974 Synod of Bishops in Rome. The topic that had been chosen for that event was the church's evangelization of the contemporary world. Due to a variety of reasons, the results of the synod were inconclusive. The bishops could not come together on a final statement, deciding instead to submit their reflections to the pope for sorting out. The result of that synthesis was *Evangelii Nuntiandi*.[30]

This is not the place for me to summarize the pope's whole statement. I would rather focus on one thing.

In a lengthy section near the end of the exhortation, the pope vigorously attacks any claim that would call into question or otherwise soften the church's mission of proclaiming the gospel to nonbelievers.[31] He points to a lack of fervor for mission among some in the church. (And by *mission*, it is clear that St. Paul VI means the proclamation of the gospel for the purpose of converting nonbelievers to Christ. He does not mean the broader reality, now called *evangelizing mission*.) This lack of fervor comes from within the church, he writes, and manifests itself "in fatigue,

30. Belgian theologian Jacques Dupuis summarized the Synod in his article "Synod of Bishops." Later in his career, Dupuis pronounced a sour judgment on the pope's exhortation that had resulted from the Synod. In his view, the pope merely resumed the "Fulfillment Theory" of religions, which Dupuis considered outdated. The pope did not reflect some of the more thoughtful and farsighted views expressed among the bishops, especially from Asia. See Dupuis, *Toward a Christian Theology*, 171–73.

31. Paul VI, *Evangelii Nuntiandi*, §80.

disenchantment, compromise, lack of interest and above all lack of joy and hope."[32]

But then there comes a shocking statement: the pope admits that some are able to defend their lack of missionary fervor by appealing to Vatican II's documents themselves! He writes, "Thus one too frequently [*saepius*] hears it said, in various terms, that to impose a truth, be it that of the Gospel, or to impose a way, be it that of salvation, cannot but be a violation of religious liberty. Besides, it is added, why proclaim the Gospel when the whole world is saved by uprightness of heart? We know likewise that the world and history are filled with 'seeds of the Word'; is it not therefore an illusion to claim to bring the Gospel where it already exists in the seeds that the Lord Himself has sown?"[33] According to Vatican II's opening message to the world, the bishops committed themselves to "take pains so to present . . . God's truth in its integrity and purity that [men and women] may understand it and gladly assent to it."[34] But then, it would seem that something had gone very wrong here, if Catholics were now finding it possible to question the church's traditional understanding of her "mission" based on the bishops' texts at Vatican II. Although the pope calls these excuses "most deceitful [*insidiosissimi*]" and based on a "thoughtless [*inconsiderate*]" reading of the council, he cannot however deny that such readings are possible since he must rebut them with his own selected texts from Vatican II.[35] But why should he have had to? This is a question for another place—indeed, another book—which I will not treat here. I mention it, though.

One might recall here the complaint that Archbishop Francesco Panfilo stated above during a question period at the symposium, about how as a young priest he had heard Catholics openly questioning the church's missionary endeavors. Why, they asked, was the church still sending out missionaries to non-Christians? Instead, their cry was, "Remove your sandals, because God is already present!" The allusion, of course, is to the story of Moses's encounter with God in the burning bush (see Exod 3). The implication is that when encountering nonbelievers

32. Paul VI, *Evangelii Nuntiandi*, §80.

33. Paul VI, *Evangelii Nuntiandi*, §80. See Paulus VI, "Episcopos, Sacerdotes et Christifideles," §80 (73).

34. See "Message to Humanity," in Abbott and Gallagher, *Documents of Vatican II*, 4.

35. See Paulus VI, "Episcopos, Sacerdotes et Christifideles," §80 (73). For example, from the council's Declaration on Religious Liberty (*Dignitatis Humanae*) and its Decree on the Missionary Activity of the Church (*Ad Gentes*).

and their religions, the Christian missionary already stands on holy ground, like Moses, in the presence of the Almighty (see vv. 5–6). While I appreciate the good will and positive outlook that (I assume) lie behind the statement, I am concerned that it could be used—and has been used—in a fashion that relativizes the unique and exclusive character not just of God's revelation to Israel but also of his revelation in Jesus, Israel's messiah. On the contrary, instead of removing their sandals, Christians ought to proclaim the One whose sandals no one is worthy to unloose (see Mark 1:7 and parr.)!

## Excursus on the "Theology of Religion(s)"

It is not my purpose here to enter into a full-blown "theology of religions." Rather, my concern is to challenge certain assumptions that one finds in some Christian religious-pluralist theologies. The main assumption is that because it might be true to say that God is somehow actively present among human beings, that presence must also necessarily amount to a kind of "revelation." What is more, it amounts to a revelation that is just as unique, definitive, and salvific as the one that the church believes has been given in Jesus Christ.

If it is taken for granted that God is already present among nonbelievers, then some questions are raised. First, where and how is God present? According to St. Thomas Aquinas, God is present to all beings as the active source and cause of their existence. He is further present through his almighty power by which he has made everything and keeps it in existence. He is also present by his all-encompassing knowledge, which wisely orders and directs all things according to their final end, which is he.[36] So it is undoubtedly true to say that God is present everywhere, among all his creation. His presence extends from the "event horizon" of a black hole to the sap-filled trunk of a maple tree, from the boson particle of an atom to the fur of the elk strutting through its forest. God made them all; and he keeps them in existence. He knows them and their needs. God is present, at the very least, in the fact that *anything* should exist in the first place. As taught in the Sacred Scriptures, God is most especially and intensely present in mankind. In the Book of Genesis, man's creation is not merely an object of divine command as it is with all of the other creatures of the cosmos. Rather, God deliberates over the

36. See Thomas Aquinas, *Summa Theologiae* 1.8. See also *CCC*, §300.

creation of the human being: "And God said: 'Let us make a man . . .'" (Gen 1:26). Moreover, he declares that man should be like him: "[made] to Our image and likeness" (v. 26; see also 1:27 and 9:6). These acts occur with no other creature. As the bishops of Vatican II have so profoundly recognized, the human being is the only creature that God has created for himself.[37]

The human soul is not an abstraction; it is not a theoretical aspect of human personhood. It is real, and it constitutes a part of a man's essence. It is a man's or woman's connection to God. Saint Thomas Aquinas recognizes that the human being has a rational soul, which allows God to actuate his image within him or her in several ways:

- In humankind's "natural aptitude for understanding and loving God" (which is common to all)
- In a man's response to God's grace by which he or she comes to know and love God
- Through a man's perfect knowledge and love of God by which he or she becomes "blessed"[38]

The *Catechism of the Catholic Church* expresses it nicely: "The human person: with his openness to truth and beauty, his sense of moral goodness, his freedom and the voice of his conscience, with his longings for the infinite and for happiness, man questions himself about God's existence. In all this he discerns signs of his spiritual soul. The soul, the 'seed of eternity we bear in ourselves, irreducible to the merely material' [Vatican II, *Gaudium et Spes*, §18], can have its origin only in God."[39] Obviously, these conditions apply to all who are called *human*—both male and female, both Christian and non-Christian. But how? I would say that it is in and through religion, whether in a developed or a more inchoate form, that human beings investigate their connection to God in the soul and search out the source and cause of their existence. As the *Catechism of the Catholic Church* teaches, "*Man is in search of God*. In the act of creation, God calls every being from nothingness into existence. 'Crowned with glory and honor,' man is, after the angels, capable of acknowledging 'how majestic is the name of the Lord in all the earth' [Ps 8:1, 5]. Even after losing through his sin his likeness to God, man remains an image

37. See Vatican II, *Gaudium et Spes*, §24.

38. See Thomas Aquinas, *Summa Theologiae* 1.93.

39. *CCC*, §33.

of his Creator, and retains the desire for the one who calls him into existence. All religions bear witness to men's essential search for God."[40]

From a certain traditional perspective, found in the Sacred Scriptures and sacred tradition and enunciated in the church's magisterium, the beliefs and practices of humankind's religions are not simply wrong but foolish (see e.g., the Book of Wisdom, chs. 11–15).[41] They are even manifestations of evil (see 1 Cor 10:20–21). The second-century-AD apologist Clement of Alexandria writes,

> But you [pagans] say it is not creditable to subvert the customs handed down to us from our fathers. And why, then, do we not still use our first nourishment, milk, to which our nurses accustomed us from the time of our birth? Why do we increase or diminish our patrimony, and not keep it exactly the same as we got it? . . . Why do we not still vomit on our parents' breasts, or still do the things for which, when infants, and nursed by our mothers, we were laughed at . . . ? Then, if excesses in the indulgence of the passions, though pernicious and dangerous, yet are accompanied with pleasure, why [should] we not in the conduct of life abandon that usage which is evil, and provocative of passion, and godless, even should our fathers feel hurt, and betake ourselves to the truth, and seek Him who is truly our Father, rejecting custom as a deleterious drug?[42]

In their Bull of Union with the Copts, the bishops of the Council of Florence declare,

> [The Catholic Church] firmly believes, professes and preaches that never was anyone, conceived by a man and a woman, liberated from the devil's dominion except by faith in our lord Jesus Christ, the mediator between God and humanity. . . . He alone by his death overthrew the enemy of the human race, cancelling our sins, and unlocked the entrance to the heavenly kingdom, which the first man by his sin had locked against himself and all his posterity. . . .
>
> It firmly believes, professes and preaches that all those who are outside the catholic church, not only pagans but also Jews or heretics and schismatics, cannot share in eternal life and will go

40. *CCC*, §2566; italics in original.

41. In the allocution *Salvete Fratres* to the bishops of Vatican II, His Holiness Pope St. Paul VI noted how the church was painfully aware that humanity's religions contained "gaps, defects, and errors" (Paulus VI, "Seconda Sessione"; my translation).

42. Clement of Alexandria, *Exhortation to the Greeks* 10 (Wilson, *ANF* 2:197).

> *into the everlasting fire which was prepared for the devil and his angels* [Matt 25:41], unless they are joined to the catholic church before the end of their lives.[43]

Of course, in the current theological climate after Vatican II, which assumes a more positive and optimistic outlook on humanity's spiritual endeavors, such traditional caveats about other religions can be for some a source of embarrassment. But they cannot be swept under the rug. They still bear the character of authority (especially the Sacred Scriptures) and cannot simply be discarded because we, moderns, do not now like what they say. On the contrary, we should endeavor to find a way to join them to the novel, albeit valid, perspective of the postconciliar church. We can still acknowledge and rejoice in truth and goodness, while still being mindful of what is imperfect, lacking, or erroneous.

I do not think that it can be claimed, as has been done sometimes in the past, that the panoply of humankind's spirituo-religious efforts has little or no value, either for humans or for God. On the contrary, the church has maintained from her earliest days that humanity's religions could serve, at the very least, as preparatory vehicles for the reception of God's saving revelation in his Son, Jesus Christ.[44] So they are not *necessarily* spiritually valueless. Perhaps they may be in the hands of men—but not for a God who wishes all to be saved and to come to the knowledge of the truth (see 1 Tim 2:4). If God can breathe his Spirit into the mud of the earth, making it into a living creature (see Gen 2:7), then I believe that he can use the elements found in mankind's religions, elementary as well as complex, no matter how erroneous or distorted by evil, to bring men to the threshold of everlasting life. This view seems to be confirmed somewhat by the declaration "On the Unicity and Salvific Universality of Jesus Christ and the Church" (2000) of the Congregation for the Doctrine of the Faith, approved by Pope St. John Paul II. In it, the CDF allows that the religious figures and positive elements of humanity's religions may act as cooperative and participated mediations in the salvation of those who accept them.[45] But I think this should be added: if God does use humanity's religions at all as instruments of his salvific will, then it is *God* who chooses to use them as pathways leading to him. Humans

43. Tanner, *Decrees*, 1:575, 578; italics in original.

44. The most famous example being Eusebius of Caesarea's fourth-century-AD work *The Preparation for the Gospel*.

45. See CDF, *Dominus Iesus*, §14.

make them for themselves—and, God may use them—but humans do not make them for God. Moreover, if they are used, they are used solely for *God's purpose*, which is to restore humanity to the divine image and likeness. Even more so, *God* chooses how he will effect his purpose. The Sacred Scriptures tell us how the Father has done this: "And a voice came from the cloud saying, 'This is my chosen Son; hear him!'" (Luke 9:35). Our father among the saints, Irenaeus of Lyons (d. ca. AD 202), writes in *Against Heresies*,

> The Son, administering all things for the Father, works from the beginning even to the end, and without Him no man can attain the knowledge of God. For the Son is the knowledge of the Father; but the knowledge of the Son is in the Father, and has been revealed through the Son; and this was the reason why the Lord declared: "No man knoweth the Son, but the Father; nor the Father, save the Son, and those to whomsoever the Son shall reveal . . . [Matt 11:27; Luke 10:22]." For "shall reveal" was said not with reference to the future alone, as if then . . . the Word had begun to manifest the Father when He was born of Mary, but it applies indifferently throughout all time. For the Son, being present with His own handiwork from the beginning, reveals the Father to all; to whom He wills, and when He wills, and as the Father wills.[46]

So humanity's religions are not valueless; they do have a certain relative value in light of God's ultimate, final, and definitive revelation in Jesus, his Son. It may be true, as some say, that God is already present among those who do not know of or believe in the gospel. Yet, it is not the same as the uniqueness of his presence in his Son, Jesus, in whom "it has been very pleasing [to God] for all the fullness to dwell" (Col 1:19).[47]

Traditionally, the church has acknowledged that God can truly be known by human beings through their rational consideration of the created world. This "natural revelation," albeit imperfect in comparison to God's positive revelation of himself, yet allows men and women to know with certainty of God's existence and what they can do in order to please him.[48] I do not think that it is completely outside the realm of possibility to think that human beings' varied experiences of this "natural revelation" cannot have been made concrete in their religions. Nor do I

46. Irenaeus, *Against Heresies* 4.6.7 (Rambaut, *ANF* 1:469).

47. See also John 10:38; 14:10–11; 17:21, 23.

48. See e.g., Wilhelm and Scannell, *Sources of Theological Knowledge*, 3–8.

think that these possible actuations—no matter how imperfect—could not have been found or could not still be found now by God to be in some way useful for the enrichment and (even) salvation of a person's soul. That is, as long as it is *God* who is making use of them. In *Dominus Iesus*, for instance, the CDF expressly affirms that humanity's many religions "contain and offer religious elements" which, although not having a direct origin in God, nevertheless do "come from God" through the activity of the Holy Spirit in human hearts.[49]

Let me say, however, that I am still unsure whether God has *directly* and *actively* willed the formation of humanity's religions for his own salvific purpose or whether he has only willed them *indirectly* and *permissively* based on the positive spiritual influence that they might have on mankind. I tend to lean towards the latter view for the following reasons:

For one, God is *truth*. He neither deceives nor can be deceived. If that claim is axiomatic, which I think it is, then I do not think or believe that God himself would actively and directly will people to be led to believe or act erroneously in what touches upon the fulfillment of their ultimate destiny. I do think and believe that he might allow or permit it, however, if for no other reason than to show us humans that all of our own efforts at saving or liberating or healing ourselves were ultimately inadequate without God's active intervention.[50]

Humanity has tried to build towers to God (cf. Gen 11:4). Some of them are quite beautiful and awe-inspiring; some may even have approached the sill of heaven. But God is also *personal* . . . and a relationship cannot be forced on a person. Humans may try through their religions to create encounters with God—to knock on the door of his dwelling—but as with any true, authentic relationship, the other person must choose to be encountered. He himself must choose to open the door. Jesus proclaims that *he* is that encounter; *he* is that opened door: "The one who has seen me, he has seen the Father" (John 14:9); "Amen, amen, I say to

49. See CDF, *Dominus Iesus*, §21. See also §6 where it states, "Faith requires us to profess that the Word made flesh, in his entire mystery . . . is the source, participated but real, as well as the fulfilment of *every salvific revelation of God* to humanity" (CDF, *Dominus Iesus*, §6; emphasis added).

50. Another question, which I will not treat here: Could God in some cases even look approvingly on beliefs or practices (e.g., polytheism, idolatry) that, while otherwise false or distorted, nevertheless express the human being's intent to search for him? Humanity's many religions reveal at the very least that there is some kind of spiritual quest that is ultimately worth making—which, I would say, is a *good* intuition to have, even if imperfectly pursued.

you: I am the door of the sheep. . . . If someone should enter through me, he will be saved and will walk in and walk out and find pasture" (10:7, 9).

Moreover, while a person *qua* person can exist in multiple relationships that are all authentic and genuine, each in its own way, a person can choose nonetheless out of all those relationships to enter into one that is unique, definitive, and exclusive. If this obtains for the human person, then it does so no less for the Divine One. Indeed, the Sacred Scriptures tell us that God has precisely made such a choice of relationship: it is with the Jews. God tells the Israelites, "You shall be holy to me, for I am holy, I the Lord, and I have separated you from the other peoples, so that you should be mine" (Lev 20:26; see also v. 24). And Moses reminds them later, "The Lord your God has chosen you, so that you should be to him a people peculiar from all the peoples who are upon the earth" (Deut 7:6; see also 14:2). It is not without reason, then, that the Sacred Scriptures describe God's relationship with Israel and, later, the church in the most deeply exclusive terms.[51] It is no happenstance that God came as the Christ of the Jews. The coming of Jesus was the fulfillment of God's manifold promises and covenants whereby he had forged a proprietary relationship with Israel. Yet, he became "present" to Israel in a way that he has never been present to any other people: he humbled himself to be born of an Israelite woman, that is, he became a Jew. Certainly, this event had consequences for all humanity since by becoming man, God fulfilled the curse that he had promised to the serpent—namely, to send one, born of Eve, who would wound his head (see Gen 3:15). As Vatican II teaches, by becoming a man, God has in some way united himself with all men, with all peoples—not just the Jews.[52] Still, it was through the seed of Abraham and his children that God chose to bless all the peoples of the world (see Gen 26:4; see also 12:2–3, 18:18, and 22:18). Of course, a person's choice of entering into an exclusive relationship with someone does not by that fact itself obliterate all other relationships that person might have had with others. But it does recontextualize them in light of

51. God is a Parent: "When Israel was a young boy, I loved him and out of Egypt I called my son" (Hos 11:1; see also Exod 4:22 and Jer 31:9); "You have not accepted a spirit of slavery again in fear, but have accepted a Spirit of adoption as sons and daughters, in which we cry out: 'Abba, Father!'" (Rom 8:15; see also Gal 3:26, 4:5–6, Heb 12:7).

He is a Spouse: "On that day, says the Lord, you will call me: 'my Husband' and you will not call me anymore: 'my Baal'" (Hos 2:18; see also Ezek 16:32); "I am zealous for you with the zealousness of God; for I have betrothed you to one Husband to present a chaste virgin to Christ" (2 Cor 11:2).

52. See Vatican II, *Gaudium et Spes*, §22.

the "other," who has become that person's sole and primary concern. (In some cases, it might even entail having to end a relationship that might conflict with the other exclusive one.)

The Second Vatican Council concedes that God can, in ways that he knows about, bring a nonbeliever to that faith by which he himself is pleased. Thus, God can associate the nonbelieving person with the mystery of the death and resurrection of his Son, Jesus.[53] True also, mankind has originally been made by God in his image and likeness (see Gen 1:26; see also 5:1–2). Our first human parents were created in perfect holiness and justice.[54] God was indeed present to them (see e.g., Gen 3:8). But on account of our first parents' disobedience due to Satan's deception, our likeness to God suffered severe injury: "God created man in an unspoiled state and he made him the image of his likeness; yet, by the Devil's envy death entered into the world of nations; and they experience it, who are on his side" (Wis 2:23–24). Man's nature now inclines towards "evil," in other words, to whatever deprives him of the good. The church calls this *concupiscence*.[55] As the Second Vatican Council describes,

> Although he was made by God in a state of holiness, from the very onset of his history man abused his liberty. . . . Man set himself against God and sought to attain his goal apart from God. Although [men and women] knew God, they did not glorify him as God, but their senseless minds were darkened and they served the creature rather than the Creator [see Rom 1:21–25]. . . . Examining his heart, man finds that he has inclinations toward evil . . . and is engulfed by manifold ills which cannot come from his good Creator. Often refusing to acknowledge God as his beginning, man has disrupted also his proper relationship to his own ultimate goal as well as his whole relationship toward himself and others and all created things.
>
> Therefore man is split within himself. As a result, all of human life . . . shows itself to be a dramatic struggle between good and evil, between light and darkness. Indeed, man finds that by

53. See Vatican II, *Ad Gentes*, §7, and *Gaudium et Spes*, §22.

54. See Council of Trent, "Decree Concerning Original Sin," §§1 and 2.

55. As the *Catechism of the Catholic Church* explains, "Etymologically, 'concupiscence' can refer to any intense form of human desire. Christian theology has given it a particular meaning: the movement of the sensitive appetite contrary to the operation of the human reason. The Apostle St. Paul identifies it with the rebellion of the 'flesh' against the 'spirit' [Gal 5:16–17, 24; Eph 2:3]. Concupiscence stems from the disobedience of the first sin. It unsettles man's moral faculties and, without being in itself an offense, inclines man to commit sins" (*CCC*, §2515; see also §§405, 418, 1264).

> himself he is incapable of battling the assaults of evil successfully, so that everyone feels as though he is bound by chains. . . . For sin has diminished man, blocking his path to fulfillment.[56]

It cannot, therefore, in my opinion be simply assumed, if God is present among men and women, that his presence has not been misapprehended or become twisted due to the effects of humanity's fall from grace. Be all that as it may, God is *still* not present to the nonbeliever in the way that he is present in the soul of the Christian. Through a person's baptism, not only is all sin removed but that human being becomes a new creature—that is, an adopted son or daughter of God. Likewise, he or she receives a share in God's nature and is attached to Christ and becomes the corecipient (!) of Christ's treasures. Thus, he or she is truly "Christ-ian." The Christian, then, is established as a dwelling place of God the Holy Spirit.[57] Saint Irenaeus writes in *The Demonstration of the Apostolic Preaching* that "[faith] bids us bear in mind that we have received baptism for the remission of sins, in the name of God the Father, and in the name of Jesus Christ, the Son of God, who was incarnate and died and rose again, and in the Holy Spirit of God. And that this baptism is the seal of eternal life, and is the new birth unto God, that we should no longer be the sons of mortal men, but of the eternal and perpetual God."[58] Whenever someone is baptized in the name of the Trinity and further chrismated with the Holy Spirit, that person receives a permanent, ineffaceable mark or seal (Greek, *charaktēr* or *sphragis*) on his or her soul. In effect, God is stamped on the baptized person's spirit, and the persons of the blessed Trinity are engraved onto his or her very being.[59]

## A Problem Starts to Emerge

Moving back to St. Paul VI's apostolic exhortation *Evangelii Nuntiandi*, the pope challenges any attempt to place the church's mission into question as drawing too superficially on the texts of Vatican II. He responds in no uncertain terms:

56. Vatican II, *Gaudium et Spes*, §13. See also *CCC*, §§374–75, 384, 403–5, 415–18, 1707, 1714.

57. See *CCC*, §§1265 and 1279 (see also §§364 and 1695).

58. Irenaeus, *Demonstration of the Apostolic Preaching* 3 (Robinson, 72).

59. See *CCC*, §§1272–74, 1280. The blessed apostle Paul reminds the Corinthian church, "You are the temple of God, and the Spirit of God dwells in you" (1 Cor 3:16; see also 6:19 and 2 Cor 6:16b).

> It would certainly be an error to impose something on the consciences of our brethren. But to propose to their consciences the truth of the Gospel and salvation in Jesus Christ, with complete clarity and with a total respect for the free options which it presents—"without coercion, or dishonorable or unworthy pressure" [Vatican II, *Dignitatis Humanae*, §4]—far from being an attack on religious liberty is fully to respect that liberty, which is offered the choice of a way that even non-believers consider noble and uplifting. Is it then a crime against others' freedom to proclaim with joy a Good News which one has come to know through the Lord's mercy?[60]

Then, he continues:

> The respectful presentation of Christ and His kingdom is more than the evangelizer's right; *it is his duty*. It is likewise the right of his fellow men to receive from him the proclamation of the Good News of salvation. God can accomplish this salvation in whomsoever He wishes by ways which He alone knows. And yet, if His Son came, it was precisely in order to reveal to us, by His word and by His life, the ordinary paths of salvation. And He has commanded us to transmit this revelation to others with His own authority.[61]

The pope adds,

> It would be useful if every Christian and every evangelizer were to pray about the following thought: men can gain salvation also in other ways, by God's mercy, even though we do not preach the Gospel to them; but as for us, *can we gain salvation if through negligence or fear or shame . . . or as a result of false ideas we fail to preach it?* For that would be to betray the call of God, who wishes the seed to bear fruit through the voice of the ministers of the Gospel; and it will depend on us whether this grows into trees and produces its full fruit.[62]

Clearly, this passage shows that there was some alarm on the pope's part at how Vatican II itself was being used to justify a softening of the

60. Paul VI, *Evangelii Nuntiandi*, §80. He continues on with a forceful recrimination: "And why should only falsehood and error, debasement and pornography have the right to be put before people and often unfortunately imposed on them by the destructive propaganda of the mass media, by the tolerance of legislation, the timidity of the good and the impudence of the wicked?"

61. Paul VI, *Evangelii Nuntiandi*, §80; emphasis added.

62. Paul VI, *Evangelii Nuntiandi*, §80; emphasis added.

church's missionary spirit. Saint Paul VI, however, categorically rejects that attempt. Indeed, the pope's comments eschew erudite distinctions. Nor does he consider even fairly the views of others. On the contrary, the matter cuts so close to the bedrock of the faith that the pope resorts to straightforward apostolic *parrhēsia*—that is, "frankness." He goes right to the heart of the problem in clear terms, rejecting it strenuously. That is so because the stakes are so high, for it touches upon God's salvation of the world in Christ. Hence, the pope seems to have felt that he must speak with absolute clarity and seriousness. He even warns with the loss of salvation (!) those who would fail in or deny their obligation to still proclaim the gospel to those who did not believe in it. One would have thought that Pope St. Paul VI's comments in *Evangelii Nuntiandi* should have forestalled—or at least given "food for thought" to—any further attempt to lessen or otherwise relativize the church's missionary spirit. But such was not the case. The next chapter addresses that situation.

# 4

# From Loss of Interest in Mission to Loss of Faith in the Lord Jesus

## The Attempt to Reinvigorate Mission

In 1990, Pope St. John Paul II issued an encyclical letter, *Redemptoris Missio*. In that missive, addressed to all the bishops and faithful, the pope felt compelled to defend the permanent validity of the missionary mandate given to the church by Jesus.

Pope St. Paul VI's exhortation on the church's missionary mandate was titled "De Evangelizatione in Mundo de Huius Temporis," which is commonly translated into English as, "On Evangelization in the Modern World."[1] This is an accurate enough translation.

But the title of Pope St. John Paul II's letter is "De Perenni Vi Mandati Missionalis."[2] This is commonly rendered, "On the Permanent Validity of the Church's Missionary Mandate." Some comment is warranted here.

A more literal and correct rendering of *Redemptoris Missio*'s title in English, I believe, would be, "On the Enduring Force of the Missionary Command." First, we might begin at the end. I think "command" is a better translation of the Latin *mandatum*, since it derives directly from the verb *mando*, which means precisely that: "to order, command, enjoin."[3] The word "mandate," though, as it is often used today, can sound

1. Paulus VI, "Episcopos, Sacerdotes et Christifideles," 5.
2. Ioannes Paulus II, "Mandati Missionalis," 249.
3. Andrews, *New Latin Dictionary*, s.v. "Mando," 1107.

more like the idea that some kind of permission has been given—not of an actual order given that might require obedience. As I aimed to show above in the chapter on Matt 28, when Jesus is on the mountain with his disciples, he does not offer a suggestion about what they might choose to do or not do. Nor does he tell what they are allowed or permitted to do. On the contrary, he tells them imperatively what he wants to be done—namely, to baptize and teach! Second, the word *vis* in Latin has the meaning or sense of "force," "power," "energy," as well as of "strength" or "vigor." It can also be used as "meaning" or "sense," in the way that I have just used those terms above.[4] Most modern translations of the encyclical (for example, in German, Italian, Spanish, etc.) have favored translating the word as "validity," which I would say is certainly a possible interpretation of the pope's meaning.[5] In my opinion, either "force" or "meaning" is the best translation, although I opt for the former. The reason is that the idea of "force" carries with it the concomitant idea of pressure—that is, it places a burden on someone and has the effect of asking something of someone. It is not a presence which simply exists before a person that he or she can choose to ignore; rather, it is a thing which has been given to that person, requiring a response. Furthermore, there is "force" behind a command when the one giving it has authority, which Jesus does: "To me is given all power in heaven and on earth. . . . Therefore . . ." (Matt 28:18b–19a).[6] Finally, we come to the word *perennis*. In Latin, it has the connotation of something that continues throughout the year or occurs year after year. So in an extended sense, it could also carry the meaning of "unceasing" or "everlasting." I, however, prefer the related notion of "enduring," since the church's missionary mandate should not be expected to continue after the parousia when Christ returns and restores all things. So to say that the "force" or "power" of the command is everlasting or perpetual would not seem appropriate. On the contrary, the church's missionary command exists until all things have been summed up in Christ (see Eph 1:10), when all will know and be subject to him: "A man will come whose name is the Dayspring; from his throne he will rule over all; he will speak of peace to the nations."[7]

4. See Andrews, *New Latin Dictionary*, s.v. "Vis," 1997.

5. The French translation preferred the word *valeur* ("value").

6. Although "meaning" could also be a valid and adequate translation, it seems to me like it would tend to weaken the import of the pope's overall statement.

7. Antiphon 1, Morning Prayer, Solemnity of Christ the King, in Catholic Church, *Ordinary Time*, 579. See also Antiphon 2, Office of Readings, for the same feast: "All

## The Problem Worsens

The title of *Redemptoris Missio* would seem to have belied a grave concern regarding the status of the church's evangelizing mission.[8] In Pope St. Paul VI's apostolic exhortation, evangelization is taken for granted. It is simply a fact of the church's existence. But for Pope St. John Paul II's encyclical letter, commitment to evangelization cannot be so simply presumed. In fact, it must now be justified and defended to members of the church herself! On the one hand, in *Evangelii Nuntiandi* St. Paul VI expresses concern over the lack of fervor for the church's evangelizing mission among some Catholics only near the end of the long document (in §80 out of 82 sections)—it is almost an afterthought that anyone should question it. On the other hand, in St. John Paul II's *Redemptoris Missio*, the problem is raised from the very start (in §2 out of 92). In *Redemptoris Missio*, Pope St. John Paul II starts by recognizing the positive fruits that

the kings of the earth will worship him; all nations will serve him" (Catholic Church, *Ordinary Time*, 572).

8. A further question, which I cannot really address here, regards what kind of (possible) magisterial value might be intended by the actual form of a document that either pope issued. In other words, did it mean something that Pope St. Paul VI used an "apostolic exhortation" to present his teaching, whereas Pope St. John Paul II used the form of an "encyclical"? Does using one kind or form of document somehow differentiate its doctrinal status as higher or lower? Moreover, did the form which either pope chose to use (perhaps) indicate the seriousness with which he viewed the matter? And consulting the indices of either the *Acta Apostolicae Sedis* (1909–present) or the previous *Acta Sanctae Sedis* (1865–1908) is of no help since neither provides any explanation as to why it lists papal and curial statements in the order that it does.

As its name implies, an exhortation's purpose is to animate or incite by words or argument—that is, to urge someone to believe or do something (*Merriam-Webster*, s.v. "exhort," https://www.merriam-webster.com/dictionary/exhort; Harris and Sturges, *Webster's New International Dictionary*, s.v. "exhort," 768). An encyclical's purpose is typically didactic: a pope seeks to extend his ordinary magisterium by expounding on some topic of doctrine. See e.g., Morrisey, "Papal and Curial Pronouncements," 102–25. So I would venture to say that, *in my own tentative opinion*, an encyclical's contents would bear more magisterial weight than those of an exhortation. An encyclical seems to be more consciously directed towards the exercise of the magisterium (that is, telling what ought to be believed), whereas an apostolic exhortation seems to be intended more for advisement and persuasion. Obviously, church teaching almost certainly appears in both. But it seems to me that an exhortation is meant more as a confirmation of what is already accepted for belief, rather than as a presentation of what is to be believed. *Evangelii Nuntiandi* seems to take for granted the church's magisterium regarding her evangelizing mission. But *Redemptoris Missio* cannot do so since that teaching was being questioned and challenged. So it had to be authoritatively reiterated.

I would like to thank Dr. Eric M. Johnston of Immaculate Conception Seminary School of Theology, Seton Hall University, and Dr. John P. Joy of Holy Apostles College and Seminary for allowing me to chew over this matter with them.

have been borne through the renewal initiated by the Second Vatican Council. Yet, in this "new spring" of the church, the pope has a worry: there is "an undeniable negative tendency" which has become apparent in the church's life.[9]

What is this tendency?

It is this: "Missionary activity specifically directed 'to the nations' (*ad gentes*) appears to be waning, and this tendency is certainly not in line with the directives of the Council and of subsequent statements of the Magisterium."[10]

Of course, Pope St. Paul VI had already pointed this out similarly above in *Evangelii Nuntiandi*—namely, that there had developed certain ideas of the church's evangelizing mission which were not in line with the doctrine of Vatican II. This, of course, begs the question of how that could possibly have been so if the bishops of Vatican II had taught so clearly on the matter of mankind's salvation. Saint John Paul II was writing fifteen years later. How could such a misconstrual of the council have been allowed to have gained a footing and remain for so long?

The pope continues: the weakening of the church's missionary efforts is a matter for concern since "in the Church's history, missionary drive has always been a sign of vitality, just as its lessening is *a sign of a crisis of faith*."[11] The pope intimates that there are Catholics who have come to question not just the church's missionary enterprise per se but also the very message about Jesus Christ that she has been sent out to bring. They disparage evangelistic missionary activity in principle because they believe that the "Principle" himself is relative or insufficient. This is clearly a problem of fundamental proportions since it directly strikes at the church's very foundation: the one who is her cornerstone (see Eph 2:20). The author of 2 Peter writes,

> Wherefore it is contained in Scripture:
> "*Behold, I lay in Zion a cornerstone, chosen, precious;*
> *and the one who believes in him shall not be confused.*"
> To you therefore who do believe, he is the honorary gift; yet to them who do not believe he is

9. John Paul II, *Redemptoris Missio*, §2.

10. John Paul II, *Redemptoris Missio*, §2.

11. John Paul II, *Redemptoris Missio*, §2; emphasis added. Almost two decades earlier, Pope St. Paul VI had already warned of a "spiritual asphyxia" that had come over the missionary spirit of some Catholics (see Paolo VI, "Giornata Missionaria Mondiale 1972"; my translation).

> "*the stone which the builders rejected*" . . .
> and "*a stone of offense and a rock of stumbling*"; they who do not believe offend against the word, for which they were purposed. (2 Pet 6–7b, 8; italics in original)

Yet, the words of this Scripture seem to have been perversely overturned by some Christians: that Jesus of Nazareth should be placed as just one stone among many others in the foundation of mankind's grand temple to God—this is acceptable. But that he ought to become the capstone, "the head of the corner" (1 Pet 2:7c)—this is unacceptable. So Christ has become even for some *believers* a stumbling block! They question the church's missionary activity precisely because they question the message. But what is the church's message other than that God has fulfilled his promises to Israel by sending the long-awaited messiah? What is it but that God has saved all humanity in his Son through the cross and glorified human beings through his Son's resurrection? What is the underlying principle of the gospel other than that God the Word out of love has humbled himself to become flesh? That Christ has established his church as the ordinary means for reconciling humankind with God? Nevertheless, to actually tell nonbelievers that Jesus is the one and only God come in the flesh, . . . that there is no other like him, . . . that God's salvation is only to be found in Jesus, . . . that God's revelation of himself in Jesus is unique, complete, and ultimate, . . . and that the establishment of the values of God's kingdom comes with the acceptance of Jesus and his body, the church—these have all now become offensive claims. Catholics may say them among themselves or say them to other Christians (although, in the latter case, they perhaps ought not to say certain things about ecclesiology), but *they should never say these things to outsiders*—that is, non-Christians. To do so would be rude. It would scandalize.

Now, I am an American. I come from a nation with a tradition, based in its core law, that the government would neither establish a national religion nor interfere in any person's practice of his or her own.[12] Papua New Guinea's constitution also affirms "the right to freedom of conscience, thought and religion and the practice of [one's] religion and beliefs, including freedom to manifest and propagate [one's] religion and beliefs."[13] I have not lived in any country where my religious beliefs and

12. The First Amendment to my country's foundational document, the US Constitution, stipulates, "Congress shall make no law respecting an establishment of religion, or prohibiting the free exercise thereof" (U.S. Const. amend. I).

13. Papua New Guinea Const., §45.1. However, in its preamble, it does state that

practices have been restricted by the government.[14] I cannot, therefore, truly understand the situation or experience of some of the speakers at the symposium, for example, of Reverend Devadass from Malaysia. While, as noted above, the right to profess and practice one's own religion, whatever that might be, is guaranteed by the Malaysian constitution, the document nevertheless makes clear that Islam is the religion of the nation.[15] Furthermore, it specifies that both federal and state laws "may control or restrict the propagation of any [non-Islamic] religious doctrine or belief among persons professing the religion of Islam."[16] Whereas Muslims in Malaysia have the unlimited right to try to convert anyone to Islam, no one may try to convert a believer in Islam to another or to no religion, under legal penalty. According to a report by the Office of International Religious Freedom of the US Department of State, "Muslims who seek to convert to another religion must first obtain approval from a sharia court to declare themselves 'apostates.' Sharia courts seldom grant such requests, especially for those born Muslims, and are reluctant to allow conversion for those who had previously converted to Islam."[17] If an application for "apostasy" is approved, then that Muslim man or woman may be subject to a penalty, ranging from a simple fine, to incarceration, to caning, to the infliction of death (all depending on which state the "apostate" lives in).[18] As Reverend Devadass proudly stated above during the question period, his local church received around eight hundred people into the church every year, despite the government's restrictions on the church's ability to preach as well as on people's conversion from Islam.[19] Indeed, if this is so, then I think that some or even many of those converts, particularly from Islam, ought to be classified under the ancient designation of "confessor," since it is possible—even probable—that they might have already had to have actually suffered for the name of Christ in some way, even *before* they were baptized into him! So *any critical*

PNG's citizens "pledge ourselves to guard and pass on to those who come after us our noble traditions and the Christian principles that are ours now."

14. As a teenager (in 1988?), I did very briefly visit the German Democratic Republic, a Socialist state that placed severe restrictions on religious practice.

15. Malaysian Federal Const. §3.1 (see also §160).

16. Malaysian Federal Const. §11.4.

17. Office of International Religious Freedom, "2019 Report."

18. Though the report adds that the death penalty has not yet been imposed on anyone for this offense.

19. Dunn, "Mr. Paolo Baleinakorodawa," 1:06:27.

*comment that I might make or seem to make below is not directed at those Catholics throughout the world who, with great prudence (see Matt 10:16), must navigate professing their faith in societies and under governments that are anti-religious or anti-Christian.* Rather, I hope my thoughts will help them think of our "common salvation" and strengthen them in their "struggle for the faith handed on once to the saints" (Jude 3).[20]

No—I am concerned with those Catholics who, instead of concerning themselves with the church's lack of freedom in parts of the world to proclaim Christ and bring people into his church, seem to bemoan rather the "exclusivism" and "triumphalism" and "fundamentalism" of the church's beliefs and the intolerance and insensitivity of her message.

Returning to *Redemptoris Missio*, the pope writes that the encyclical's aim is "to invite the Church *to renew her missionary commitment*."[21] So he wants to call for the renewal of both the faith and the life of Christians who (apparently) have succumbed to this lessening or weakening of missionary fervor.[22] Yet, one might reflect on whether his response comported with the gravity of the situation. For it is not a mere lack of fervor for missionary activity. (He calls that just a "sign.") On the contrary, the expression used by the pope is a "crisis of faith." Just how did he think that Catholics' enthusiasm for mission could be stoked when the very basis of the church's missionary enterprise was no longer being assumed—even being attacked and rejected? It could be put parabolically like this: A ship's crew sees ripples in the waters around the ship. The officers and crew think they have merely hit a rough patch of ocean. It will pass. But the ripples indicate something far more worrisome: they have inadvertently run the ship into an iceberg, and the hull has been

20. I ask Holy Mary the Queen of all Christians to pray to her divine Son for all of my brothers and sisters who, in many places throughout the world, feel that they cannot proclaim Christ openly to their people without experiencing suffering or death. May she protect them and encourage them for better times, when they might be able to announce and proclaim her Son, Jesus, freely!

21. John Paul II, *Redemptoris Missio*, §2; emphasis original.

22. A further matter that could be addressed—but will not be here—is the extent to which the activities of the sainted pope himself might have contributed to the lessening of missionary resolve among Catholics. Or, at least, might have caused confusion regarding the "permanent validity" of the church's missionary mandate. One could think, for example, of the pope's convocation of the 1986 interreligious prayer gathering in Assisi, Italy, which some viewed as the Catholic Church's equivalent of the 1893 "World's Parliament of Religions." It was among the last straws for Archbishop Marcel Lefebvre, who called it "an insult" to Christ and began plans to initiate his own schism from Rome by ordaining several men as bishops for his religious group, the Society of St. Pius X (see e.g., Roy-Lysencourt, "Traditionalist Catholics," 369–70).

torn open. They are sinking. It would be one thing if the officers and crew did not realize the danger because they were simply unenthusiastic and lacked fervor in their work. It would be quite another—and far more serious—if they did not notice because they did not even care. Hopefully, the ship's captain would notice and would care, sounding the alarm: "All hands on deck!" What a tragedy if, instead, he just contented himself with putting a memo on the board: "To all hands—In the unlikely case that we might be sinking . . ."

## *Dominus Iesus*—The Problem Explodes

Despite St. John Paul II's hopes, it would have seemed that the pope's "invitation" in *Redemptoris Missio* was not met with generosity. Ten years later, St. John Paul II charged the Congregation for the Doctrine of the Faith with composing the declaration *Dominus Iesus* (2000).[23] The declaration sought to assert as clearly as possible certain essential points of the Christian faith—many of which had already been covered by the pope's encyclical a decade earlier:

- The full and definitive value of God's revelation in Jesus (§§5–8)
- The exclusivity of God's salvation in Christ (§§9–11)
- The essentially christological orientation of the Holy Spirit's salvific activity (§12)
- Jesus' unique and comprehensive status as the Savior of humankind (§§13–15)
- The unitary nature of Christ's body, the church, and the unique presence of his body in the Catholic Church (§§16–17)
- The inseparable relationship between Jesus, the church, and the kingdom of God (§§18–19)
- The church's salvific relationship to other religions (§§20–22)

The declaration's notes are stuffed full of citations from the documents of the Second Vatican Council and the pope's encyclical letter, *Redemptoris Missio*. Moreover, it is replete with references to the Sacred Scriptures. The document's contents are based not just on the

23. The cardinal-prefect of the dicastery at the time was Archbishop Joseph Ratzinger, who later became Pope Benedict XVI in 2005. He abdicated in 2013, however, and fell asleep in the Lord in 2022.

magisterium of the most recent ecumenical council (viz., Vatican II) but also on some of the most antique statements of the church's faith (viz., Nicaea I, Constantinople I, Chalcedon—even Trent makes an appearance several times!).[24] The various points it makes could not have been deemed—one would have imagined—anything but "settled doctrine" (or, nearly so). From the perspective of the church's traditional and oft-stated teaching, it would have seemed that there was nothing at all controversial in the statement. On the contrary, its assertions were just *re*assertions.

Then, the debacle ensued.

Consider, for example, a lecture given on *Dominus Iesus* by J. Augustine DiNoia, OP.[25] At the time of the declaration, he was working in the Secretariat for Doctrine and Pastoral Practices of the National Conference of Catholic Bishops (NCCB). He described the "furor" created by *Dominus Iesus*:

> When the document came to the [US] bishops' conference . . . the General Secretary of the conference [Monsignor Dennis M. Schnurr] asked us, some of the staff, to read it and to prepare any assistance that it might require for the bishops. . . . We went back and reported to the General Secretary: "There's absolutely nothing new in this document. It's just a lot of quotations . . . from Vatican II. . . . The first three chapters are about the salvation that comes through Christ, and the second third is about the place of the Church in salvation. . . . There's absolutely nothing controversial or unfamiliar here." Well. *The Los Angeles Times* as well as practically every other person in the media, thought differently. . . . And, so, was launched, this firestorm. . . . I think what it revealed was that we were very wrong at the bishops' conference. We thought that everything in [*Dominus Iesus*] was self-evident. But, the crisis clearly is that after thirty years of the [Second Vatican] Council, there is a lot of confusion about these two apparently central topics of our faith.[26]

24. As a matter of fact, I have made the argument, which (I believe) is well substantiated, that *Dominus Iesus* was ultimately based on a short address given by Pope St. John Paul II to the CDF on Jan. 28, 2000. See Dunn, "CDF's Declaration," 61–64.

25. DiNoia has since been ordained a "titular bishop." The NCCB was reorganized in 2001 and renamed as the US Conference of Catholic Bishops (USCCB).

26. DiNoia, "Dominus Iesus," 5:45–8:33. A copy of the talk has been placed on my YouTube channel (see Dunn, "Fr. Augustine DiNoia"). My thanks to the people at the site Riverside (https://riverside.fm) for providing a helpful transcription tool, used for this talk.

Contrary to Reverend DiNoia's implication, I do not believe that the controversy over *Dominus Iesus* came about due to the reactions of a skeptical, hostile media. (Although, the media's coverage of it may have exacerbated it.) No, the media did not launch the "firestorm." Rather, the "firestorm" was already blowing through the church. It was only smoldering in some places, but in others it had consumed the church: hierarchies, schools of theology, missionary orders. In a short article on *Dominus Iesus*, Robert P. Imbelli, a professor of theology at Boston College, Massachusetts, makes some incisive points. For him, "the robust Christocentrism" of Vatican II's documents now seems like an embarrassment to some. *Dominus Iesus*, however, "intends to recapitulate the church's faith in the uniqueness and universal salvific significance of Jesus Christ, the incarnate Word of God: the article of faith upon which the Church itself stands or falls. What is crucially important about this document is that *this article of faith*, everywhere professed and presumed by Vatican II, *can no longer be taken for granted*."[27] He continues,

> Put bluntly: There is abroad a measure of innocent and sometimes quite intentional apostasy. Among some Catholic theologians, there is advanced the idea of "multiple incarnations" of the Christ, or that Jesus is Savior only for Christians, or that the salvific role of the Spirit is more universal than that of Jesus Christ, or that [the] Trinity is but one "model" for speaking of the incomprehensible mystery of God. Such "unitarianism of the Spirit" is no figment of some overheated Roman imagination. It appears in print, both at popular and more sophisticated theological levels.[28]

The "furor" over the claims in *Dominus Iesus* was not a phantom of journalists' own making. It had already been roaming around the halls of bishops' chanceries, commanding the podium at missiological conferences, acting as *Pontifex Maximus* at interreligious gatherings, staring out from the pages of "agreed statements."

For me, the document's negative reception among the "press" is not so much a problem since for a world that is perishing, the message of the gospel indeed appears as foolishness (see 1 Cor 1:18).

No—I am more concerned about two groups: the church's faithful and her interlocutors. For there were many Catholics, both lay and clerical, who were also shocked, confused, and (even) hostile to *Dominus*

27. Marty et al., "Rome and Relativism," 13; emphasis added.

28. Marty et al., "Rome and Relativism," 13.

*Iesus*'s claims about Jesus and the church. For example, Catholic theologian Francis X. Clooney, SJ, summarized his own ambivalence towards the document:

> Potential [non-Christian] dialogue partners will probably have already read *Dominus Iesus* when they come for dialogue. . . . One wonders what they will think about the declaration. They will be a tough audience to please or subdue. Centuries of missionary work have not convinced them that their souls are in peril; they are not worried about their lack of union with Rome; they have no reason to revere the document as the work of a flawless magisterium; they will be amused or upset by its characterization of their traditions as gravely deficient; and they will want to know whether there are still good reasons why they should engage in dialogue with Roman Catholics, whatever reasons Catholics themselves might have.[29]

The document was challenged in even stronger terms by a fellow Jesuit, Masashi Masuda, from Japan. He wrote,

> [The CDF's declaration] is just a theological monologue that reiterates old truth claims formed in the circle of Western-centric paradigms expressed in traditional theological language. Such a monologue, *to which no one is listening*, has no power to solve problems; it lacks even the ability to point the way toward a solution. If a document issued by the teaching authority of the Catholic church does not appeal to people's hearts, if it merely succeeds in causing despair and confusion through being too far removed from reality, then surely it indicates a crisis in the magisterium of the Catholic church. That was the situation confronting the Catholic church immediately prior to Vatican II. It seems the Catholic Church of our era is about to find itself in the same position. It is trying to close again the windows that had once been opened onto the world.[30]

Many non-Catholics involved in official dialogues with the Catholic Church also reacted with disappointment and bewilderment at the CDF's declaration. According to them, during their conversations with members of the church—even at the highest levels (!)—the points laid out in *Dominus Iesus* were not insisted upon by their Catholic interlocutors.

29. Clooney, "*Dominus Iesus*," 18. For full disclosure, Clooney was the external reader of my doctoral dissertation, and hence, he sat on my defense committee. Obviously, I am grateful to him for having voted to pass my thesis!

30. Masuda, "*Dominus Iesus*," 281–82; emphasis added.

The general experience was expressed by British rabbi Jonathan Romain of Maidenhead Synagogue (Reform). Replying to a question from a journalist of *The National Catholic Reporter*, he said, "I've yet to encounter an English Catholic who takes [the CDF's declaration's] position in real life. . . . My sense is that the reaction among Catholics here will be, 'This is the official line and we have to dredge it up every 25 years or so, but don't worry, lads, we'll just carry on.' The Catholic bishops with whom I've spoken all say they're extremely embarrassed, extremely sorry."[31]

There was even a "schism" of sorts within the Holy See. Edward Idris Cassidy, the cardinal-prefect of the Pontifical Council for Promoting Christian Unity (now, a "Dicastery"), gave an interview to the Italian newspaper *Corriere della Sera*. He clearly criticized the document both for its tone and timing, which he described as inopportune.[32] At an interfaith meeting in Lisbon, Portugal, Cassidy was asked by reporters about the pope's approval of the declaration. His reply was reproduced in an article for *The National Catholic Reporter*: "Certainly, [Pope St. John Paul II] approved [*Dominus Iesus*] like he approves all the declarations of the Congregation for the Doctrine of the Faith. . . . But the encyclicals *Ut Unum Sint* or *Redemptoris Missio*, which treated these themes with different language, actually carry his own signature. And this is a beautiful difference."[33] Cassidy was joined in his criticism by the secretary at

31. Allen, "Gap Between Theory, Reality," 6. An overview of just a few of these criticisms, both from inside and outside the Catholic Church, can be found in my article: Dunn, "CDF's Declaration," 51–57. One can also look at Chia, "*Dominus Iesus*," 278–83.

In 1968, His Excellency Charles Helmsing, the bishop of Kansas City–St. Joseph, Missouri, in whose diocese *The National Catholic Reporter* is located, issued an official statement condemning this publication "for its disregard and denial of the most sacred values of our Catholic faith." He stated,

> Inasmuch as The National Catholic Reporter does not reflect the teaching of the church, but on the contrary, has openly and deliberately opposed this teaching, I ask the editors in all honesty to drop the term "Catholic" from their masthead. By retaining it they deceive their Catholic readers and do a great disservice to ecumenism by being responsible for the false irenicism of watering down Catholic teachings. . . .
>
> I make this statement with apostolic freedom as given by Our Lord to his followers; I make it conscious of the heavy burden that is mine as a Bishop, as one enjoined by the Holy Spirit. (*St. Louis Review*, "Bishop Helmsing's Statement")

The publication's board of directors rejected the bishop's request and has continued to present itself as a "Catholic" publication in good standing.

32. Accattoli, "Religioni." (Cardinal Cassidy fell asleep in the Lord in 2021. RIP.)

33. Allen, "Oceans of Peace," 14. The cardinal's mention of *Ut Unum Sint* refers to

the dicastery, Bishop Walter Kasper.[34] He also viewed *Dominus Iesus* as problematic, especially in its final sections on the church (i.e., §§16–22). In an interview with an Austrian journal, he complained that those sections were composed in "abstract" and "doctrinaire" language whose tone was not effective. He continued, "Insofar as this statement is regrettable, it is not successful and misleading."[35] He was apologetic for the offense *Dominus Iesus* had caused. In another interview with Lutheran World Information, Kasper noted that the declaration's language differed not only from that of Vatican II but also of Pope St. John Paul II.[36] As a matter of fact, the situation became so overwrought that Cardinal Ratzinger himself of the CDF came out with a public rebuke of both Cassidy and Kasper. In a German newspaper interview, he addressed the matter head on. Ratzinger pointed out that both Cardinal Cassidy and Bishop Kasper were members *ex officio* of the CDF. As such, they "took an active part in drafting the document," whose text had been presented for comment to all of the CDF's members several times. Any recommendation made for the document by either prelate (called, a *votum*) was discussed "thoroughly" by the CDF's membership. In fact, "almost all the proposals of the two persons in question [viz., Cassidy and Kasper] were accepted."[37]

Eventually, the pope got involved!

Pope St. John Paul II's 1995 encyclical letter "On the Commitment to Ecumenism."

34. The Catholic Theological Society of America held a roundtable discussion on *Dominus Iesus* at its 2001 meeting. According to one of its participants, John T. Pawlikowski, OSM, "both . . . Cassidy and Kasper have done everything possible to marginalize the impact of *Dominus Iesus* on ecumenical and interreligious affairs" (Pawlikowski et al., "*Dominus Iesus*," 97).

35. Kasper, "Keine Änderung," 9; my translation. Please note that Kasper's interview, which was given in German, suffered mistranslation into English, which unfortunately found its way into all of the quotations from it. According to the current translation reproduced in most English-language journals, Kasper is supposed to have said that *Dominus Iesus* was "an unfortunate affirmation—clumsy and ambiguous" (see e.g., Allen, "Cardinal Kasper").

However, Kasper's German goes thus: "Insofern ist diese Aussage bedauerlich, sie ist nicht geglückt und missverständlich." *Bedauerlich* means that something is to be regretted—but what? Does he mean the whole document or just particular sections of it? Kasper is not altogether clear. Nevertheless, it does not mean "unfortunate." The word *geglückt* does not mean "clumsy"; it means "successful." *Missverständlich* can mean "ambiguous." But it more properly refers to the misunderstanding of the sense of a statement. One thing *Dominus Iesus* was not generally accused of was a lack of clarity, which makes "misleading" a more accurate translation in my view.

36. Lutheran World Information, "Cardinal Kasper."

37. Ratzinger, "Answers to Main Objections."

During an interview for a book on St. John Paul II, Pope Benedict XVI (who, as Cardinal Ratzinger, had overseen the writing of *Dominus Iesus*) recounted how the pope told him that he himself, the pope, wanted to make a public statement on the declaration in which he would clearly affirm both his acceptance of *Dominus Iesus*'s contents and his own special approval of the document.[38] Ratzinger agreed and obligingly prepared a statement for the pope to deliver. The pope delivered it at his Angelus address on October 1, 2000.[39]

Personally, I was overjoyed when *Dominus Iesus* came out. And yet . . . I was as completely shocked and surprised by it as any of its critics! I think it is true to say that, as a statement of the modern Catholic Church, *Dominus Iesus* is indeed an outlier. It is the exception—not the rule. One could have imagined something like it having come out of the Holy Office of the 1920s—but not after Vatican II. There was just nothing analogous to it in the contemporary church, not even in the magisterium of Pope St. John Paul II. So there was no preparation for it. Few would have predicted it. It said clearly and boldly things that were hardly ever said anymore by the church's leadership. On the contrary, *Dominus Iesus* said things that Catholics (one had the impression) were *not supposed* to say anymore, unless one were some kind of "fundamentalist" or *intégriste*.

Of course, I assume that the church's dialogue partners expect her to state her doctrine candidly and without artifice—and to hold to it and defend it, even if it is hard for them in many cases to accept. They recognize that true dialogue cannot happen if their Catholic partners are being willfully inauthentic with them. So then one can understand, and even sympathize with, the anger, frustration, and confusion felt by some non-Catholics and non-Christians over *Dominus Iesus*. For what the CDF now said in *Dominus Iesus* and what they had been led to believe by other church authorities did not seem to agree. So whom should they believe?

## Vatican II and *Dominus Iesus*

Both Cassidy and Kasper did not attack so much the contents of *Dominus Iesus*, which I do believe that they accepted. Instead, each criticized the

38. Benedict XVI, "It Became Increasingly Clear," 23.

39. Benedict XVI, "It Became Increasingly Clear," 23. Interestingly, St. John Paul II did not think that Ratzinger's statement was clear enough. But the CDF prefect assured him that it would suffice ("It Became Increasingly Clear," 23). See also John Paul II, *Angelus*.

*language* of the declaration. They claimed that its language differed significantly from the language used by the bishops of Vatican II and of Pope St. John Paul II (especially in his encyclical *Redemptoris Missio*).

Since neither ever specified what he actually meant by this, it is difficult to actually know. Did they mean, for instance, that the CDF did not rely enough on the texts of Vatican II or *Redemptoris Missio* for the contents of *Dominus Iesus*? Yet, most of the citations of the declaration come from both Vatican II's documents (referenced fifty-nine times!) and *Redemptoris Missio* (referenced twenty-five times!). Over 80 percent of the declaration's content comes from these two sources.[40]

Or did they mean that the declaration did not use the actual words of those documents?

Well, this last is easily checked: one can simply look at all the times that *Dominus Iesus* refers verbatim to the texts of Vatican II or *Redemptoris Missio*—which I will do now. My process is thus: I will follow the outline of the various topics as they are covered in the declaration. I will focus on what is actually quoted. In reproducing what is actually quoted in each section, I will give a privileged place to the statements of Vatican II, since it was an ecumenical council. They will be presented first. Then, I will include anything from the pope's encyclical *Redemptoris Missio*, since it is brought up.

On God's revelation in our Lord Jesus Christ, we have Vatican II's dogmatic constitution, *Dei Verbum*:

> The deepest truth about God and the salvation of man shines out for our sake in Christ, who is both the mediator and the fullness of all revelation.[41]
>
> Jesus Christ . . . the Word made flesh, was sent as "a man to men" [*Letter to Diognetus*, chapter 7]. He "speaks the words of God" (John 3:34), and completes the work of salvation which His Father gave him to do. . . . To see Jesus is to see His Father. . . . For this reason Jesus perfected revelation by fulfilling it through his whole work of making himself present and manifesting himself: through His words and deeds, His signs and wonders, but

40. As Kilian McDonnell, OSB, writes, "A look at the documents of Vatican II and also of the ecumenical accords of the past 30 years demonstrates that the declaration contains nothing new. These claims have been part of the theological conversations between churches. The shock comes from having them all gathered in one place" (McDonnell, "Imperial Claims?," 1041).

41. Vatican II, *Dei Verbum*, §2.

> especially through His death and glorious resurrection from the dead and final sending of the Spirit of truth. Moreover He confirmed with divine testimony what revelation proclaimed. . . . The Christian dispensation, therefore, as the new and definitive covenant, will never pass away and we now await no further new public revelation before the glorious manifestation of our Lord Jesus Christ.[42]

From Pope St. John Paul II's encyclical *Redemptoris Missio*: "In [Jesus, who is] this definitive Word of his revelation, God has made himself known in the fullest possible way. He has revealed to mankind who he is. This definitive self-revelation of God is the fundamental reason why the Church is missionary by her very nature. She cannot do other than proclaim the Gospel, that is, the fullness of the truth which God has enabled us to know about himself."[43]

On the divine inspiration of other religions' sacred writings, *Dei Verbum* is quoted:

> For holy mother Church, relying on the belief of the Apostles . . . holds that the books of both the Old and New Testaments in their entirety, with all their parts, are sacred and canonical because written under the inspiration of the Holy Spirit, they have God as their author and have been handed on as such to the Church herself.[44]

> [The Bible] must be acknowledged as teaching solidly, faithfully and without error that truth which God wanted put into sacred writings for the sake of salvation.[45]

On Jesus as the only Son of God and unique mediator of God's salvific will, we have this from Vatican II's pastoral constitution, *Gaudium et Spes*:

> For God's Word, by whom all things were made, was Himself made flesh so that as perfect man He might save all men and sum up all things in Himself. The Lord [Jesus is he] . . . Whom the Father raised from the dead, lifted on high and stationed at His right hand, making Him judge of the living and the dead.[46]

42. Vatican II, *Dei Verbum*, §4.
43. John Paul II, *Redemptoris Missio*, §5.
44. Vatican II, *Dei Verbum*, §11.
45. Vatican II, *Dei Verbum*, §11.
46. Vatican II, *Gaudium et Spes*, §45.

From *Redemptoris Missio*:

> To introduce any sort of separation between the Word and Jesus Christ is contrary to the Christian faith. . . . Jesus is the Incarnate Word—a single and indivisible person. . . . Christ is none other than Jesus of Nazareth: he is the Word of God made man for the salvation of all. . . . In the process of discovering and appreciating the manifold gifts—especially the spiritual treasures—that God has bestowed on every people, we cannot separate those gifts from Jesus Christ, who is at the center of God's plan of salvation.[47]

On the indissoluble relationship between Christ and the Holy Spirit, the CDF quotes from the encyclical *Redemptoris Missio*:

> The [Holy] Spirit's presence and activity affect not only the individuals but also society and history, peoples, cultures and religions. . . . The risen Christ "is now at work in human hearts through the strength of his Spirit" [citing *Gaudium et Spes*, §38]. . . . Again, it is the Spirit who sows the "seeds of the Word" [see St. Justin Martyr, *Second Apology*] present in various customs and cultures, preparing them for full maturity in Christ.[48]
>
> This is the same Spirit who was at work in the Incarnation and in the life, death and resurrection of Jesus, and who is at work in the Church. [The Holy Spirit] is therefore not an alternative to Christ, nor does he fill a sort of void which is sometimes suggested as existing between Christ and the Logos. Whatever the Spirit brings about in human hearts and in the history of peoples, in cultures and religions serves as a preparation for the Gospel and can only be understood in reference to Christ, the Word who took flesh by the power of the Spirit "so that as perfectly human he would save all human beings and sum up all things" [citing *Gaudium et Spes*, §45].[49]
>
> No one . . . can enter into communion with God except through Christ, by the working of the Holy Spirit.[50]

On the universality and uniqueness of Christ's mediation of God's salvation, Vatican II's *Gaudium et Spes* states,

47. John Paul II, *Redemptoris Missio*, §6.
48. John Paul II, *Redemptoris Missio*, §28.
49. John Paul II, *Redemptoris Missio*, §29.
50. John Paul II, *Redemptoris Missio*, §5.

> The Church firmly believes that Christ, who died and was raised up for all, can through His Spirit offer man the light and the strength to measure up to his supreme destiny. Nor has any other name under the heaven been given to man by which it is fitting for him to be saved. She likewise holds that in her . . . Lord and Master can be found the key, the focal point and the goal of man, as well as of all human history.[51]

From Pope St. John Paul II's *Redemptoris Missio*:

> Although participated forms of mediation of different kinds and degrees are not excluded, they acquire meaning and value only from Christ's own mediation, and they cannot be understood as parallel or complementary to his.[52]

> It is precisely this uniqueness of Christ which gives him an absolute and universal significance, whereby, while belonging to history, he remains history's center and goal: "I am the Alpha and the Omega, the first and the last, the beginning and the end" (Rev 22:13).[53]

On the unity of Christ's body, the church, and its unique presence in the Catholic Church, there is this from Vatican II's dogmatic constitution *Lumen Gentium*:

> This is the one Church of Christ . . . which our Saviour, after His Resurrection, commissioned Peter to shepherd, and him and the other apostles to extend and direct with authority, which He erected for all ages as "the pillar and mainstay of the truth" [1 Tim 3:15]. This Church constituted and organized in the world as a society, subsists in the Catholic Church, which is governed by the successor of Peter and by the bishops in communion with him.[54]

From Vatican II's Decree on Ecumenism, *Unitatis Redintegratio*, there is the following quotation:

> It follows that the separated Churches and Communities as such, though we believe them to be deficient in some respects [*etsi defectus illas pati credimus*], have been by no means deprived of significance and importance in the mystery of salvation. For

51. Vatican II, *Gaudium et Spes*, §10.
52. John Paul II, *Redemptoris Missio*, §5.
53. John Paul II, *Redemptoris Missio*, §6.
54. Vatican II, *Lumen Gentium*, §8.

> the Spirit of Christ has not refrained from using them as means of salvation which derive their efficacy from the very fullness of grace and truth entrusted to the Church.[55]

And since it is mentioned above, we have this from St. John Paul II's encyclical *Ut Unum Sint*: "The [positive and gracious] elements of . . . [the] Church exist, found in their fullness in the Catholic Church and, without this fullness, in the other [Christian] Communities."[56]

On the Catholic Church and the kingdom of God, *Lumen Gentium* states,

> [The Church's mission is] to proclaim and to spread among all peoples the Kingdom of Christ and of God and to be, on earth, the initial budding forth [*germen et initium*] of that kingdom.[57]

From *Redemptoris Missio*:

> The kingdom [of God] cannot be detached either from Christ or from the Church. . . . If the kingdom is separated from Jesus, it is no longer the kingdom of God which he revealed. The result is a distortion of the meaning of the kingdom, which runs the risk of being transformed into a purely human or ideological goal, and a distortion of the identity of Christ, who no longer appears as the Lord to whom everything must one day be subjected. . . . Likewise, one may not separate the kingdom from the Church. It is true that the Church is not an end unto herself, since she is ordered toward the kingdom of God of which she is the seed, sign and instrument. Yet, while remaining distinct from Christ and the kingdom, the Church is indissolubly united to both.[58]

On Christ and the church in relation to humanity's religions, the CDF quotes Vatican II's *Lumen Gentium*:

> The Church, now sojourning on earth as an exile, is necessary for salvation. Christ, present to us in His Body, which is the Church, is the one Mediator and the unique way of salvation. In explicit terms He Himself affirmed the necessity of faith and

55. Vatican II, *Unitatis Redintegratio*, §3. See Tanner, *Decrees*, 2:910.

56. John Paul II, *Ut Unum Sint*, §14.

57. Vatican II, *Lumen Gentium*, §5. See Tanner, *Decrees*, 2:851. Perhaps a better translation of *germen et initium* would be "the sprouting-forth and beginning."

58. John Paul II, *Redemptoris Missio*, §18.

> Baptism and thereby affirmed also the necessity of the Church, for through Baptism as through a door men enter the Church.[59]
>
> [The church is] the universal sacrament of salvation.[60]

And from Vatican II's missionary decree *Ad Gentes*, it takes the following:

> Though God in ways known to Himself can lead those inculpably ignorant of the Gospel to find that faith without which it is impossible to please Him . . . yet a necessity lies upon the Church . . . and at the same time a sacred duty, to preach the Gospel. And hence missionary activity today as always retains its power and necessity.[61]

From Vatican II's declaration *Nostra Aetate*, we have this:

> [The church] [truly][62] proclaims, and ever must proclaim Christ "the way, the truth, and the life" (John 14:6), in whom men may find the fullness of religious life, in whom God has reconciled all things to Himself.[63]

And again from *Redemptoris Missio*:

> It is necessary to keep these two truths together, namely, the real possibility of salvation in Christ for all mankind and the necessity of the Church for salvation.[64]
>
> For [nonbelievers] salvation in Christ is accessible by virtue of a grace which, while having a mysterious relationship to the Church, does not make them formally part of the Church but enlightens them in a way which is accommodated to their spiritual and material situation. This grace comes from Christ; it is the result of his Sacrifice and is communicated by the Holy Spirit.[65]

Finally, the CDF quotes from Vatican II's Declaration on Religious Freedom, *Dignitatis Humanae*:

59. Vatican II, *Lumen Gentium*, §14.

60. Vatican II, *Lumen Gentium*, §48.

61. Vatican II, *Ad Gentes*, §7.

62. I have supplied for the Latin word *vero* (truly), which for some reason is not translated (see Tanner, *Decrees*, 2:969).

63. Vatican II, *Nostra Aetate*, §2.

64. John Paul II, *Redemptoris Missio*, §9.

65. John Paul II, *Redemptoris Missio*, §10.

> We believe that this one true religion subsists in the Catholic and Apostolic Church, to which the Lord Jesus committed the duty of spreading it abroad among all men. Thus He spoke to the Apostles: "Go, therefore, and make disciples of all nations, baptizing them in the name of the Father and of the Son and of the Holy Spirit, teaching them to observe all things whatsoever I have enjoined upon you" (Matt. 28: 19–20). On their part, all men are bound to seek the truth, especially in what concerns God and His Church, and to embrace the truth they come to know, and to hold fast to it.[66]

The above comprise almost every direct, verbatim quotation in *Dominus Iesus* from the documents both of Vatican II and Pope St. John Paul II's encyclical *Redemptoris Missio*. Looking at them, it is honestly incomprehensible to me how anyone could genuinely maintain that the statement's language differs from that of Vatican II or *Redemptoris Missio*. In many places, it *is* their language!

## Dialogue: Both Respect and Candor

Still, there is another interpretation. Perhaps Cassidy and Kasper did not mean that the CDF was remiss in quoting from Vatican II but that in quoting from Vatican II the CDF did not convey the same tone or feeling as the conciliar documents. In other words, *Dominus Iesus* does not reflect the "style" of the council. So the criticism shifts to how the declaration has used or interpreted the documents of Vatican II. It is that usage or interpretation which is claimed to be unreflective of Vatican II's "tone." Whereas the declaration's exposition of Vatican II's magisterium is accurate and undeniable, the council's doctrine is presented in such a way as to trample on the feelings of non-Catholics. In other words, the declaration's message does not reflect the deeper understanding and necessary sensitivity which the postconciliar church has achieved through ecumenical and interreligious dialogue.

Personally, I appreciate a tone or style that is clear and precise, candid and frank. It lets me know exactly where I stand with another person. He or she respects me enough to tell me what he or she really believes or thinks. It also gives me a frame of reference from which to work when approaching dialogue with the "other." It warns me not to make undue

66. Vatican II, *Dignitatis Humanae*, §1.

assumptions. I do not consider such a "style" or "tone" to be either rude or insensitive, if the other person is sincere in his or her frankness.

Obviously, one should not use language that one knows will hurt or offend another person. And we should remember the Lord Jesus' severe judgment on those who do: "You have heard that it was said to the ancients: 'You shall not kill; he who yet has killed, he shall be subject to the judgment.' Yet I say to you: Everyone, who is angry with his brother, will be subject to the judgment; he who yet has said to his brother: 'Racha,' will be subject to the council; he who yet has said: 'Fool,' will be subject unto the Gehenna of fire" (Matt 5:21–22). Still, I am not sure that a change in tone or style necessarily entails an actual change of meaning. Whether one says "schismatic" or "a person lacking in full communion with the Catholic Church," the reality still remains. Whether one says "heresy" or "it does not reflect the fullness of the church's faith," the reality still remains. Whether one says "false religion" or "it does not offer the fullness of truth as Christianity does," the reality still remains. Perhaps it is prudent to opt for more irenic language which, albeit not as explicit, has the psychological effect of softening the harsh blow of doctrinal reality for the church's interlocutors—like putting a fluffy cozy on a hot teapot. But that does not change the fact that the person receiving the cup might still find the tea to be too hot and too bitter to drink!

But I know that it is not just about "words." It is also about demeanor and attitude. We are morally obliged to avoid rash judgment and should interpret another person's words or actions in as favorable a light as possible.[67] As St. Ignatius Loyola advises in his *Spiritual Exercises*, "It should be presupposed that every good Christian ought to be more ready to give a good sense to the doubtful proposition of another than to condemn it; and if he cannot give a good sense to it, let him inquire how the other understands it, and if he is in error, let him correct him with charity [*con amor*]; and if this does not suffice, let him seek all suitable means in order that being brought to a right understanding of it he may save himself from error."[68] The bishops of Vatican II tried to do this: they evinced an attitude that, while sometimes acknowledging and never denying the negative theological or ecclesiological realities that existed in the church's relationship with other Christians and non-Christians, nevertheless expressed a hopefulness in the effectiveness of God's grace as well as in

67. See *CCC*, §2478.

68. Ignatius of Loyola, *Spiritual Exercises*, 24–25. Ignacio de Loyola, *Ejercicios espirituales*, 6.

the good will of human beings to address—and even resolve (!)—these realities in a positive manner. The bishops' assumption being, of course, in favor of the only Savior of humankind, Jesus Christ, and his body, the Catholic Church. Obviously, such an attitude of hopefulness required a more positive reappraisal of the religious "other"—that is, it required the church to seek where God might be present and working, instead of highlighting where he was absent or resisted. The Jesuit historian John W. O'Malley describes Vatican II's difference in style as "panegyric" or "epideictic":

> The purpose of the genre . . . is not so much to clarify concepts as to heighten appreciation for a person, an event, an institution, and to excite emulation of an ideal. . . .
>
> The documents of Vatican II fit this mold. That is their "style." They hold up ideals and then often draw conclusions from them and spell out consequences. . . .
>
> The epideictic genre is a form of the art of persuasion and thus of reconciliation. While it raises appreciation, it creates or fosters among those it addresses a realization that they all share (or should share) the same ideals and need to work together to achieve them. This genre reminds people of what they have in common rather than what might divide them, and the reminder motivates them to cooperate in enterprises for the common good, to work for a common cause.[69]

But there is a danger with this, as described by the late Jesuit theologian, Avery Dulles:

> Since the council, the popes and the synods of bishops have been laudably conscious of their responsibility to guard the deposit that has been entrusted to them. . . . They have found the council documents very helpful for that purpose, when those documents are read for their substance rather than their style. At times the Roman authorities have found it necessary to speak more plainly and less diplomatically for the sake of truth and fidelity. *Dominus Iesus* did precisely that in its treatment of the uniqueness of Christ and of the Catholic Church. The Congregation for the Doctrine of the Faith seems to have learned from hard experience that when you couch unpopular teachings in

69. O'Malley, "Vatican II," 25–26. Reverend O'Malley fell asleep in the Lord in 2022: requiescat in pace!

> "polite" language, people easily conclude that you didn't really mean what you said.[70]

Does a change in tone or style necessarily mean a change in one's beliefs or opinions? Does it mean previous disagreements have gone away, or were no longer of any matter (i.e., they are set aside)? The answers to these questions are fundamentally important, especially when the claim is made that—yes—Vatican II's change in tone has meant also a change in the church's magisterium. As O'Malley puts it, "The council *wanted* something to happen."[71]

Dialogue is essentially an encounter between persons—not beliefs. Beliefs are grasped and held by persons, by human beings, who bring them to their dialogue. Man "is the only creature . . . which God willed for itself," and which was created to share in God's everlasting life.[72] Hence, the human person is dignified. And the dignity of dialogue comes from the persons involved; it does not rest on their beliefs. A person can be wrong, but he or she is not "false." Religions, however, as belief systems created by human beings can be "false." I think that needs to be recalled by the Catholic every time he or she enters into dialogue.

*Dominus Iesus* expressly reminds its audience that equality in dialogue refers only to the dignity afforded to the human persons—of whatever belief—who are involved in it.[73] But the teachings of other Christian churches and communities or of other religions are not equal in quality to the doctrines of the Catholic Church. Nor is any religious figure in any way equivalent to Jesus of Nazareth.[74] Indeed, it is because of that respect for the human person that the church is bound to tell others what the truth is and how they can be saved by it.[75] Of course, this necessarily involves telling others that what they have come to believe is not true

70. Dulles, "Vatican II," 15–16. Dulles fell asleep in the Lord in 2008. May Christ remember his priesthood in his kingdom!

71. O'Malley, "Vatican II," 33; emphasis original. But could the quarrel about *Dominus Iesus*'s tone and style just be a "red herring"? Could not a person disagree with the manner in which someone else stated his own opinions, without being necessarily offended by it? As DiNoia remarked during his lecture on *Dominus Iesus* above, while he heard many focus on the declaration's "tone," he could not help but notice that it was *the content* of the document that people really did not seem to like (see DiNoia, "Dominus Iesus," 8:38).

72. Vatican II, *Gaudium et Spes*, §24. See also *CCC*, §§355–60.

73. CDF, *Dominus Iesus*, §22.

74. CDF, *Dominus Iesus*, §22.

75. CDF, *Dominus Iesus*, §22.

and that the paths which they have chosen to follow do not ultimately lead to salvation. The Catholic dialogue partner knows that he or she has the fullness of the truth of salvation in Christ and his church. He or she can then enter into dialogue with non-Catholics in a spirit of humble confidence. It is that confidence which makes the Catholic unafraid of dialogue with those who do not believe. But it should never be allowed to become the arrogant "sin of presumption" that he or she has nothing to learn from the religious beliefs, practices, or experiences of others.

Dialogue between the church and the various Christian churches and communities is viewed today by many as a necessary task. Dialogue between the church and the world's nonbelievers is even more so, since at least non-Catholic Christians have Christ. True, Christ wills the unity of all of his disciples (see John 17:11, 21). But he states in the same context that his followers' union must be one of holiness *in the truth* (v. 17). True also, God wills all men and women to be saved (see 1 Tim 2:4a). But the Pauline author adds that this happens by "com[ing] to an acknowledgment of truth" (4b). Even if a dialogue tries to be open, inoffensive, and respectful, I believe that it will eventually run up against the reality of the "non-negotiables." There are just some things—even of the most basic and essential kind—that neither group can say to the "other" or about the "other" because it does not believe them to be true. There just are some beliefs and practices of humanity's religions that will always be unacceptable to the church since they either distort or reject something of the authenticity of the Christian religion, which is the truth. One of the two sides has to be wrong. And if wrong, one of them has to change, whether in whole or in part. *Dominus Iesus* was a statement of some of those "non-negotiables" about which the Catholic Church cannot ever just "agree to disagree."

## The Missionary Mandate Goes Down the "Memory Hole"

If the missiological conference that I attended in Papua New Guinea were any indication, the declaration *Dominus Iesus* has left little, if any, overall impact on the church's missiological enterprise. Rather, it seems to have been just a jarring pothole on the road to further dialogue which, once passed over, could be forgotten.

And forgotten it was.

Even years later, some within the Holy See still seemed to have been piqued by *Dominus Iesus*. So they quietly packed it away with the Catholic Church's other magisterial oddities, like the Syllabus of Errors. In 2006, for example, the Pontifical Council for Interreligious Dialogue (PCID) published an updated edition of its book *Interreligious Dialogue: The Official Teaching of the Catholic Church*. It is a thick volume containing statements, both excerpted and complete, from Vatican II, the popes (even the very short reign of Pope Bl. John Paul I!), and curial offices—even the *Code of Canon Law*. The CDF's *Dominus Iesus* is nowhere to be found there; it has been "memory-holed."[76]

I used the PCID's volume extensively when writing my doctoral dissertation on the work of theologian Jacques Dupuis. I also consulted it thoroughly when writing an article on *Dominus Iesus*, which was eventually published (see the bibliography below). Honestly, if one looks through the collection of St. John Paul II's speeches after the declaration, there is not much mention of it. This might not have been notable had the pope at least mentioned *Dominus Iesus*'s core principles, like Jesus as the definitive revelation of God, Jesus as the unique mediator of God's salvation, and the salvific necessity of belonging to Christ's church. But, typically, he does not.[77]

Given the various interreligious contexts of the meetings, it might have seemed out of place for the pope to bring up matters that his listeners would have severely objected to. The situations (it might have been thought) were not the right ones for asserting what the church really believed about others' religious beliefs. Yet, I ask this: What *would* have been the right situation for the pope to have spoken about Jesus Christ or the church to nonbelievers?

The pope is generally regarded by the world at large as the spokesman of the Christian religion. Only he among all Christian leaders can, by his very presence, bring together so many thousands and even millions of people, whether Catholic or Christian or not, to hear his message. Who better to proclaim the gospel to so many, especially to those who may have only an elemental acquaintance with Jesus or the church? Pope

76. See Dunn, Review of *Interreligious Dialogue*, 410–12. Strangely enough, Pope St. John Paul II's defense of *Dominus Iesus* in his Angelus address of October 1, 2000, is included in the volume.

A new, updated edition of this volume came out in 2013. It is over two thousand pages long. The CDF's declaration still does not appear in it!

77. Nor did his successor, Pope Benedict XVI (Cardinal Ratzinger), who himself had been intimately involved with the publication of *Dominus Iesus*.

St. John Paul II opens his encyclical *Redemptoris Missio* with St. Paul's cry, "Woe is me then, if I will not have brought good news!" (1 Cor 9:16c). Still, among all the many times when the sainted pope sat or stood before groups of non-Christians during his frequent journeys and meetings, I have to ask, *When did he?* To Catholics—yes. To other Christians—usually only about what they believed together about Christ; little about the church. To all others—usually nothing about Christ or the church at all. Again, I come away with the impression, mentioned above, that the message of the gospel is only intended to be kept "intra-ecclesially"—that is, Catholics talk about it among Catholics and, perhaps, with other Christians. But the message is not proclaimed to outsiders. So how then can the popes wonder at a lack of missionary fervor when they themselves do not lead by example?

# 5

# The King Without Kingship or Kingdom

In his encyclical letter *Redemptoris Missio*, Pope St. John Paul II writes that "the kingdom of God is the manifestation and the realization of God's plan of salvation in all its fullness."[1] This plan is stated with sublimeness by the Gospel of John:

> For God has thus loved the world, that he gave his only begotten Son, that everyone, who believes in him, may not be lost, but may have eternal life. For God did not send the Son into the world, that he should judge the world, but that the world may be saved through him. (John 3:16–17)

In its essence, the "kingdom" is something that has come from God, has been effected by Jesus Christ, his Son, and is manifested in Christ's community of believers, the church. This is the argument that I will make below.

## Israel's God as King of the Cosmos

The idea of God's kingdom runs throughout the Sacred Scriptures of Israel. Biblical scholar John P. Meier acknowledges that *as a mythic story* the "kingdom of God" stretches from the opening pages of the Old Testament to the last:

> If we were to construct an artificial summary of the story of the kingdom, it would include God's creation of His good and ordered universe, creation's corruption by human sin and

1. John Paul II, *Redemptoris Missio*, §15.

> rebellion, God's gracious choice of the people Israel to be His very own, His liberation of them from slavery in Egypt, the experiences of sin and salvation at the Reed Sea and Mt. Sinai, the desert journey, and entrance into the promised land. The story might include the kingdom of . . . King David, God's choice of Jerusalem and Mt. Zion for His dwelling place alongside the king, the disasters caused by David's less than ideal successors, the descent of Israel into ever greater idolatry and sin, Israel's rejection of the prophets' warnings, the destruction of Jerusalem and the Babylonian exile, the promise of future restoration that would include a rebuilt Jerusalem and a new, purified temple, the subjection of the hostile Gentiles, and the establishment among human beings of God's eternal kingdom of peace and justice (with or without a human vicegerent or intermediary). Depending on how apocalyptic a given storyteller might be, the final kingdom might be envisioned as a restoration-but-vast-improvement of David's original kingdom, or a return to paradise on earth, or a heavenly kingdom beyond this world of time and space.[2]

But the phrase "kingdom of God," as well as the idea, seems to achieve prominence only in the preaching of Jesus of Nazareth. So let us start by asking, What is the image or concept of the "kingdom of God" in the Sacred Scriptures? How did Jesus use it? What did he mean by it? What is its relationship to the church's evangelizing mission?[3]

The literature on the subject of the "kingdom of God" is vast, as we scholars are wont to say. As such, it is not my purpose here to present all, or even most, of the biblical and scholarly data on the subject.[4] It is,

2. Meier, *Mentor, Message, and Miracles*, 241.

3. In this chapter, I am indebted to a couple of works by the late Avery Cardinal Dulles: The first is a paper that then–Reverend Dulles presented to a 1991 symposium sponsored by the National Conference of Catholic Bishops (now the USCCB). See Dulles, "Church and the Kingdom." The second is a chapter in his 1977 book *The Resilient Church* (pp. 9–27). With his typical clarity, concision, and insightfulness, he helped me both to understand the issues involved and to organize my own thoughts.

4. Dulles provides a basic bibliography on the topic (see "Church and the Kingdom," 14n1). It would include the following:

- Carmignac, *Le Mirage de l'Eschatologie*
- Chilton, *The Kingdom of God in the Teaching of Jesus*
- Perrin, *Jesus and the Language of the Kingdom*
- Perrin, *The Kingdom of God in the Teaching of Jesus*
- Schnackenburg, *God's Rule and Kingdom*
- Willis, *The Kingdom of God in 20th-Century Interpretation*

however, helpful to review some of the data in order to build a foundation on which I can then establish my own thoughts.

It is commonplace among scholars, when discussing the idea of the "kingdom of God," to point out that it appears only very rarely in the Old Testament. This is true . . . depending on what one means.

If one means *the exact phrase* "kingdom of God," then—yes—its use is very infrequent. It appears in that exact form only once in the Old Testament: in the Book of Wisdom (10:10; *basileian theou*).[5] This Scripture was composed in Greek, maybe fifty to one hundred years before the time of Christ.[6] The next closest instance that we have—and the only one in the Hebrew language—is from 1 Chronicles (see 28:5). There, it speaks of the "kingdom of Yahweh" (Hebrew, *malkut Yhwh*).[7] Of course, the statement is not exactly the same as "kingdom of God," but it is nevertheless clearly the exact same idea, since "Yahweh" was believed to be God's name, and should be taken as the phrase's equivalent. So we have two relatively clear examples of the statement in the Old Testament Scriptures.[8]

Yet why should one be bound to the exact phrase "kingdom of God"? Why is it not possible to accept also any and all statements that

---

*Nota bene*: In volume 2 of his mammoth series on the "Historical Jesus" titled *A Marginal Jew*, John P. Meier gives a more extensive bibliography (see Meier, *Mentor, Message, and Miracles*, 272–73n3). Meier fell asleep in the Lord just a few years ago, leaving his excellent work (alas) unfinished.

5. Rahlfs, *Septuaginta*, 2:359.

6. See Wright, "Wisdom," §2.

7. *BHS*, 1510.

8. A few words need to be said about the proper translation and understanding of the words *malkut* and *basileia*. The word "kingdom" has traditionally been the preferred translation into English for the Hebrew and Greek words *malkut* and *basileia*, respectively. Scholars have long recognized, though, that it is maybe not the best translation since it tends to convey the idea of a boundaried "realm" wherein a person exercises his or her own rule. Or it could be understood as indicating something that has already been completely realized (the difference between the [present] reign of God versus the [future] kingdom of God). The word as used in both the Hebrew and Greek, however, seems to want to convey more the abstract sense of "reigning" or "ruling." Some scholars prefer, then, to speak more accurately about the "reign [or kingship] of God" rather than of his "kingdom." The word, both in its meaning and in its usage in the Old Testament, highlights the state of "rulership" or "dominion" or (one might say) "kingly power" that God has over all creation. See e.g., Schnackenburg, *God's Rule and Kingdom*, 9–10, 354–57; Perrin, *Kingdom of God*, 23–24; see also Meier, *Mentor, Message, and Miracles*, 240; Robert and Feuillet, *Introduction to the New Testament*, 753–66; and McKenzie, *Dictionary of the Bible*, 480. So in the Jews' most basic and generalized usage of the expression "kingdom of God" (and related statements), the Jews meant to acknowledge *the unquestioned sovereignty of God over all things*, both in heaven and on earth and under the earth.

mean or say essentially the same thing? For example, the sons of Korah call God a "King" in Ps 47:

> The Lord is the most high, the fearful one,
> a great king over every land. . . .
> Because God is the king of every land,
> sing a psalm in a skillful way.
> (Ps 47:3, 8)[9]

The sacred writings say that God possesses a "kingdom," as the pagan ruler Nebuchadnezzar must admit in the Prophecy of Daniel:

> [God's] signs, how great they are,
> and his wonders, how mighty!
> And his kingdom is an everlasting kingdom,
> and his power is from generation to generation.
> (Dan 3:100)[10]

The prophet Zephaniah declares,

> Praise, daughter of Zion;
> shout, you of Israel!
> Rejoice and leap about with all your heart,
> daughter of Jerusalem!
> The Lord has taken away your judgment,
> He has turned away your enemies;
> the King of Israel, the Lord, is in your midst,
> you shall not fear evil anymore.
> (Zeph 3:14–15)

God is said to actually "rule" or "reign," as Asaph and his brothers sing:

> Let the heavens rejoice, and the earth leap about,
> and let them say among the nations: "The Lord reigns."

9. See also Ps 10:16.

10. In the book of Tobit, the eponymous character blesses God and "his kingdom" (13:2). Psalm 103 declares that "His own kingdom [viz., God's] will rule over everyone" (v. 19b). In the Prophecy of Daniel, Darius, the pagan king, sends out a decree to the people of his empire declaring that "they should tremble at and fear the God of Daniel: For he is the living God and endures unto the ages, and his kingdom shall not be scattered, and his power is even unto eternity" (Dan 6:27). Moreover, when talking to God directly, the inspired authors refer to "your kingdom," which obviously means God's (see e.g., Ps 45:7 and Dan 3:54). There also appears the more circumlocutory statement, namely, "the thing ruled by Yahweh" (*laYhwh hamlukah*), which does seem to evoke the idea of a specific place where God reigns—a "realm." It is rarely used, though, found only in Obadiah's prophecy (v. 21) and Ps 22 (v. 29). See *BHS*, 1030 and 1105.

(1 Chr 16:31)[11]

God's "dominion" or "lordship" is equated with having a "kingdom," as in Ps 145:

> Your kingdom [*malkuteka*] is a kingdom [*malkut*] for all ages,
> and your dominion [*memshelteka*] is from every generation to generation (Ps 145:13)[12]

God is said to sit upon a seat from which he rules—a "throne"—as declared in the Church Book, composed by Jesus ben Sira:

> One is the most high, the creator almighty
> both a powerful king and greatly to be feared,
> sitting upon his throne and dominating: God!
> (Sir 1:8)[13]

I fail to see in *any* of these statements given above how neither the idea nor the language of the "kingdom of God" is not in some way being equivalently expressed. The language in most instances is almost the same; the idea is surely the same. If looked at this way, I think, the general scholarly opinion needs revision.[14]

11. The last expression, "The Lord reigns [or rules]," occurs several times throughout Psalms (see 93:1, 96:10, 97:1, 99:1, 146:10). It also appears expressed in other places (see e.g., Exod 15:18, 1 Sam 12:12, Isa 24:23, 52:7, Lam 5:19, Mic 4:7).

12. See *BHS*, 1223. Another translation of the Hebrew *memshelteka* is "your place of reigning," which also evokes the possibility of God's rule having a spatial characteristic (i.e., it is somewhere). See Koehler and Baumgartner, *Lexicon in Veteris Testamenti Libros*, 531 and 534.

13. As a matter of fact, the image of God's kingly seat—his "throne"—is exceptionally present throughout the Sacred Scriptures, from the earliest to the latest writings (especially in Psalms): Exod 17:16; 1 Sam 4:4; 2 Sam 6:2; 1 Kgs 22:19; 2 Kgs 19:15; 1 Chr 13:6, 29:23; 2 Chr 9:8; 18:18; Job 36:7; Pss 9:4, 7, 11; 11:4; 22:3; 29:10; 33:14; 45:6; 47:8; 55:19; 80:1; 89:14; 93:2; 97:2; 99:1; 102:12; 103:19; 123:1; Wis 9:4, 10; 18:15; Sir 1:8; Isa 6:1; 37:16; 66:1; Jer 3:17; 14:21; 49:38; Lam 5:19; Ezek 43:7.

14. And yet, such a careful scholar as John P. Meier can write that the claims of God's kingship in the Old Testament, whether in the expression "kingdom of God" or in similar ones, is "hardly overwhelming" (Meier, *Mentor, Message, and Miracles*, 244). On the contrary, he continues, "there are whole parts of the [Old Testament] that have no explicit reference to God as king or to God's kingship" (244). I am not sure what to make of such an argument: First, what does he mean by "whole parts"? And why is that indicative of anything? Second, what about *implicit* references to God as king or his kingship? If not explicit, then is he saying that a reference does not count? Third, is no other kind of language possible except "king" or "kingdom"?

Old Testament scholar Lawrence Boadt takes a different view: "Many of the testimonies of early Israel proclaim that Yahweh was king over Israel" (*Reading the Old Testament*, 242; see 242–43). And the idea of God's kingship is a line of continuity

While the ancient Israelites might have been a generally trivial and undistinguished group (as even their own Scriptures sometimes admit: see e.g., Deut 7:7–8 and Amos 7:1–6), their God most definitely was not. He was supreme and unique. The God of Israel retains a dominion, or mastery, over all things that is direct, complete, eternal, and unchallenged.[15] Israel's belief in God's "kingdom," or sovereignty, is powerfully expressed, for example, in Mordecai's prayer in the Book of Esther where he cries out,

> Lord, Lord, all-powerful King,
> for under your sovereignty are all things placed,
> and there is no one who can resist your will. . . .
> For you have made the sky and the earth
> and whatever marvel is contained under the ambit of heaven.
> You are Lord of everything,
> nor is there is one who could resist your majesty.
> (Esth 4:17c–e)

We can also see the same idea at play in the prayer of the biblical heroine Judith, who prays to God, addressing him as "the king of the entirety of your creation" (Jdt 9:12).

Yet sovereignty, or "kingly power," does not exist in a vacuum: there must actually be someplace and something upon which such dominion is exercised—even if it is everywhere and on everything (as in God's case). Therefore, as David M. Stanley notes in *The Jerome Biblical Commentary*, while "kingdom" understood as a "realm" does not represent the primary sense of either the Hebrew or Greek word, "the secondary meaning . . . [of] the territory or subjects ruled by the king, is closely cognate to the idea of the king's rule, dominion, or reign, inasmuch as territory and subjects symbolize concretely royal power."[16] This begs the question of where God's sovereignty might be exercised. In other words, is there someplace where God has centered his lordship specifically?

Yes—in Israel.

The psalmist declares, "Upon Israel's going forth from Egypt, the House of Jacob from a barbarous people, Judah was made [God's] sanctuary, Israel his power [*mamshelotao*]" (Ps 114:1–2).[17] In a vision,

---

between the Old Testament and Jesus' preaching (*Reading the Old Testament*, 539–40).

15. See Robert and Feuillet, *Introduction to the New Testament*, 755.

16. Stanley and Brown, "Aspects of New Testament Thought," §96.

17. See *BHS*, 1196. The Nova Vulgata opts to translate the Hebrew *memshalah* in the sense of "power" or "might" (Latin, *potestas*), instead of "dominion" or "place of

the prophet Ezekiel sees the Lord God entering the restored temple in Jerusalem: "And he said unto me: 'Son of Man, [this is] the place of my throne and the place for the soles of my feet, where I will dwell in the midst of the children of Israel unto eternity'" (Ezek 43:7).

Of course, the demolition of the kingdoms of Israel and Judah (in 721 and 587 BC, respectively), the displacement of their citizens to other lands, and the destruction of the Jerusalem temple posed serious challenges to the Jews' faith in their sovereign God. In the time of Judah's captivity in Babylon as well as after, there started to appear a development in Jewish theology regarding God's sovereignty: God's sovereignty is not just something that God *qua* God has absolutely—his "reign"—but it is also something that he will exert definitively over all creation—his "kingdom." The statement of the "kingdom of God" becomes more than just an affirmation of God's absolute sovereignty, or dominion, over his creation; it becomes understood to mean that God will actually, concretely, and finally establish his sovereignty over all things that stand up against or oppose themselves to his will.[18] How God would do this was a matter of opinion: some believed it would be through God's destruction of all of Israel's foes and the reestablishment of the ancient monarchy of David, others saw it more as God's placement of his Spirit into all flesh and the writing of his law on every heart, still others believed that it would happen through God's bringing an end to all time and history, when everything that opposed his will (e.g., death, sickness, sorrow) would be vanquished.[19]

## God's "Kingdom" and Jesus Himself

I think that it is fair to say that this idea of the "kingdom of God" found its full flowering in the imagination of an early first-century-AD charismatic

---

dominion" (see also Koehler and Baumgartner, *Lexicon in Veteris Testamenti Libros*, 534). This is a possible meaning of the Hebrew term. Nevertheless, the verse could also be understood to mean that Israel became God's "place of power."

18. The Jews' belief in God's eventual and final "in-breaking" (as scholars like to call it) starts to appear in Jewish literature that was composed during the period from their return from exile in Babylon and the rebuilding of the Jerusalem temple to that temple's subsequent destruction by Roman armies in the first century of Christ. Scholars call this historical time the "Second Temple Period." It runs ca. 539 BC–AD 70. See Wright et al., "History of Israel," §§186–87.

19. See e.g., Schnackenburg, *God's Rule and Kingdom*, 41–75, and Perrin, *Jesus and the Language*, 24–29.

Jew, a woodworker-cum-rabbi, who was called by his followers, "Jesus the Christ." Its use continued in the movement that had gathered around him, which came to be called *Christianity*. Whereas the specific expression of the "kingdom of God" had already started to appear in Jewish literature, the idea veritably burgeons in the writings about Jesus.

Historically, can we say that Jesus of Nazareth spoke about "the kingdom of God"? The question admits of two interpretations: First, did Jesus use the actual phrase?[20] Second, did he talk about the idea? Almost all New Testament scholars would say yes to each question. I would agree with them.

The Gospel According to Mark is believed to be the earliest written Gospel, composed sometime in the AD 60s.[21] It is notable, then, that Mark places a reference to God's kingdom on the lips of Jesus from the very start of his ministry. According to Mark, almost the first words to come out of Jesus' mouth speak about it:

> Jesus came into Galilee, proclaiming the gospel of God and saying: "The time is fulfilled, and the kingdom of God [*hē basileia tou theou*] has come near; repent and believe in the gospel." (Mark 1:14b–15)

This, of course, could have been Mark's own redactional activity—that is, he intentionally placed speech about the "kingdom" into Jesus' teaching. It could also indicate the influence of Mark's community in how it

20. *Nota bene*: I have no intention whatsoever here of wading into the morass of a question about the *form* of the phrase that Jesus might have actually used. Anyone who has read the Gospels knows that Matthew the Evangelist records Jesus as using almost exclusively the expression "the kingdom of [the] heaven[s]" (*hē basileia tōn ouranōn*). The practice would seem to have been due to the Jewish tendency to respectfully avoid any direct mention of the Divine. Though, just to add to our puzzlement, Matthew does record Jesus also using the phrase the "kingdom of God" a few times (see 6:33; 12:28; 19:24; 21:31, 43). So scholars ask, Which one did Jesus really use? Which is genuine? Are both genuine? The great majority of New Testament scholars accept that "kingdom of God" is most likely the expression that Jesus actually used. I think this consensus has good reasons behind it (e.g., it appears throughout the Gospel traditions, even in Matthew, who typically avoids it), so I am comfortable in accepting it. "Kingdom of God" will, therefore, be the preferred way that I refer to it in Jesus' doctrine.

21. See Harrington, "Gospel According to Mark," §2. The Gospels of Matthew and Luke seem to depend on Mark's Gospel's contents and, hence, logically should have been written later—that is, sometime after the AD 60s. (Most scholars think in the AD 70s or later.) John's Gospel is like a platypus: one of a kind. John does not seem to have copied from any of the other canonical Gospels. Most scholars place his Gospel as the latest (ca. AD 90s). See also Viviano, "Gospel According to Matthew," §4, Karris, "Gospel According to Luke," §3, and Perkins, "Gospel According to John," §18.

constructed the tradition about Jesus. Except, the expression is found on Jesus' lips across the board of traditions about Jesus, at every level of the Gospel tradition: from Mark's Gospel, to the ancient "Sayings Gospel Q,"[22] to the "special material" of the Gospels of Matthew and Luke,[23] to the Gospel of John. All of them agree that Jesus mentioned specifically the "kingdom of God." So it does not appear to have been something that just Mark himself or his church had created. It is also notable that the expression appears across the various kinds of tradition derived from Jesus: it appears in his aphorisms and sayings (see e.g., Mark 10:15 and John 3:5); it is explained in his parables (e.g., in Matt 13:47–50); it is connected to his wonder-working (see e.g., Luke 11:20). The coming together of these different kinds of evidence makes New Testament scholars confident in asserting that the phrase "kingdom of God" does in fact go back to Jesus himself. He used it; the expression was his own.[24] I would tend to agree with this assessment.

Scholars are also generally united in their belief that not only did Jesus himself use the expression the "kingdom of God" but that he also expatiated on its meaning. He did not just name it—that it was at hand—rather, he also spoke about it and explained it: What did it mean? What was it like? I think that this assessment is also accurate, and quite obvious to anyone who has read any of the Synoptic Gospels. (Again, John is a special case!)

Where I would tend to diverge, however, is on the question of whether Jesus made the "kingdom of God" his *primary* topic of discourse. Many, if not most, New Testament scholars would agree that the topic of God's kingdom was the central theme of Jesus' preaching—indeed, his

22. *Simply put*, the "Sayings Gospel Q" is all of the material that the Gospels of Matthew and Luke share but that does not appear in Mark. Once you isolate all of this material, its contents amount primarily to sayings of Jesus. (Though, some scholars claim that it did include some stories. The debate rages on!) "Q" also designates material that, while appearing in Matthew, Mark, and Luke, appears in both Matthew and Luke in a version that agrees against Mark's version in many respects. In such cases, scholars think it more likely that Matthew and Luke have used a common source, which is not Mark (i.e., "Q").

Most scholars believe that "Q" was a written document all by itself (now lost), which was used independently by Matthew and Luke. See e.g., Kloppenborg, Q, 12–15, 55–57.

23. These are materials that occur exclusively in either Matthew or Luke. In other words, they comprise stories or sayings of Jesus that are specific either to Matthew (hence, called "M") or Luke ("L"). For the classic statement of this idea, see Streeter, *Four Gospels*, 199–270 (chs. 8 and 9).

24. See Meier, *Roots of the Problem*, 174–75.

supreme message. For instance, in his book *Rediscovering the Teaching of Jesus*, the esteemed New Testament scholar Norman Perrin writes with no apparent fear of contradiction,

> The central aspect of the teaching of Jesus was that concerning the Kingdom of God. *Of this there can be no doubt and today no scholar does, in fact, doubt it.* Jesus appeared as one who proclaimed the Kingdom; all else in his message and ministry serves a function in relation to that proclamation and derives its meaning from it. The challenge to discipleship, the ethical teaching, the disputes about oral tradition or ceremonial law, even the pronouncement of the forgiveness of sins and the welcoming of the outcast in the name of God—all these are to be understood in context of the Kingdom proclamation *or they are not to be understood at all.* Of all the descriptive titles that have been applied to Jesus through the centuries, the one that sums up his historical appearance best is . . . : Jesus is the Proclaimer of the Kingdom of God.[25]

I do not have the stature of Professor Perrin; nor would I claim to. But I think his assessment above might be wrong. Rather, I agree with the

25. Perrin, *Rediscovering*, 54; emphasis added. The problem with such a categorical claim as Perrin's is that it does not really fit the evidence. While it is true that Jesus of Nazareth talks about the "kingdom of God," he does not talk about it as much as Perrin and other scholars assume that he does. The two earliest sources that we have for the teaching of Jesus are the Gospel According to Mark and the "Sayings Gospel Q." How many times does Jesus actually mention the "kingdom of God" (Greek, *hē basileia tou theou*) in them?

Mark's Gospel is traditionally divided into 678 verses in Greek (Just, "New Testament Statistics"). Of those, 284 verses actually purport to record the words of Jesus. (There is always the possibility that I have miscounted, but I think that my enumeration is accurate.) In those verses, Jesus uses the expression the "kingdom of God" thirteen times in total out of thirteen verses (see Mark 1:15; 4:11, 26, 30; 9:1, 47; 10:14–15, 23–25; 12:34; 14:25). This means that in only around *5 percent* of Jesus' teaching in the Gospel of Mark does he mention it.

What about "Q"? The "Sayings Gospel Q" is almost wholly comprised of sayings of Jesus. The International Q Project generally assigns the contents of "Q" to around 260 distinct verses (see Kloppenborg, Q, 123–63). In it, Jesus mentions the "kingdom of God" a total of twelve times in eleven verses (Q 7:28; 9:62; 10:9; 11:52; 12:31; 13:18, 20, 28; 16:16; 17:20–21). (*Nota bene*: This versification of "Q" follows the versification of the Gospel of Luke.) This equals *4.2 percent* of the total verses.

This is a somewhat puzzling result (to say the least) for something that is claimed to be the "central aspect" of Jesus' teaching—something, which Norman Perrin says, no scholar denies or can (!) deny. Indeed, Perrin says, it is the context by which all of Jesus' words and actions are to be understood—or they are not to be understood at all! How, then, does one explain such a meager result? Well, the consensus would appear to be wrong—or, at least, in need of substantial revision.

judgment of scholar John P. Meier who, while agreeing with Perrin that the "kingdom of God" was part of Jesus' doctrine, was less convinced that it was the only concern of Jesus' ministry. A major theme for Jesus? Meier says yes. But *the* central and overriding theme? No.[26]

What did Jesus of Nazareth mean by the "kingdom of God"?

It is not so easy to tell. When Jesus does talk about it, he almost always conveys his teaching through the use of similes and metaphors.[27] Thus, someone as thorough and meticulous a scholar as John P. Meier can write plaintively for his article in *The New Jerome Biblical Commentary*, "It is almost impossible to define what Jesus meant by the kingdom . . . of God" because it has so many "allusive resonances" and is not "a clearly defined doctrine or abstract concept."[28]

In his book *Jesus and the Language of the Kingdom*, Norman Perrin famously applied the ideas of "steno-symbol" and "tensive symbol" to Jesus' preaching about the "kingdom of God." A steno-symbol represents an exact, one-to-one equivalence to something else, whereas a tensive symbol can be used with a wide variety of meanings. Perrin maintained that Jesus' language about the kingdom should be interpreted as a tensive symbol—that is, an image or symbol which can have a set of widespread and variegated meanings.[29] Perrin's contribution, albeit not without its critics, is nevertheless of critical importance as a reminder that we should not casually assume that Jesus always used the expression the "kingdom

26. See Meier, *Mentor, Message, and Miracles*, 237–43. Meier writes, "Jesus seems to have seized upon imagery and language that was present but hardly central to the [Old Testament] and intertestamental traditions of Judaism and consciously decided to make the symbol of God's kingly rule one of the central themes of his own message" (Meier, *Mentor, Message, and Miracles*, 269).

27. As a matter of fact, it is recorded in the Gospels that sometimes Jesus *refused* to elucidate the meaning of his teaching about the kingdom for those outside his circle of discipleship: see e.g., the parable of the sower in Mark 4:10–12 and parallels. Yet, as John P. Meier points out, many exegetes believe that vv. 10–12 have been inserted by Mark from another place into the original context of Jesus' discussion of the parable of the sower (see Meier, *Mentor, Message, and Miracles*, 491–92n177; see also Harrington, "Gospel According to Mark," §27). If so . . . so what? Even if one could show that Mark placed a *logion* of Jesus into the parable of the sower in ch. 4, I still do not see how it makes a huge change in meaning: Jesus uses "riddle speech" when teaching the crowds so that they may "see" and "not see," "hear" and yet "not understand" (v. 12). But to his own followers he gives "the mystery of the kingdom of God" (v. 11).

28. Meier, "Jesus," §17.

29. See Perrin, *Jesus and the Language*, 29–32. (Perrin is using the previous work of Philip Wheelwright, *Metaphor and Reality*.)

of God" in exactly the same way every time he spoke about it.[30] This seems to fit the evidence of Jesus' preaching found in the Gospels. For while in many cases Jesus attributes the "kingdom" to God, in several instances he also attaches a "kingdom" to himself and to his community of disciples.

For Jesus, I think, his intention was to make present and actual the full sovereignty of God. As Rudolf Schnackenburg explains, the "kingdom of God" was not for Jesus simply a reexpression of or a reminder to his fellow Jews of God's sovereign power over creation or his "kingship" of Israel. To any Jew, either of these ideas would have been obvious and unquestionable! Rather, Jesus announces "God's kingship in its full realization, fully active, eschatologically irrevocable."[31] This is different because with Jesus it is not the expression of a firmly held belief: it is the confirmation that it is true. God was effectively bringing a final end to anything within man and in creation that was not how God wanted it to be.

The "kingdom" was one image among several others (e.g., the Son of Man, Son of God, Messiah) that Jesus used in his overarching program of bringing God's salvation fully to the world.[32] But salvation was not merely a topic of discussion for Jesus or a message that he proclaimed (a *kērygma*). The salvation brought by the kingdom was an action. True, he described it in his parables and taught about it in his aphorisms, but he also made it completely patent and real in his healings, exorcisms, and other deeds of power. As the "kingdom" represented the activity of God himself, it was by definition *personal*: it involved a "Someone," who was directly intervening to bring it about. I think it is undeniable that Jesus believed that *he* was that "someone"! It was through him, the woodworker from Nazareth, that God was finally and definitively establishing his everlasting reign. The "kingdom" was not for Jesus some kind of generic, ephemeral presence. It was *real*. Jesus yearned for it: "I have come to send fire upon the earth and what do I want? That it be kindled already! I

30. As John P. Meier observes, "Perrin's emphasis on kingdom as a tensive symbol is a salutary warning against treating a mythic archetype like a mathematical formula" (Meier, *Mentor, Message, and Miracles*, 242).

31. Schnackenburg, *God's Rule and Kingdom*, 82.

32. See e.g., the comment of Rudolf Schnackenburg: "From Jesus we hear nothing about vengeance. One outstanding feature of his preaching is that salvation is proclaimed also and indeed especially for sinners. In his eyes the reign of God is in the first place the realization of God's redeeming will, the fulfilment of the prophecies of Deutero-Isaias. . . . The content of his preaching is a message of salvation, joy and peace on the lines of Isa. 52:7" (Schnackenburg, *God's Rule and Kingdom*, 87–88).

have yet to be baptized with a baptism and how I am agitated until it be accomplished" (Luke 12:49–50).

Of course, for Jesus to bring about God's sovereignty meant that he had to reclaim anything and everything that resisted the will of his Father (like, unclean spirits) or manifested itself against it (like, sickness or disability). Jesus then is the "captain" (Luke 9:49) who leads that attack on whatever opposes God's holy will in some way:

> The Lord appointed seventy-two others and sent them two-by-two before his face unto every city and place that he was going to come. And he said to them: . . . "Into whatever city you enter, and they receive you . . . cure the sick who are there, and say to them: 'The kingdom of God has come near to you.'" . . .
>
> Now the seventy-two returned with joy saying: "Lord, even the demons are subjected to us in your name!" And he said to them: "I saw Satan like a flash of lightning falling from the sky. Behold, I have given you the power to trample upon serpents and scorpions and upon every power of the enemy; and nothing shall harm you. However, do not wish to rejoice in this, that the spirits are subjected to you; yet rejoice that your names have been written in the heavens." (Luke 10:1–2a, 8–9, 17–20)

As Scripture scholar André Feuillet writes in the *Introduction to the New Testament*, "When Jesus speaks of the reign of God, He has in mind first of all, it seems clear, what the prophets and the psalmists mean by the phrase, namely, a personal, all-powerful, wholly gratuitous intervention of God who (through his Son) asserts his rights as the master of history, changing its course, effecting the complete triumph of his will over the entire human race, and destroying the empire of Satan."[33] In a word, it entailed *salvation*. As the famed New Testament scholar Rudolf Bultmann describes it, "The dominant concept of Jesus' message is the *Reign of God*. . . . It means the regime of God which will destroy the present course of the world, wipe out all the contra-divine, Satanic power under which the present world groans—and thereby, terminating all pain and sorrow, bring in salvation for the People of God which awaits the fulfilment of the prophets' promises."[34]

The ultimate enemy of God's will is death (see 1 Cor 15:22–26; see also Rom 5:12–21). So I do not think that it was unclear at all to Jesus that the plan of salvation—the fulfillment of the *kairos* and the bringing

33. Robert and Feuillet, *Introduction to the New Testament*, 756–77.

34. Bultmann, *Theology of the New Testament*, 4; emphasis original.

near of the kingdom—should entail a "ransom" (see Mark 10:45), which would be the giving of his own life: "And [Jesus] said to them: 'With desire I have desired to eat this Passover with you before I should suffer. For I say to you: I will not eat it, until it be fulfilled in the kingdom of God'" (Luke 22:15–16).

## The "Kingdom" of Christ and of His Church

Some progressive, liberal missiologists want to challenge the church's view of evangelizing mission, that has seen extending the "kingdom of God" primarily through converting people to Christ and baptizing them into his church. Hence, it became needful for them to look at the biblical record again—but in such a way as they could distance the expression both from Christ and from the community derived from him. So they accept unquestioningly the biblical scholarship that fits their purpose, such as Jesus coming solely to proclaim the kingdom of God as his central theme or that Jesus meant the "kingdom of God" only in one way. If that is so, then he necessarily did not intend to proclaim himself (*pace* "Christocentrism"). Further, if Jesus saw his mission as establishing God's kingdom, then he did not see his mission as founding a church (*pace* "ecclesiocentrism"). I think that both of these views are wrong because they rely on questionable assumptions, which often claim to be based on the results of modern biblical exegesis. Furthermore, they present the expression "kingdom of God" as uninterpretable as anything except

- *the kingdom* of God—and hence, not the church; and
- the kingdom *of God*—and hence, not Christ's.

In their view, then, the kingdom really has little or nothing to do with Jesus per se, for (as per his own expression) it is *God's*—never his or the church's! They take for granted a "scholarly consensus" that claims that Jesus came to proclaim God's kingdom—not the church and not himself—without ever having actually asked for themselves whether or not this consensus is correct or accurate. Some do this, I think, in all sincerity because they trust in the bona fides of the members of the biblical guild. Others, however, seem to do it precisely *because they need to*. It fits their theological agenda. For if the kingdom is only attributable to God—and not to Christ or the church—then both Christ and his church can be de-centered from the missiological debate. Working for the "kingdom" and its values can take the place of making conversions to Christ, and discerning the presence of the "kingdom" can be substituted for planting the church. American theologian Richard P. McBrien, for example, was refreshingly honest about his underlying agenda to change the church's understanding: "Breaking the long-standing tendency in Catholicism to identify the Church and the Kingdom of God while developing an understanding of the Church's mission in relationship always to the Kingdom has been a central priority of my writings on the Church from my earliest years as a theologian. . . . [Which writings have] call[ed] for a 'Copernican Revolution' in ecclesiology, displacing the Church from the center of the history of salvation in favor of the Kingdom of God."[35]

## The Jesus Who Will Not Be Gotten Rid Of

It should be pointed out immediately that the belief that Jesus himself has an everlasting "kingdom" is, in my opinion, a nonnegotiable part of the Christian faith. It has been solemnly defined in the creedal statements that were presented and approved by the holy fathers at the Council of Chalcedon (AD 451): "[Christ's] kingdom will have no end."[36] Chalcedon, however, was only confirming a belief that had been inserted into the creed (according to historical tradition) by the bishops of the First Council of Constantinople (AD 381). Thus, we have not just a previous ecumenical council's affirmation of it but also another's confirmation of it. I would consider the belief, then, to be *dogma de fide divina et catholica definitum*.

Some argue for de-centering Jesus from the church's evangelizing mission. They claim that the church should emulate the way in which Jesus seemed to conceive of his mission. For Jesus, his mission was not to proclaim himself but the kingdom of God. Since Jesus was "all about" the "kingdom," then (it would seem to follow) the church should also be primarily or only about God's kingdom. It is not about making conversions to Jesus; it is about converting people to the values of God's reign—just as Jesus tried to do! The kingdom ought to be the focus. So it is assumed that, if Jesus were not focused on himself in his preaching, then the church should not be so focused on him either. In fact, by placing Jesus

35. McBrien, *Church*, 376n10. Reverend McBrien is now dead. May he rest in peace!

36. Tanner, *Decrees*, 1:24 (see also 84).

at the center of her practice of mission, the church has actually falsified Jesus' original intention.

All of this can sound quite sensible precisely because there is some truth in it. As already noted above, there is little question from the data found in the Sacred Scriptures that the "kingdom" (of some sort) was an important part of Jesus' preaching.

However.

There is a massive fallacy here.

For it assumes that by focusing on the practice and intent of Jesus' preaching, one has somehow got around Jesus—or at least put him in his proper place vis-à-vis the church's mission. In fact, one has not left Jesus by the wayside at all; rather, he or she has just approached him from a different angle! If it is true that Jesus saw his purpose as to proclaim God's kingdom—as, I think, he did—that does not therefore make *the kingdom* the central point of focus. On the contrary, it is still *Jesus* who lies at the center. For if the kingdom is of utmost importance to the church, it is because the Master thought so. And if I proclaim the Master's message, I am in some way yet proclaiming something about the Master himself: how *he* interpreted it, why *he* thought it was important, how *he* saw his role in bringing it. So even by trying to reorient mission away from Jesus and onto his message of the "kingdom of God," one comes back nevertheless to that woodworking peasant of Galilee. The instruction *Dialogue and Proclamation* (1991) states,

> Jesus proclaimed the Gospel from God saying: "The time is fulfilled, and the Kingdom of God is at hand; repent and believe in the Gospel" (Mk 1:14–15). This passage sums up the ministry of Jesus. Jesus does not proclaim this Good News of the Kingdom by word alone, but also by his actions, attitudes and options, indeed by means of his whole life and finally through his death and resurrection. His parables, his miracles, the exorcisms he works, all are related to the Kingdom of God which he announces. This Kingdom moreover is not just something to be preached, quite unrelated to his own person. Jesus makes it clear that it is through him and in him that the Reign of God is breaking through into the world . . . that in him the Kingdom has already come upon us, even though it still needs to grow to its fullness.[37]

37. Congregation for the Evangelization of Peoples and Pontifical Commission for Interreligious Dialogue, *Dialogue and Proclamation*, §56.

That is why proclamation of the kingdom must include proclamation of the one who brought its message, Jesus the Christ. Indeed, the values of the kingdom of God are ordered to and find their decisive fulfillment only in Christ.[38] Jesus is not merely the "bringer" of the "kingdom." He is also the "brought." *He* is the "good news of the kingdom" which is to be proclaimed to the whole world.[39] We can see this especially in Matthew's retelling in his Gospel of the story of Jesus' anointing at the house of Simon the Leper in Bethany (see Matt 26:6–13).[40] A woman in the house takes a jar of perfumed ointment, which was very expensive, and pours it on Jesus' body. His other disciples become angry: they see it as a waste of the ointment since the money that was expended on having bought the ointment could have been given to help the poor. So they complain about it. But Jesus responds, "Why are you making trouble for the woman? For she has worked a good work for me. . . . For she, putting forth this ointment upon my body, has made preparation for my burial. Amen I say to you: Wherever this gospel will be preached in the whole world, that which she has done will also be said in her memory" (Matt 26:10, 12–13). The woman did not do it for the "kingdom"; she did it for Jesus. The "gospel" already seems to have become synonymous with telling stories about Jesus: it is the church's message about Jesus. Wherever the church will bring the "gospel," she will recall this woman's generous, compassionate action that she worked on behalf of Jesus. Jesus and the kingdom have become one and the same.

One frequently finds Jesus inserting himself into the message about the kingdom. Jesus tells parables about the kingdom (see e.g., Mark 4:26–34), but he also tells parables about himself (12:1–12). Moreover, it is by Jesus' own activity—and that which he delegates to his followers—that he believes the kingdom of God is being inaugurated: "Yet if in the Spirit of God I cast out demons, then the kingdom of God has come to you" (Matt

38. See e.g., CDF, *Dominus Iesus*, §§18–19.

39. In Matt 24:3–14, the disciples ask Jesus what "the sign of your coming" will be before the end of the age (v. 3). Jesus mentions several happenings, like people falsely claiming to be the Christ, wars, earthquakes (see vv. 5–7). Then all races of peoples will hate his followers and kill them "on account of my name" (v. 9). But, ultimately, the sign of his future arrival will be that "this gospel of the kingdom" had been preached throughout all the world (v. 14). The message and messenger are one.

40. Matthew bases his account on the story found in Mark 14:3–9. John (surprisingly) shares the story with Matthew and Mark, albeit independently (see 12:1–8). Luke does not have it all—though scholars posit that his story of Jesus' pardoning of the sinful woman (see 7:36–50) is a related version of it.

12:28 // Luke 11:20). If the "kingdom" was understood to be an intervention initiated by God himself—that is, a truly divine "in-breaking" without the use of any artifice or mediator—then what indeed did Jesus think he was up to? Why did he seem to think that it was he who specifically had to take up the initiative for God? Why would he have even dared to think that he could force God's hand by accepting a grisly death?[41]

Jesus exercises full possession over the kingdom: he explains it to whomever he wants, and to those he deems unworthy he does not: "And with many such parables, he spoke to [the people] the word, according as they were able to hear; yet without a parable he did not speak to them. Yet separately, he explained everything to his disciples" (Mark 4:33–34).[42] Moreover, it is something that Jesus possesses as his own, which he can give to whomever he wishes: "[Jesus said to the apostles:] 'I set aside for you, just as my Father has set aside for me, a kingdom, that you may eat and drink at my table in my kingdom and sit upon thrones judging the twelve tribes of Israel'" (Luke 22:29–30). Jesus expects those who do hear him, particularly his disciples, to understand the kingdom as *he* understands and proclaims it. The concept or image of the "kingdom of God" is not something that Jesus sets before the crowds or his disciples as a topic for discussion. He is not another Socrates. Jesus defines what the kingdom is: "[Jesus] was saying therefore: 'To what is the kingdom of God like, and to what shall I value it?'" (Luke 13:18; cf also v. 20). Jesus alone evaluates whether someone understands God's kingdom correctly: "And Jesus seeing that [the scribe] had answered wisely said to him: 'You are not far off from the kingdom of God'" (Mark 12:34). Jesus decides whom belongs to the kingdom: "Blessed are the poor, because yours is the kingdom of God" (Luke 6:20), and "Blessed are the ones who suffer persecution on behalf of justice, since theirs is the kingdom of heaven"

41. As Albert Schweitzer so rightly perceived about Jesus, yet ultimately misinterpreted: see Schweitzer, *Historical Jesus*, 385–90.

42. Pilate therefore entered again into the praetorium and he called Jesus and said to him: "You are the king of the Jews?" Jesus responded: "Do you say this of yourself, or have others spoken to you of me?" Pilate responded: "Am I a Jew? Your race and the high priests have handed you over to me; what have you done?" Jesus responded: "My kingdom is not of this world; if my kingdom were from this world, my servants would fight, so that I not be handed over by the Jews; yet now my kingdom is not from here." For that, Pilate said to him: "Therefore, you are a king?" Jesus responded: "You say that I am a king. I was born for this and unto this have I come into the world, that I should give testimony for the truth; everyone, who is from the truth, hears my voice." (John 18:33–37)

(Matt 5:10). And Jesus is the king-judge who shall determine whom does not belong to it:

> [Jesus said:]"Yet when the Son of Man shall come in his glory, and all the angels with him, then he will sit upon the throne of his glory. And all the races shall be gathered together before him; and he will separate them from each other, just as the shepherd separates the sheep from the goats, and he shall stand the sheep truly on his right, yet the goats on the left. Then the King shall say to those who will be on his right: 'Come, you blessed of my Father; possess the kingdom made ready for you from the foundation of the world. For I hungered, and you gave me to eat; I thirsted, and you gave me to drink; I was a stranger, and you took me in; naked, and you covered me; sick, and you visited me; I was in chains, and you came to me.' . . . Then he shall also say to those, who will be on the left: 'Depart from me, you accursed, into the eternal fire, which is prepared for the Devil and his angels. For I hungered, and you did not give me to eat; I thirsted, and you did not give me a drink; I was a stranger, and you did not take me in; naked, and you did not cover me; sick and in chains, and you did not visit me.' . . . And these will go unto eternal punishment, yet the Just unto eternal life."
> (Matt 25:31–36, 41–43, 46)

He outlines the moral code that one must follow in order to be part of the kingdom of God. We see some of the hallmarks of that code enunciated above in Christ's parable—namely, caring for the suffering and vulnerable (i.e., the starving and infirm, the foreigner and prisoner, the poor). Matthew the Evangelist has encapsulated this code in a collection of Jesus' sayings that has come to be called the Sermon on the Mount (chs. 5–7). It has been described as "the charter of the kingdom."[43] His Holiness Pope St. John Paul II observes in his encyclical letter *Veritatis Splendor*, "In the New Covenant the object of the promise is the 'Kingdom of Heaven,' as Jesus declares at the beginning of the 'Sermon on the Mount'—a sermon which contains the fullest and most complete formulation of the New Law. . . . This same reality of the Kingdom is referred to in the expression 'eternal life,' which is a participation in the very life of God."[44] In short, it is always Jesus who is deciding what anyone must do in order to be a part of the kingdom of God.

43. See Atterbury, "Many-Sided Christ," 451.

44. John Paul II, *Veritatis Splendor*, §12.

So it is indeed not surprising at all that the Proclaimer, Jesus, did become—and really ought to have become—the Proclaimed, for they are really one and the same. In fact, we can see that this development has already occurred in the earliest traditions about Jesus. For example, look at Luke's telling of Jesus' sending out of the seventy-two disciples:

> The Lord appointed seventy-two others and sent them two-by-two *before his face* into every city and place *that he was going to come*. And he was saying to them: . . . "Now into whatever city you enter, *and they receive you*, eat what is set out for you. And cure the sick, who are in it, and say to them: '*The kingdom of God has come near to you*.' Into whatever city you enter, *and they do not receive you*, going out into its squares say: 'Even the dust, that adheres to us on our feet from your city, we wipe off against you; however know this, that *the kingdom of God has come near*.' I say to you that it will be more tolerable for Sodom on that day than for that city. . . .
>
> *The one who hears you, hears me; and the one who despises you, despises me*; the one who despises even me, despises him who has sent me." (Luke 10:1–2a, 8–12, 16; emphasis added)[45]

Jesus sends out groups of his disciples to thirty-six different towns, villages, and cities in order to herald his future coming to each. They do not say, "Jesus is coming!" Rather, Jesus tells them to proclaim that the "kingdom" is nearby. It is coming; it is on its way. Yet, was the kingdom still no closer when Jesus did actually arrive in the places he intended to visit? Did it not arrive with Him? In Jesus, we again see that the "proclaimer" and "proclaimed" are tightly united. It is, in truth, the "kingdom" both of God and of Christ.[46] Yes, the kingdom does not come in lieu of Jesus; they come together. And they must come together since without Jesus the kingdom of God does not make sense.

We see something else in Luke's story above: the "kingdom," which is Christ's, also becomes associated with the church. For Jesus does not say that the townspeople have either received or rejected the kingdom by their acceptance or not of the disciples' *message*. On the contrary, the townspeople show their reception or denial of the kingdom of God by their acceptance or not of Jesus' *followers* themselves! Just as Jesus' coming

45. Luke has reworked "Q" material here. Also, other very reputable manuscripts give the number of disciples as seventy. Either number (i.e., seventy or seventy-two) is defensible. See Karris, "Gospel According to Luke," §122.

46. See Eph 5:5 and Rev 11:15.

to each town or village would embody the coming of God's kingdom, so also Jesus' disciples themselves embodied his own presence—and, therefore, the kingdom as well—wherever they were. Whoever listens to their message hears Jesus. So the church, Jesus, the kingdom of God, they are already so interrelated as to be the same.

## "Come, and I Will Show You the Bride, the Wife of the Lamb" (Rev 21:9)

The concepts of "ecclesiocentrism" and "regnocentrism" made their appearance at the symposium. Reverend Devadass alluded to the shift from "church-centered" mission to a "kingdom-centered" one. Although he did not fully explain the terminology, he nonetheless seemed to agree with it, telling Archbishop Panfilo that the church had been too "ecclesiocentric" in the past and needed to "de-center" by going out. Reverend Javier was more forthright: he admitted that whereas he had once been ecclesiocentric and exclusivist in his religious views, wanting to convert others to Christianity, he now embraced religious pluralism. Christianity is about Jesus Christ—not the church. Christ proclaimed God's kingdom, which includes all peoples. The church, therefore, cannot monopolize it since even non-Christian religions can be part of building up God's kingdom on earth. Both speakers seemed to assume that their listeners knew what they meant. But what in fact do these terms mean?

*Ecclesiocentrism* (Greek, *ekklēsia*; "assembly, church") refers to a viewpoint or activity that is judged to focus excessively on the church. In terms of contemporary missiology, this can mean the attempt to convert nonbelievers and bring them to baptism. *Regnocentrism* (Latin, *regnum*; "kingdom, reign") refers to the kingdom of God, which Jesus came to preach (see Mark 1:14–15; also, v. 38) and which he established the church to serve. The kingdom of God is, then, a broader and more basic reality than the church and is the genuine center and focus of her existence. For missiology, a "regnocentric" perspective means uncovering and effectuating the values of the kingdom (that is, peace, justice, fraternity, etc.) wherever and among whomever they may be found.

There are certainly benefits to a regnocentric view, not least of which is to constantly challenge the church against a sense of privilege and self-preservation. The kingdom requires the exclusive promotion of God's activity, which means the liberation of the world from any and all forms of evil. The values of the kingdom include human values like peacemaking and social development. It is, therefore, the concern of all well-minded and well-intentioned individuals and not just of the church alone. As such, the church stands at the service of the kingdom, no matter where it might be found and whoever its agents might be.[47] Javier is right that the church does not have a monopoly on building up God's kingdom; rather, it belongs to all men and women of good will. The church stands at the service of the kingdom's values by spreading them in the world. This she does "by establishing communities and founding new particular churches, and by guiding them to mature faith and charity in openness toward others, in service to individuals and society, and in understanding and esteem for human institutions."[48] The church's role, then, is not a static one. By increasing her own presence in the world, she can locate and promote these values more readily and abundantly than if she just stayed present within herself—that is, within her own preexisting institutions. Thus, we see the whole purpose of the "Baptized and Sent" symposium: it is only by *going out* that the church can do those things.

But while there is a beneficial understanding to *regnocentrism*, one can also see some of the problematic: the church can be portrayed as occupying a subservient position to the kingdom . . . which is *not* the same as a position of service! Thus is damaged the interrelated character of their relationship as well as the intention which Christ had for the church in relation to the kingdom that he came to inaugurate. The distinction between the church and God's kingdom is highlighted so strongly that they are almost placed in opposition. The church becomes an opponent and—perhaps, *even*—an impediment to the kingdom, at least to the extent that the church can take a central role. That central role is epitomized by the church's missionary enterprise by which nonbelievers are called to believe in Jesus and become her members. Thus, proclamation in order to convert is looked askance at or minimized since conversion to the values of the kingdom of God is enough—and indeed more important—than explicit conversion to Christ and his church. Yet, it is to his community of disciples that Jesus hands over the charge of actuating further the kingdom: "These Twelve Jesus sent, instructing them and saying: . . . 'Going, preach saying, "The kingdom of heaven has drawn near." Heal sick persons, raise dead men, cleanse lepers, cast out demons; freely you

47. See John Paul II, *Redemptoris Missio*, §15.

48. John Paul II, *Redemptoris Missio*, §20.

have received, freely give' " (Matt 10:5a, 7–8). This community has come to be called "the church." I do not think it is untoward to identify the church phenomenologically with *the means purposely created by Christ to fully manifest and realize the kingdom* that he himself was sent to preach. Hence, she can be called the kingdom's "sacrament," its servant, and its "sign and instrument."[49] This is why the church's magisterium can and must insist that the kingdom is intrinsically related to the church. While distinguishable, they cannot be detached. As *Dialogue and Proclamation* summarizes, "The Church has been willed by God and instituted by Christ to be, in the fullness of time, the sign and instrument of the divine plan of salvation . . . the centre of which is the mystery of Christ. She is the 'universal sacrament of salvation' . . . and is 'necessary for salvation'. . . . The Lord Jesus himself inaugurated her mission 'by preaching the good news, that is, the coming of God's Kingdom.'"[50]

Devadass spoke of the church's "de-centering." If understood to mean that Catholics should transcend the safe and self-satisfied complacency of their social and institutional life, then I think that there is merit to his view. For Pope Francis states in his apostolic exhortation, *Evangelii Gaudium*, that Catholics must go out to bring the joy of the gospel to others. He writes there, for example, "The Church which 'goes forth' is a community of missionary disciples who take the first step, who are involved and supportive, who bear fruit and rejoice. An evangelizing community knows that the Lord has taken the initiative, he has loved us first (see 1 John 4:19), and therefore we can move forward, boldly take the initiative, go out to others, seek those who have fallen away, stand at the

49. Vatican II, *Lumen Gentium*, §48; *Redemptoris Missio*, §20; *Evangelii Nuntiandi*, §59. As Alfred Loisy famously wrote in his book *The Gospel and the Church*, "Jesus foretold the kingdom, and it was the Church that came" (166). But for Loisy, that was to have been expected: not even the message of Jesus could have stayed the same! As with anything "historical," the gospel would have needed to have been developed and adapted to new circumstances. Jesus' community of followers, the church, would be the vehicle for doing that. Loisy writes immediately after, "[The church] came, enlarging the form of the gospel, which it was impossible to preserve as it was, as soon as the Passion closed the ministry of Jesus. There is no institution on the earth or in history whose status and value may not be questioned if the principle is established that nothing may exist except in its original form. Such a principle is contrary to the law of life, which is movement and a continual effort of adaptation to conditions always new and perpetually changing. Christianity has not escaped this law, and cannot be reproached for submission to it. It could not do otherwise than it has done" (Loisy, *Gospel*, 166).

50. Congregation for the Evangelization of Peoples and Pontifical Commission for Interreligious Dialogue, *Dialogue and Proclamation*, §33.

crossroads and welcome the outcast."[51] Still, in its declaration *Dominus Iesus*, the CDF warns against "one-sided accentuations" when considering the kingdom, or reign, of God in relation to the church herself. It cautioned against regnocentric views which "stress the image of a Church which is not concerned about herself, but which is totally concerned with bearing witness to and serving the Kingdom."[52] One sees this in Javier's declaration that the church needs to be placed within a broader regnocentric perspective. There is nothing wrong with this per se, given that the church is the seed, sign, and instrument of God's kingdom.[53] The church is not an end unto herself but exists always and only in relationship to Christ, the Bringer of God's kingdom. It stands to reason, then, that since the church owes her existence to Jesus' inauguration of the kingdom of God, she is ordered to it. Yet, she is also its peculiar servant. The church retains her unique identity as that which makes God's kingdom present and real in the world.

This is so, I think, even though the kingdom of God is not identified in its totality with the visible church. Christ and the Holy Spirit can act outside the church's visible boundaries.[54] Yet the two are of such an interrelated reality that that reality by its nature necessitates an inseparable relationship between them. As Pope St. John Paul II said to a group of Indian bishops making their regular *ad limina* visit to the Holy See,

> The kingdom is inseparable from the Church, because both are inseparable from the person and work of Jesus himself. He established the Church to be the revelation and instrument of the kingdom. It is therefore not possible to separate the Church from the kingdom as if the first belonged exclusively to the imperfect realm of history, while the second would be the perfect eschatological fulfilment of the divine plan of salvation. Nor can the kingdom be considered a purely interior or spiritual reality, in contrast with the Church considered as an historical and social realization of Jesus's intention to establish a community of

51. Francis, *Evangelii Gaudium*, §24 (see also §§21 and 120). The pope writes, "To go out of ourselves and to join others is healthy for us. To be self-enclosed is to taste the bitter poison of immanence, and humanity will be worse for every selfish choice we make" (Francis, *Evangelii Gaudium*, §87).

52. CDF, *Dominus Iesus*, §19.

53. See John Paul II, *Redemptoris Missio*, §18.

54. See John Paul II, *Redemptoris Missio*, §18.

> faith and salvation. Consequently it is not possible to relativize the Church's role in bringing all to union with Christ.[55]

Granted—and it is true—Jesus did not come proclaiming the church; he proclaimed the kingdom of God. So the distinction between the two must be respected and attended to. In the apostolic exhortation *Ecclesia in Asia*, Pope St. John Paul II states, "Empowered by the Spirit to accomplish Christ's salvation . . . the Church is the seed of the Kingdom of God and she looks eagerly for its final coming. Her identity and mission are inseparable from the Kingdom of God which Jesus announced and inaugurated in all that he said and did, above all in his death and resurrection. The Spirit reminds the Church that she is not an end unto herself . . . she exists to serve Christ and the salvation of the world."[56] Yet Jesus does inaugurate both. He establishes the church—that is, his own special community, which, albeit distinct, is not unrelated to the kingdom of God that he proclaimed. The values of Jesus' kingdom are the church's values as well. The church is intended as the catalyst for extending God's kingdom among all men and women. So the church is not the center; that must always remain Christ the Lord himself and his proclamation of God's kingdom. But she is central and fundamental since she has been established as such by her center. Again, it should be enough to point out that the Sacred Scriptures call the church Christ's body and even his wife (see e.g., 1 Cor 12:27 and Rev 21:9).

## Either/Or? The Church and the Kingdom's "Values"

Missiologist Edmund Chia outlines a view of mission which gears itself towards proclaiming the gospel and bringing people into the church. These are (what he calls) the *kērygma* (preaching) and *koinōnia* (communion) aspects of mission. But there is also the *diakonia* model, which highlights and focuses on the doing of good works. He writes,

> There is a school of thought that views mission as consisting primarily and even solely of *diakonia*. Mission, as the Lord's Prayer teaches, is enabling God's Kingdom to come and doing

55. John Paul II, "To the Bishops of India," §3. According to church law, every five years, a bishop is required to go to Rome "to venerate the tombs of the Blessed Apostles Peter and Paul and to present himself to the Roman Pontiff" (Catholic Church, *Code of Canon Law*, canon 400, §1; see also canon 399).

56. John Paul II, *Ecclesia in Asia*, §17.

> God's will "on earth" as in heaven. The missioner's task therefore is not so much the institutional conversion of the beneficiaries but their holistic and spiritual conversion as evidenced in their being able to live whole and holy lives before death. This perspective of mission focuses on the teaching and practice of Jesus on the coming of the reign of God and especially his preferential option for the poor and commitments to justice, peace and the integrity of creation.[57]

Chia continues,

> Taking seriously Matthew 6:33 to "seek first the Kingdom of God," [a *diakonia* aspect] shifts the focus from a church-centered or ecclesiocentric understanding of mission to a kingdom-centered or regnocentric perspective of mission. . . . Mission is seen as essentially the building up of the reign of God and not that of the church. The aim of mission is not so much the conversion of the *gentes* but the alleviation of the suffering, oppression and inhuman conditions that keep people from living in dignity and integrity.[58]

Surely, the alleviation of suffering and liberation from evil are paramount projects for promoting the kingdom of God. In practical terms, I can see how they are viewed as the most urgent needs to be addressed when searching for and promoting the kingdom of God. For the Letter of James itself warns, "If a brother or sister is poorly clothed and lacking in daily food, and one of you says to them, 'Go in peace, be warmed and filled,' without giving them the things needed for the body, what good is that? So also faith by itself, if it does not have works, is dead" (2:15–17). Indeed, such a paradigm of service is commanded by Christ as the litmus test for his disciples (see Matt 25:31–46 above). One can see Chia's *diakonia* aspect at work in Javier's comment at the symposium that the church must be a church "of the poor" and "for the poor." Surely, this is true, for who would argue against helping the poor? So it might not always happen that the "preaching" and "community" aspects of the kingdom of God are highlighted, at least not at first; rather, the focus is first of all on the alleviation of suffering and liberation from evil.[59] Some of the precious values of God's kingdom were also discussed by the symposium's

57. Chia, "Mission as Inter-Religious Dialogue," 217.

58. Chia, "Mission as Inter-Religious Dialogue," 217.

59. See Chia, "Mongolia," for his account of the actual, real-world benefits of a *diakonia* model.

speakers: peacemaking, environmental healing, preferential concern for the poor, rehabilitation of the outcast, and so forth. Certainly, as the servant of the kingdom, the church must be involved in such concerns.

Yet surely the church's mission also extends beyond just addressing humankind's purely natural needs. As Pope St. John Paul II recalls, "The missionary Church['s] . . . primary task lies elsewhere: the poor are hungry for God, not just for bread and freedom. Missionary activity must first of all bear witness to and proclaim salvation in Christ, and establish local churches, which then become means of liberation in every sense."[60]

I would say that a *diakonia* model cannot exist in isolation from the *kērygma* and *koinōnia* aspects. On the contrary, *diakonia* only strengthens the church's need for proclamation. For it is Christ himself and his own message of the kingdom which underlie the church's search to locate and promote the values of that kingdom in the first place. It includes explicit proclamation, for the kingdom does not come in secret; it comes in the footsteps of the one heralding the good news of peace (see Isa 52:7). The kingdom of God does not and cannot exist in isolation from the church, or *koinōnia*. If the kingdom's values are to be located and promoted, then there must be a group of people which is doing the locating and promoting. When Jesus lays upon his followers the "sweet" yoke of service to the kingdom (see Matt 11:30), he does so with the authority of one empowered to bring that kingdom about—an authority which he passes onto his community. And it is not some generic, nonspecific "kingdom" whose values are being searched for and identified. Rather, it is the kingdom which Jesus of Nazareth preached to his disciples. It is his followers—Christians—who are called to identify and promote this kingdom and its values. The followers of Jesus, who have been baptized into his death (see Rom 6:3–4), are also called "the church." There is, then, no "ecclesiological vacuum" whereby the kingdom and its values are simply identified and promoted apart from Christ's community. The work of Christ's disciples, who are the church, is always and necessarily involved.

I agree wholeheartedly with Javier's comments above during the symposium that the promotion of the values of God's kingdom involves not only the church but also all men and women of good will, who together seek to rid the world of evil in all its forms. This makes locating and promoting the values of the kingdom the concern of all humanity—not

60. John Paul II, *Redemptoris Missio*, §83.

just the church's concern alone. But the ultimate purpose of this activity should be remembered—namely, "the manifestation and the realization of God's plan of salvation in all its fullness."[61] The church's evangelizing mission is meant for all men and women, as all are in the process of being led towards God's kingdom yet to come—that is, in the *eschaton*. The values of that kingdom are already mysteriously present, albeit incompletely, throughout the world, particularly in humanity's religious traditions. The Second Vatican Council recognized this in its Decree on the Missionary Activity of the Church, when it spoke of *semina Verbi* ("seeds of the Word") existing in the cultures and religions of non-Christians.[62] If present, then it is not surprising when some or many non-Christians have found these "seeds," these values of the kingdom of God, and have reacted to them. By recognizing them, the church is only discovering what is already hers by right, since Christ told his followers to "seek . . . the kingdom of God and his justice" (Matt 6:33). That command was not made to outsiders, even though the kingdom might yet be present to them in certain ways.[63] By fervently advocating for the kingdom's seeds or values, the church is only pouring out the grace of Christ on them so that they might grow in men's hearts and souls.

Still, I was disturbed by Javier's view that it is enough that non-Christians promote the kingdom and its values without also intending to be converted to Christ and his church. Not that Javier necessarily excluded the latter, although it was certainly not a priority. Yet his attitude runs counter to Pope St. John Paul II's observation in *Redemptoris Missio*:

> Nowadays the call to conversion which missionaries address to non-Christians is put into question or passed over in silence. It is seen as an act of "proselytizing"; it is claimed that it is enough to help people to become more human or more faithful to their own religion, that it is enough to build communities capable of working for justice, freedom, peace and solidarity. What is overlooked is that every person has the right to hear the "Good News" of the God who reveals and gives himself in Christ, so that each one can live out in its fullness his or her proper calling.[64]

61. John Paul II, *Redemptoris Missio*, §15.

62. See Vatican II, *Ad Gentes*, §11 (see also §§15 and 18).

63. Jesus was not hesitant to recognize the presence of faith even outside of Israel, for example, in the centurion (Matt 8:5–13) and the Canaanite woman (15:22–28).

64. John Paul II, *Redemptoris Missio*, §46. As Pope Francis states in *Evangelii Gaudium*, "An authentic faith . . . always involves a deep desire to change the world, to

Pope St. John Paul II reminds us in *Redemptoris Missio* that the proclamation of Christ cannot be detached from proclamation of the kingdom or its values. Nor can the kingdom be separated from the community which Christ established—that is, the church. This is so because "Christ not only proclaimed the kingdom, but in him the kingdom itself became present and was fulfilled. This happened . . . through his words and his deeds. . . . The Kingdom of God is not a concept, a doctrine, or a program subject to free interpretation, but it is before all else a person with the face and name of Jesus of Nazareth, the image of the invisible God."[65] It is the selfsame Jesus, who proclaimed the kingdom, who also created the church. Hence, the relationship between the church and God's kingdom is as inseparable as their source.

## When the Church Starts to Forget Who She Is and What She Is For

Christ endowed the church with the fullness of all of the means and benefits of salvation.[66] In other words, only she perfectly and truly effectuates the kingdom's presence. That is not to deny that elements of God's kingdom can be found outside the visible church. But those elements represent an incomplete reality, which only finds fulfillment in Christ and his church.[67]

In 1979, the bishops of South America and the Caribbean Islands met together in Puebla, Mexico, for their Third General Conference.[68] The theme of the conference was the church's present and future evangelization efforts in those regions. It is commonly referred to as the "Puebla Conference."

In his opening address to the gathering, Pope St. John Paul II commented that while going over the large amount of documentation that had been submitted in preparation, "one sometimes notices a certain uneasiness in interpreting the nature and mission of the Church."[69] He continued,

transmit values, to leave this earth somehow better than we found it" (§183).

65. John Paul II, *Redemptoris Missio*, §18.

66. John Paul II, *Redemptoris Missio*, §18.

67. See John Paul II, *Redemptoris Missio*, §20.

68. The grouping is called Consejo Episcopal Latinoamericano y Caribeño, or CELAM.

69. John Paul II, "Puebla Conference," §1.8 (62). Another English translation can be

> Allusion is made, for example, to the separation that some set up between the Church and the Kingdom of God. Emptied of its full content, the Kingdom of God is understood in a rather secularist sense: i.e., we do not arrive at the Kingdom through faith and membership in the Church but rather merely by structural change and sociopolitical involvement. Where there is a certain kind of commitment and praxis for justice, there the Kingdom is already present. This view forgets that "the Church . . . receives the mission to proclaim and to establish among all peoples the kingdom of Christ and of God. She becomes [*constituye*] on earth the initial budding forth [*el germen y el principio*] of that kingdom" [quoting *Lumen Gentium*, §5].[70]

Nevertheless, the pope reminded the bishops, "Without a well-grounded ecclesiology, we have no guarantee of a serious and vigorous evangelizing activity."[71] In other words, if the church does not know at the most basic level who or what she is, then how can she know what she is supposed to be? What does she exist to do?

As the medieval Scholastics used to say, "agere sequitur [ad] esse."[72] In other words, a thing acts in the way that it is supposed to. Doing follows upon, and is necessarily linked to, being.

But there is a problem—a very serious one—when something does not act as it is or how it is supposed to be. It becomes an especially serious problem when that thing is a *person*—namely, a human being.

Other animals do not seem to have this problem. Cats, for example, simply act according to how they are, without even (apparently) giving much thought to it. A cat's *esse* is to be a cat (very much so, as any cat will tell you . . . and with much pride!). A cat does not flap its paws and try to fly in the air like a bird. It does not even try to.

Human beings do try, though.

They try to be what they are not and to make other things what they are not, too. Humans dress up animals in all sorts of humanlike clothing. They play music for them and make them dance for the crowds. They talk to them and try to teach them their language. It would never, ever

found on the Holy See's website (see John Paul II, "Latin American Episcopate," §1.8).

70. John Paul II, "Puebla Conference," §1.8 (62). The Spanish text of the pope's speech can be found online (see Juan Pablo II, "Conferencia General del Episcopado Latinoamericano").

71. John Paul II, "Puebla Conference," §1.7 (62).

72. See e.g., Thomas Aquinas, *Summa Contra Gentiles* 1.24, 2.35, and 3.69; also, Thomas Aquinas, *Commentary on the Sentences* 3.3.2.1.

occur to an animal to try to do similarly to a human. An elephant could not conceive of stripping a man of his clothing and making him wander about the bush; or a chimpanzee, of placing a human in a tree where he would climb and swing throughout the day; or a gorilla, of trying to teach the meaning of his grunts and body movements to an animal psychologist. Only the *human* animal seems to be able to forget who he is—with dire consequences for how he acts, both to himself and to others.

The church is not an abstraction. She is comprised of human beings.

Yes, people may at times speak of the "institutional" church of the "hierarchy" or "magisterium" in contradistinction to the "people," who are seen to be the real, flesh-and-blood believers and practitioners of the faith. But that is not really so at all. Even the physical structures hold persons within them; and positions are given to someone.

No, the church recognizes herself as a "society"—that is, a population of real men and women united by their beliefs, their practice of the faith, their common worship, and their submission to certain persons who are recognized as authorities.[73] The church is not an "institution" per se but a system of interactions. In other words, a *relationship*.[74] Anyone who believes in Christ and has accepted baptism has become a *socius* (an ally or partner—a kinsman, even!) to all others who have done the same.[75]

As such, the "church," as comprised of people, can sometimes forget who and what she is. She can dress up in a hat and suit, like people do to monkeys, and dance around for the crowds. But the church is not a monkey: "Do you not know that you are the temple of God, and the Spirit of God dwells in you?" (1 Cor 3:16). And dancing for the crowds is not her mission:

> Yet to whom shall I reckon this generation? It is like children sitting in the market place, who calling to their companions say:
> "We piped for you, and you did not dance;
> we wailed, and you did not beat your breast." (Matt 11:16–17)

73. See e.g., Vatican II, *Lumen Gentium*, §8: "Christ . . . established and continually sustains here on earth His holy Church, the community of faith, hope and charity, as an entity with visible delineation through which He communicated truth and grace to all. . . . This Church constituted and organized in the world as a society, subsists in the Catholic Church, which is governed by the successor of Peter and by the bishops in communion with him." See also Vatican II, *Gaudium et Spes*, §§14 and 40.

74. See Coser, "Society," 436.

75. Andrews, *New Latin Dictionary*, s.v. "Socius," 1715–16.

At Puebla, I think the Roman authorities started to see further indications of a developing crisis within the church about her nature and mission in the world. The church was starting to forget herself! Whether or not the bishops attending the conference took the pope's cautions with utter seriousness and responded accordingly is for the reader ultimately to judge. If statistics mean anything, I do not think that they did, on either score (see the epilogue to this book).

Even at the 2019 symposium which I attended (and which was the event that impelled me to write this book), I sensed a similar disorder. The symposium's panel discussion was a time to show how the church's mission could serve the "kingdom values" of justice and peace, reconciliation and compassion. I wondered how each of these topics would be treated from the perspective of Christ and his church. How would the gospel be brought to bear on each (admittedly) important issue? Alas, each area was viewed almost from a purely secular and practical standpoint. It seemed like the church's transcendent and supernatural purpose was lost sight of, to some extent. At times, I did not see where the values of God's kingdom were being located or promoted.

Not that this was always the case: Paul Harricknen of the Catholic Professionals' Society was a standout in demonstrating how to make Pope Francis's encyclical *Laudato Si'* more widely known and applicable among even secular groups. Donatus Nahak spoke about ecumenical initiatives to make the plight of climate change more broadly understood from a religious perspective, in other words, Bible study.

But other aspects showed much less religious focus: Nongkas, for example, tried to impart the importance of care for the earth to her students at Port Moresby's Don Bosco Tech. But I would imagine that the same insight could also have been found at a secular school. Although a priest, Glynn's group exists almost exclusively to address the material needs of the urban poor living around Port Moresby. Cardinal Ribat is certainly a religious figure—but I am not sure that his ability to judge the benefits or the disadvantages of experimental seabed mining comes under the purview of the magisterial office.

Members of the panel listed several new concerns for evangelizing mission: environmental damage, poverty, migration, gender inequality. These, we were told, were the areas where the church's mission must now take place. Of course, none of these is without consequence for the church's evangelizing mission. As Pope St. John Paul II writes in *Redemptoris Missio*, "The Church is the sacrament of salvation for all mankind, and her activity is not limited only to those who accept her message. She is a dynamic force in mankind's journey toward the eschatological kingdom, and is the sign and promoter of gospel values."[76] The church contributes to humanity's journey towards God and his plan for it. She does this not just through her witness but also through activities like dialogue, "human promotion," commitment to justice and peace, education, and caring for the sick, the poor, and children. All the while, the church does not lose sight of the priority of the transcendent and supernatural realities which characterize salvation in the kingdom to come.[77] As Vatican II teaches, the church shares humankind's joys and hopes, sorrows and anxieties[78] and, as such, anything that concerns humanity's happiness or flourishing. But the church's mission is also clear: "The Apostles, their successors, and those who cooperate with them are sent to announce to mankind Christ, the Savior."[79] And Pope St. John Paul II said to PNG's bishops during his 1984 visit to the nation, "There are profound links between evangelization and human advancement, for the people we evangelize are at the same time subject to social and economic factors. Thus, it is important to face together questions of the social order. . . . In the light of the Gospel, the Church always has something to say on matters touching the common good of society."[80] The operative phrase is "in the light of the gospel." The pope reiterated this when he arrived in PNG again in 1995. He said, "May all the people who live in this land strive to build a society in which the dignity and rights of each individual will be respected by everyone. In this great task the Catholic Church will continue to do her part, *in accordance with her religious nature and mission*, and will generously co-operate with all sectors of the population."[81] In *Redemptoris Missio*, Pope St. John Paul II writes,

> Nowadays the kingdom is much spoken of, but not always in a way consonant with the thinking of the Church. In fact, there are ideas about salvation and mission which can be called "anthropocentric" in the reductive sense of the word, inasmuch as they are focused on man's earthly needs. In this view, the kingdom tends to become something completely human and secularized;

76. John Paul II, *Redemptoris Missio*, §20.
77. John Paul II, *Redemptoris Missio*, §20.
78. See Vatican II, *Gaudium et Spes*, §1.
79. Vatican II, *Gaudium et Spes*, §76.
80. John Paul II, "To the Bishops of Papua New Guinea," §5.
81. John Paul II, "Welcome Ceremony," §4; emphasis added.

> what counts are programs and struggles for a liberation which is socio-economic, political and even cultural, but within a horizon that is closed to the transcendent. Without denying that on this level too there are values to be promoted, such a notion nevertheless remains within the confines of a kingdom of man, deprived of its authentic and profound dimensions. Such a view easily translates into one more ideology of purely earthly progress. The kingdom of God, however, "is not of this world . . . is not from the world" (Jn 18:36).[82]

The question could be asked if whether by piling up new missional concerns for the church—none of which is spiritual or supernatural in and of itself—there is not the danger of losing focus of the church's properly spiritual end. For instance, are climate change, migration, or gender equality such overriding concerns as to place the salvation of souls in a secondary or even tertiary position of importance? Or are they concerns because they harmfully affect mankind's supernatural end, which is to seek God so as to be happy with him in this life and in the next?[83]

Let me say that I think that none of the concerns discussed by the panel was unimportant. Climate change is a threat to human flourishing, whose flourishing is God's will.[84] One cannot overlook the unjust structures which cause migration as well as the suffering of migrants. Gender equality is a value to be worked towards so that the inherent dignity of the voice and work of women is affirmed. Again, perhaps the practical must sometimes come first before the "theoretical," or spiritual. But if it comes at the neglect of the spiritual or supernatural, then have we not reduced the kingdom of God, as Pope St. John Paul II says above, to just another secular ideology? Have we not distorted the gospel message, which is, "This is yet eternal life, that they may know you, the only true God and the one whom you have sent, Jesus Christ" (John 17:3)?

Moreover, there was little discussion of how the bare performance of social projects—the "works of mercy," to be sure—necessarily requires the church. Reverend Devadass admitted that as the Malaysian government took up more and more of the social needs of its citizens, the church was left trying to discover her continued purpose in Malaysian society. This shift in focus from supernatural to natural goals may explain in part the moribundity of missionary fervor among Catholics. For if the

82. John Paul II, *Redemptoris Missio*, §17.

83. See *CCC*, §1721.

84. See John 10:10.

hungry are fed and migrants welcomed, if girls are educated and carbon emissions reduced, then what really is there left to do? God's work has been done!

Done, perhaps . . . but finished?

# 6

# Witness and Dialogue Versus Proclamation and Conversion

One might recall that during the second question period, two bishops, Francesco Panfilo and Rolando Santos, stated their concern about the continued lack of missionary zeal among the Catholic faithful. Reverend Devadass gave an articulate and nuanced response. But his proposal was indicative of a trend that, I think, needs to be addressed. That trend seeks to place witness and interreligious dialogue on a separate and superior plane in regards to proclamation and conversion. While the mandate to proclaim the gospel is affirmed and not denied, it is presented almost as a lesser reality. Whereas witness and dialogue are affirmed almost without qualification, proclamation is affirmed less so—and almost always with caveats.

## Witness Is Necessary . . . and Proclamation?

In his encyclical *Redemptoris Missio*, Pope St. John Paul II recalls the statement made by Pope St. Paul VI in *Evangelii Nuntiandi* that people put more trust in witnesses than in teachers.[1] "The witness of a Christian life," writes St. John Paul II, "is the first and irreplaceable form of mission."[2] He continues,

1. John Paul II, *Redemptoris Missio*, §42. See Paul VI, *Evangelii Nuntiandi*, §41. (The reference, however, comes ultimately from St. Paul VI's general audience of October 2, 1974; see Paul VI, "Audience Générale.")

2. John Paul II, *Redemptoris Missio*, §42.

> The first form of witness is the very life of the missionary, of the Christian family, and of the ecclesial community, which reveal a new way of living. The missionary who, despite all his or her human limitations and defects, lives a simple life, taking Christ as the model, is a sign of God and of transcendent realities. But everyone in the Church, striving to imitate the Divine Master, can and must bear this kind of witness; *in many cases it is the only possible way of being a missionary.*[3]

Christian witness entails concern for people as well as love for the poor, weak, and suffering. "A commitment to peace, justice, human rights and human promotion is also a witness to the Gospel when it is a sign of concern for persons and is directed toward integral human development."[4] So Pope St. John Paul II proposes a broad understanding of witness—that is, as the Christian way of life. In its concern for the poor and suffering, for justice and peace, its focus seems centered mostly on the corporal works of mercy.

Generally, a person is expected to practice what that person says he or she believes—for religious people, no less than for others. Without an authentic witness, that person's avowal of his or her beliefs becomes questionable; the beliefs themselves, doubtful. Certainly, the witness of a holy life is the *sine qua non* of the Christian message. For if goodness and wisdom and peace do not derive from following it, then why accept it? And if Christians themselves do not follow Christ, why should anyone else? As Sacred Scripture testifies, "Whoever says 'I know him' but does not keep his commandments is a liar, and the truth is not in him" (1 John 2:4).[5] Obviously, then, the faithful living of a Christian life is essential for

3. John Paul II, *Redemptoris Missio*, §42; emphasis added.

4. John Paul II, *Redemptoris Missio*, §42.

5. Consider, for example, the following severe assessment from Methodist missionary, E. Stanley Jones:

> A penetrating, but kindly old philosopher of India, Bara Dada [namely, Dwijendranath Tagore] . . . pronounced this judgment: as we sat in the evening talking for long hours . . . he thoughtfully said, "Jesus is ideal and wonderful, but you Christians—you are not like him."
>
> If we should be like him, if we should catch his spirit and outlook, what would happen? A Hindu lecturer on educational subjects was addressing an audience of educationalists in South India when he paused and said: "I see that a good many of you here are Christians. Now, this is not a religious lecture, but I would like to pause long enough to say that, if you Christians would live like Jesus Christ, India would be at your feet to-morrow." He said nothing less than the very truth. (Jones, *Christ of the Indian Road*, 141–42)

the authentic proclamation of the gospel to others. This view is described admirably in the Final Statement of the Seventh Plenary Assembly of the Federation of Asian Bishops' Conferences (FABC), where it asserts, "The most effective means of evangelization and service in the name of Christ has always been and continues to be the witness of life. The embodiment of our faith in sharing and compassion (sacrament) supports the credibility of our obedience to the Word (proclamation). . . . Asian people will recognize the Gospel that we announce when they see in our life the transparency of the message of Jesus and the inspiring and healing figure of men and women immersed in God."[6]

I would agree that witness is, on the practical level, surely the most effective means for demonstrating the credibility of one's stated beliefs. But it is not the only means. As Pope St. Paul VI clarifies in the apostolic exhortation *Evangelii Nuntiandi*, while witness is essential, witness *alone* never suffices for the church's evangelizing mission, which should normally and naturally lead to proclamation. On the contrary, he explains,

> Even the finest witness will prove ineffective in the long run if it is not explained, justified—what Peter called always having "your answer ready for people who ask you the reason for the hope that you all have" [1 Pet 3:15]—and made explicit by a clear and unequivocal proclamation of the Lord Jesus. The Good News proclaimed by the witness of life sooner or later has to be proclaimed by the word of life. There is no true evangelization if the name, the teaching, the life, the promises, the kingdom and the mystery of Jesus of Nazareth, the Son of God are not proclaimed. . . . This proclamation—kerygma, preaching or catechesis—occupies such an important place in evangelization that it has often become synonymous with it.[7]

Witness and proclamation are not, then, an "either-or" reality; rather, they interpenetrate. The Second Vatican Council already noticed this necessary connection when it described *evangelization* in the Dogmatic Constitution on the Church as the proclamation of Christ through both "living testimony" and "spoken word."[8] While witness should certainly be present, and is undeniably paramount, its trajectory ought to arc

6. FABC, "Renewed Church in Asia," §3.C.1. A copy of the statement can be found online (see UCA News, "Final Statement").

7. Paul VI, *Evangelii Nuntiandi*, §22.

8. Vatican II, *Lumen Gentium*, §35. See also Vatican II, *Ad Gentes*, §§11–12, 20, 24, 41, and *Gaudium et Spes*, §§23 and 41.

towards proclamation of the "good news" of God's grace to those who do not believe in Christ (see Acts 20:24). Pope St. John Paul II writes in *Redemptoris Missio*, "The proclamation of the Word of God has *Christian conversion* as its aim: a complete and sincere adherence to Christ and his Gospel through faith."[9]

Witness ought not to be placed at loggerheads with proclamation, as if the latter were not also a necessary aspect of missionary work. For Pope St. John Paul II states in *Redemptoris Missio* that "proclamation is the permanent priority of mission."[10] He writes further,

> The Church cannot elude Christ's explicit mandate, nor deprive men and women of the "Good News" about their being loved and saved by God. "Evangelization will always contain—as the foundation, center and at the same time the summit of its dynamism—a clear proclamation that, in Jesus Christ . . . salvation is offered to all people, as a gift of God's grace and mercy" [citing *Evangelii Nuntiandi*, §27]. *All forms of missionary activity* are directed to this proclamation, which reveals and gives access to the mystery hidden for ages and made known in Christ (cf. Eph 3:3–9; Col 1:25–29), the mystery which lies at the heart of the Church's mission and life, as the hinge on which all evangelization turns.[11]

Even in mission's complex reality, *Redemptoris Missio* affirms that proclamation plays "a central and irreplaceable role" since it leads to conversion to Jesus Christ: "Just as the whole economy of salvation has its center in Christ, so too all missionary activity is directed to the proclamation of his mystery."[12] But the attempt to disconnect proclamation from witness can be found in the FABC's Final Statement of the Seventh Plenary Assembly mentioned above. It states, "One common mission unites all: to proclaim 'the Good News of Jesus Christ through Christian witness, works of charity and human solidarity. . . . The many positive elements found in the local churches . . . strengthen our expectation of a "new springtime of Christian life" [citing *Ecclesia in Asia*].'"[13] The FABC quotes

9. John Paul II, *Redemptoris Missio*, §46; emphasis original.

10. John Paul II, *Redemptoris Missio*, §44. The point is made with more forcefulness in the Latin. It should go (my translation), "Proclamation holds an everlasting pre-eminence in mission [*Nuntius principatum in missione tenet perennem*]" (Ioannes Paulus II, "Mandati Missionalis," §44 [290]).

11. John Paul II, *Redemptoris Missio*, §44; emphasis added.

12. John Paul II, *Redemptoris Missio*, §44.

13. FABC, "Renewed Church in Asia," §3.

from §9 of Pope St. John Paul II's apostolic exhortation *Ecclesia in Asia*, which was issued after a "Special Assembly for Asia" of the Synod of Bishops. There is, however, a lacuna in FABC's text with something that is not quoted, something that is left out, from this document. The FABC has decided to leave out the following from the pope's statement: "Whatever the circumstances, the Church in Asia finds herself among peoples who display an intense yearning for God. The Church knows that this yearning can only be fully satisfied by Jesus Christ, the Good News of God for all the nations. The Synod Fathers were very keen that this Post-Synodal Apostolic Exhortation should focus attention on this yearning and encourage the Church in Asia to proclaim with vigour in word and deed that Jesus Christ is the Saviour."[14] Why the Asian bishops chose to pass over this particular part of the pope's statement in silence—indeed, to cut it out—is indicative. For there one can see the problematic of witness versus proclamation played out even in an official statement of the Asian Catholic bishops.

The apostolic exhortation *Evangelii Gaudium*, the first document written by Pope Francis, is devoted specifically to reinvigorating the church's missionary calling. He declares,

> The new evangelization calls for personal involvement on the part of each of the baptized. Every Christian is challenged, here and now, to be actively engaged in evangelization. . . . Every Christian is a missionary to the extent that he or she has encountered the love of God in Christ Jesus: We no longer say that we are "disciples" and "missionaries" but rather that we are always "missionary disciples."[15]

But what is *evangelization* for Pope Francis? The pope states, "Evangelization is first and foremost about preaching the Gospel to those who do not know Jesus Christ or who have always rejected him."[16] The pope is very clear, then, that the church's mission is outward directed; it is *ad gentes*. It is not just about the witness of a Christian life but also about bringing the gospel message explicitly.

If *witness* means living out faithfully the will of Christ, then how can it be claimed to be truly genuine when it refuses to fulfill the express will of the Lord Jesus regarding proclamation and making disciples (see Matt

14. John Paul II, *Ecclesia in Asia*, §9.

15. Francis, *Evangelii Gaudium*, §120 (see also §17).

16. Francis, *Evangelii Gaudium*, §14.

28:19–20, Mark 16:15, Luke 24:47)? It is not even a question of one or the other: living a Christian life is the necessary condition for anyone who has been baptized. Nevertheless, Christ did not send out his disciples to live a Christian life—which was certainly implied—but to sound forth the gospel, to lead people out of error and to the living and true God (see 1 Thess 1:8–9). The church's missional paradigm is not one or the other; it is both. Choosing to neglect one diminishes perforce the other. It is like when Jesus chided the Pharisees and the scribes for their minute attention to the Law while neglecting other more important things: "These things *you ought to have done* and not to have omitted the others" (Matt 23:23; emphasis added).

## A Missiology of Beauty?

Reverend Javier claims that God's language is the language of silence, and that the church should pursue a "missiology of beauty and silence."[17]

Surely, he is right that the God of Israel is a beautiful god, as the Sacred Scriptures themselves testify: "Greatness and beauty are in his sight, power and delightfulness in his sanctuary" (Ps 96:6); God has "put on grandeur and beauteousness" (104:1).

In 2006, the Holy See's Pontifical Council for Culture issued a document on the "Way of Beauty" (*Via Pulchritudinis*).[18] "The way of beauty," it states, "replies to the intimate desire for happiness that resides in the heart of every person. Opening infinite horizons, it prompts the human person to push outside of himself . . . to the Transcendent and Mystery, and seek, as the final goal of the ultimate quest for wellbeing and total nostalgia, this original beauty which is God Himself, creator of all created beauty."[19] The same point is made wonderfully by the inspired author of the book of Wisdom, who writes,

> If delighting in the appearance of [created things], [human beings] took them to be gods,
> let them know how much better their Ruler is than they:
> for the Source and Author of their ornament fixed them.
> Yet if they wondered at their power and working,

17. Dunn, "Fr. Edgar Javier," 45:39.

18. In 2022, both the Pontifical Council for Culture and the Congregation for Catholic Education were collapsed into each other, thus forming the "Dicastery for Culture and Education."

19. Pontifical Council for Culture, "*Via Pulchritudinis*," §2.3.

let them understand from them how much mightier than they is
the One who made them:
For by the greatness and beauty of created things,
the Creator of them can be seen in a recognizable way.
(Wis 13:3–5)[20]

As the *Catechism of the Catholic Church* teaches, since all creatures bear some resemblance to God, their source and maker, we can know something even about the excellence of God from the consideration of the perfections of those things that he has created. For the truth, goodness, and beauty that one finds in the created world are seen to be but reflections of the same truth, goodness, and beauty which are in God himself, albeit eternally and preeminently.[21] Of course, the Pontifical Council warns against the idolization of creation and its excellences. The universe appears beautiful to us; it reveals truths; it benefits our existence. But it is not to be idolized.[22] It is not ever or in any way comparable to God himself. As Asaph and his brethren sang out in the temple,

Sing to the Lord, all the earth. . . .
Tell his glory among the races,
among the entire peoples his wonders,
because the Lord is great and exceedingly praiseworthy
and he is fearful above all the gods.
For all the gods of the peoples are worthless,
yet the Lord made the skies.
Greatness and beauty are before him,
strength and joy are in his place.
(1 Chr 16:23a, 24–27)

God is the source and origin of the world's beauty, but it is in Christ, his Son, that his beauty is revealed in a singular way. And the beauty of Christ

20. The NABRE provides in some ways a better translation of the passage:

Now if out of joy in [created things'] beauty [human beings] thought them gods,
let them know how far more excellent is the Lord than these;
for the original source of beauty fashioned them.
Or if they were struck by their might and energy,
let them realize from these things how much more powerful is the one who made them.
For from the greatness and the beauty of created things
their original author, by analogy, is seen.

21. *CCC*, §41.

22. Pontifical Council for Culture, "*Via Pulchritudinis*," §3.1.

comes to the world through the witness and worship of his believers in the church: "It lets us experience God alive among His people attracting to Him those who let themselves be taken up in this meeting of joy and love."[23] The church, as witness of Christ's own beauty, "reveals herself as his spouse made more beautiful by her Lord when she makes acts of charity and preferential choices, when she engages in the promotion of justice and building up the great common house where every creature is called to live, especially the poor."[24] Through the witness of her members' acts of love (*caritas*) on behalf of justice and peace, the church seeks to offer to all men and women "the true beauty," to announce always to them "the beauty that saves," to give them "the final meaning of life."[25]

Reverend Javier is correct, in my view, to look for the presence of God in the signals of beauty that appear among men and women in their religious beliefs and practices. During his 2009 pilgrimage to the Holy Land, His Holiness Pope Benedict XVI gave an address at Al-Hussein bin Talal Mosque in Amman, Jordan. He declared, "Places of worship . . . stand out like jewels across the earth's surface. From the ancient to the modern, the magnificent to the humble, they all point to the divine, to the Transcendent One, to the Almighty. And through the centuries these sanctuaries have drawn men and women into their sacred space to pause, to pray, to acknowledge the presence of the Almighty, and to recognize that we are all his creatures."[26] Thus, humanity's religious structures indicate a surpassing thirst for God. In the search for beauty, they also evince mankind's search for the one who is transcendently beautiful. As such, it is appropriate to view aspects—many of them, even—as delightful and precious jewels, dotting the face of the earth, through which the ray of truth that enlightens all men and women is refracted.[27] Yet none of that appreciation should relativize the gospel witness, for as the prophet declares, "How beautiful upon the mountains are the feet of one announcing, preaching peace, of one announcing a good thing, preaching salvation, saying to Zion: 'Your God reigns!'" (Isa 52:7). In his apostolic exhortation *Evangelii Gaudium*, His Holiness Pope Francis speaks of the "beauty" of proclaiming the gospel about Jesus to others: "Proclaiming Christ means showing that to believe in and to follow him is not only

23. Pontifical Council for Culture, "*Via Pulchritudinis*," §3.3.

24. Pontifical Council for Culture, "*Via Pulchritudinis*," §3.3.

25. Pontifical Council for Culture, "*Via Pulchritudinis*," §3.3.

26. Benedict XVI, "Meeting with Muslim Religious Leaders."

27. See e.g., Vatican II, *Nostra Aetate*, §2.

something right and true, but also something beautiful, capable of filling life with new splendor and profound joy."[28] He continues,

> Every expression of true beauty can thus be acknowledged as a path leading to an encounter with the Lord Jesus. This has nothing to do with fostering an aesthetic relativism that would downplay the inseparable bond between truth, goodness and beauty, but rather a renewed esteem for beauty as a means of touching the human heart and enabling the truth and goodness of the risen Christ to radiate within it.[29]

As Pope St. Paul VI writes in *Evangelii Nuntiandi*,

> Neither respect and the surpassing esteem given to such religions nor the kind of possible questions raised by them delude the Church into passing over in silence what is of concern to non-Christians: the proclamation of Jesus Christ. On the contrary, she is of the opinion these very multitudes of men and women have the right to know the riches of the mystery of Christ in which . . . all humanity can find in full measure—and not rather with fearful longing—all the things which . . . it asks diligently about God, about men and women and their future lot, about life and death, and about truth.[30]

Not all societies are fully open or receptive to the transcendent message found in the revelation of Christianity, and "not all expressions of beauty . . . favour an acceptance of the message of Christ and the intuition of His divine beauty."[31] In fact, due to sin, human society can use beautiful things wrongly: "Although accessible to all, the Way of Beauty is not exempt from ambiguity, deviations, errors, detours. . . . Always dependent on human subjectivity, it can be reduced to ephemeral aestheticism and let itself be instrumentalised and made servile to the captivating fashions of . . . [a] society."[32] Saint Paul VI continues in the apostolic exhortation that even though the forms of these "natural religions" should be

28. Francis, *Evangelii Gaudium*, §167.

29. Francis, *Evangelii Gaudium*, §167.

30. Paulus VI, "Episcopos, Sacerdotes et Christifideles," §53 (41); my translation. I have not found any "official" translation of this text to be completely suitable (see Paul VI, *Evangelii Nuntiandi*, §53).

31. Pontifical Council for Culture, "*Via Pulchritudinis*," §2.1.

32. Pontifical Council for Culture, "*Via Pulchritudinis*," §2.1. The document's authors have in mind here specifically "consumer culture." Still, I think the statement can be applied more broadly, without doing any violence to the original context.

"most outstanding," only "by the power of the religion of Jesus, which she proclaims through evangelization, is humankind truly joined with the plan of God, with his living presence and with his action."[33] The pope concludes, "In other words, through our religion an undeniably true and living fellowship with God is really established, which other religions are unable to establish, even though, one might say, they be seen lifting their hands to heaven."[34]

Beauty, salvation, meaning—these are found in Jesus Christ. "Beginning with the simple experience of the marvel-arousing meeting with beauty, the *via pulchritudinis* can open the pathway for the search for God, and disposes the heart and spirit to meet Christ, who is the Beauty of Holiness Incarnate, offered by God to men for their salvation. It invites contemporary . . . unquenchable seekers of love, truth and beauty, to see through perceptible beauty to eternal Beauty, and with fervour discover Holy God, the author of all beauty."[35] If other religions are mankind's beautiful search for God, it does not take away from the fact that Christianity is the fulfillment of these searches. In Christ, God reaches down from heaven and grabs the non-Christian's searching hand, raised in prayer. Only Christianity definitively places men and women in their

33. Paulus VI, "Episcopos, Sacerdotes et Christifideles," §53 (42); my translation.

34. Paulus VI, "Episcopos, Sacerdotes et Christifideles," §53 (42); my translation. Belgian theologian Jacques Dupuis, SJ, especially disliked this portion of the exhortation. He believed the pope swept aside the suggestion that humanity's religions could constitute in some way God's approach to humankind through them. Instead, what we get is "the 'fulfillment theory' . . . exposed in its rigid form, without the refinements by which it has been softened in recent years thanks to much theological thinking" (Dupuis, "Apostolic Exhortation," 230).

What I think Dupuis fails to consider, though, is that the so-called "Fulfillment Theory" *does seem* in fact to be the church's traditionally preferred theological view of the world's religions. At least, it seems to be the one most consistent with the church's beliefs. The bishops of Vatican II, for example, use the idea explicitly when they declare that Jesus Christ is the one "in whom men may find the fullness of religious life, in whom God has reconciled all things to Himself [see 2 Cor 5:18–19]" (Vatican II, *Nostra Aetate*, §2). The theory seems to have been assumed throughout Vatican II's documents, which even Dupuis himself admits (see Dupuis, *Toward a Christian Theology*, 168). And he further acknowledges that it continues in the teachings of both Pope St. Paul VI and St. John Paul II (see *Toward a Christian Theology*, 172–73 and 177–79). So he may not like it, but . . . there it is.

35. Pontifical Council for Culture, "*Via Pulchritudinis*," §2.1. As Pope Benedict XVI declared at the start of his pontificate, "There is nothing more beautiful than to be surprised by the Gospel, by the encounter with Christ. There is nothing more beautiful than to know Him and to speak to others of our friendship with Him" (Benedict XVI, "Beginning of the Petrine Ministry").

true relationship with God. But none of this removes the church's great honor for the world's religions, whose forms are "even . . . most outstanding." So on the one hand, we must recognize and respect the beauty of mankind's varied searches for God while, on the other hand, recognizing that the forms of these searches point to the goal of humanity's search, which is found ultimately only in our Lord Jesus Christ.

## A Missiology of Silence?

Both Devadass and Javier propose a kind of "quietistic missiology," albeit in different ways. Each one favors a more silent witness which does not seem to make much room for proclamation. Devadass even maintains above that proclamation does not always entail talking. He enlists the support of St. Francis of Assisi's dictum, "Preach the gospel always; if necessary, use words!"

But there are problems with this appeal:

It is an apocryphon. Saint Francis of Assisi never said it. It does not appear in any of the official Franciscan records collected about St. Francis.[36] The nearest one comes to any statement of the kind is in St. Francis's first (unapproved) Rule of 1221. In his first rule for his community, the Rule of 1221 (sometimes called the *regula non bollata*), St. Francis covers the preaching activities of his members. He mandated that his friars could not preach wherever church law or their local superior forbade it. Then he adds, "All the friars . . . should preach by their example."[37]

If Devadass's point is that Christians ought always to preach through witness, then St. Francis's statement is certainly pertinent here. But it leaves unanswered the question of when and if the friars should ever preach. Were they just restricted by St. Francis to giving good example to non-Christians? Or were they expected to try to actively convert

36. The saying's doubtful provenance is apparently well-known among the Franciscans. Reverend Pat McCloskey, OFM, the editor of the Franciscan magazine *St. Anthony's Messenger*, writes,

> I had been a Franciscan for 28 years—and had earned an M.A. in Franciscan studies—before I heard the "Use words if necessary" quote. . . . [A] friend of mine . . . contact[ed] some of the most eminent Franciscan scholars in the world, seeking the source. . . . It is clearly not in any of Francis' writings. After a couple weeks of searching, no scholar could find this quote . . . written within 200 years of Francis' death. (McCloskey, "Great Saying")

37. Rule of 1221, ch. 17 (Habig, *St. Francis of Assisi*, 44).

them as well? This is also addressed in the Rule of 1221, where St. Francis describes missionary work "among the Saracens [that is, Muslims] and other unbelievers."[38] Saint Francis proposes two ways: In one way, the friars ought to live peaceably among men, "avoid[ing] quarrels and disputes," thus bearing witness to their Christianity.[39] In the other, when they believe it to be God's will to do so, they should proclaim the gospel openly, telling men and women about God and Christ and offering them baptism, "because unless a man be born again of water, and the Spirit, he cannot enter into the kingdom of God (Jn 3:5)."[40] Neither way, neither witness nor proclamation, is prioritized to the disadvantage of the other; rather, witness and proclamation are interconnected. But lest there be any misunderstanding about this last way, St. Francis reminds his friars in chapter 16 of the rule of Christ's warning about being ashamed to proclaim him before men (see Luke 9:26; see also Matt 10:32)![41]

Francis composed another rule in 1223, which was approved by Pope Honorius III (d. AD 1227) and which the several Franciscan groups follow to this day. The statement about preaching by example is lacking in the 1223 rule; it has been removed. But there is again the provision for doing missionary work among Muslims and other non-Christians.[42] Far from advocating silent or recondite mission, in *both* rules, St. Francis makes provision for direct missionary activity. So St. Francis was surely not averse to converting others to the faith—and from using words to do it! What is more, St. Francis of Assisi's example is specifically invoked in Pope Francis's *Evangelii Gaudium* for exactly the *opposite* purpose that Devadass intends above—that is, the pope uses him as an example of the need to actively share the faith. The pope writes,

> No one can demand that religion should be relegated to the inner sanctum of personal life, without influence on societal and national life, without concern for the soundness of civil institutions, without a right to offer an opinion on events affecting society. Who would claim to lock up in a church and silence the message of St. Francis of Assisi . . . ? [He] would have found this

38. Rule of 1221, ch. 16 (Habig, *St. Francis of Assisi*, 43).

39. Rule of 1221, ch. 16 (Habig, *St. Francis of Assisi*, 43).

40. Rule of 1221, ch. 16 (Habig, *St. Francis of Assisi*, 43). We can see, then, that St. Francis was no pluralist: salvation came only through being baptized into the name of the Lord Jesus!

41. Rule of 1221, ch. 16 (Habig, *St. Francis of Assisi*, 43–44).

42. Rule of 1223, ch. 12 (Habig, *St. Francis of Assisi*, 57–64, at 64).

> unacceptable. . . . An authentic faith—which is never comfortable or completely personal—always involves a deep desire to change the world, to transmit values, to leave this earth somehow better than we found it.[43]

I have trouble agreeing with Javier's statement that Israel's God is a god of silence. On the contrary, his first act in the Bible is *to speak*: "And God said . . ." (Gen 1:3)![44]

The God of the Old Testament is far from silent. As it proclaims in the psalm,

> The voice of the Lord is over the waters;
> the God of majesty has thundered,
> the Lord over many waters.
> The voice of the Lord with power,
> the voice of the Lord in majesty.
> The voice of the Lord tearing apart the cedars;
> yes, the Lord will tear apart the cedars of Lebanon. . . .
> The voice of the Lord dividing the flame of fire,
> The voice of the Lord shaking the desert,
> yes, the Lord will shake the desert of Kadesh.
> The voice of the Lord hastening the birth of the deer,
> and he will lay bare the thickets;
> and in his temple all shall speak glory.
> (Ps 29:3–5, 7–9; see also Ps 18:13)

The God of Israel is "the God of gods . . . [who] has spoken and summoned the earth from the rising of the sun all the way to its setting" (Ps 50:1). He does not keep silence, but he comes in fire and tempest (v. 3; see also v. 7).

Then, there is the garrulous God of prophecy: "The *word* of the Lord was given to Gad the prophet . . . *saying*: 'Go and *speak* to David: Thus *says* the Lord . . .'" (2 Sam 24:11b–12; emphasis added).[45] Indeed, it is only for the prophet Elijah that God lowers his voice. While Elijah is hiding

43. Francis, *Evangelii Gaudium*, §183.

44. See the book Ecclesiasticus:

> I will be mindful, therefore, of the works of the Lord
> and what I have seen, I will announce:
> By the words of the Lord are his works,
> and judgment is made according to his will. (Sir 42:15)

45. Indeed, it is a commonplace throughout the incipits of the Bible's prophetical books that God speaks to his people (i.e., in the phrase "the word of the Lord came to X"). See e.g., Jer 1:2, Ezek 1:3, Hos 1:1, Joel 1:1, Jon 1:1, Mic 1:1, Zeph 1:1, Hag 1–2, Zech 1:1, Mal 1:1.

in a cave on Mount Horeb (Sinai) for fear of his enemies, God comes and appears to him: "And behold the Lord went by, and there was a great and strong wind overturning the mountains and grinding apart the rocks before the Lord; the Lord was not in the wind. And after the wind, a tumult; the Lord was not in the tumult. And after the tumult, a fire; the Lord was not in the fire. And after the fire, the soft whisper of a sound [*sibilus aurae tenuis*; Hebrew, *qol demamah daqqah*]. When Elijah had heard that, he covered his face with a cloak and going out he stood at the mouth of the cave" (1 Kgs 19:11b–13a).[46] Quiet at times God may be—yet never fully silent. On Moab's plain, when the Israelites are about to enter the promised land, Moses reminds them, "The Lord spoke to you from the midst of the fire; a sound of words you heard, yet a form inside you did not see. And he showed you his covenant, which he commanded that you should do, and the Ten Words, that he wrote on two tables of stone" (Deut 4:12–13). Then this holy "man of God" (see e.g., 2 Chr 30:16) continues, "Ask of the days of old . . . if ever there was done such a great thing, or has it been known at any time, whether a people has heard the voice of God speaking out of the midst of fire, as you have heard, and lived? . . . It has been shown to you so that you might know that the Lord himself is God, and there is no other besides him. From heaven he made you to hear his voice that he might teach you . . . and you heard his words from the midst of the fire" (Deut 4:32–33, 35–36).

What can the above tell us?

Perhaps the most important thing—at least for the author, whom scholars have named the "Deuteronomist"—is to emphasize that the Israelites saw no physical body or shape on Mount Horeb (Sinai).[47] The text hesitates even to say that they heard God's actual words, since saying so could have implied a speaker with a mouth. Rather, the Deuteronomist has edited the original tradition to make clear that the Israelites heard only *a sound* of the words (*qol debarim*) that God spoke to Moses.[48] By repeatedly stating that the Israelites only perceived a "voice" or "sound" (*qol*) coming from the cloud of God's glory on the mountain, a theological point is brought home—God is bodiless; he has no form—as well as an ethical consequence: there is nothing at all that the Israelites should

46. See *BHS*, 608. The traditional rendering, "a still small voice," found in the King James Version is even now probably the best translation of the Hebrew.

47. The Deuteronomist source almost always prefers the name "Mount Horeb" for the site whereat God made the covenant of his law with the Israelites (Brown and North, "Biblical Geography," §27).

48. See *BHS*, 291 and 293.

use to represent him. God is not like anything that the nations of men—even the Israelites themselves!—might have thought him to be: with a body that could be recreated in stone, wood, or metal or with a form that could be physically seen and adored.[49] The nations of men, then, have been ignorant as to God's true nature and are wrong to continue in their idolatry. But the remedy for such ignorance is knowledge, which God himself must give. This we call *revelation*. But even that is not enough since he further sends his prophets, like Moses, to make explicit what the Israelites have only experienced. (Even the word *voice* means something deeper about God.)

Contrariwise, it is the *false* gods that remain silent. Unlike Israel's God, it is the gods of the peoples—the "no-gods" that do not even deserve to be called *god* (see Jer 5:7)—that do not speak. Thus, the author of the Letter of Jeremiah mocks relentlessly the notion that humanity's idols could be gods. Even though the idols' tongues are covered with precious metals, they are false because they cannot speak (Bar 6:7). The Judahite prophet Habakkuk derides the nations' idols' inability to speak:

> What does it profit a statue
> so that its maker has carved it;
> a molten and lying oracle,
> why has its maker hoped in a forgery,
> that he should make mute idols?
> Woe, who says to wood: "Awaken!"
> "Arise!" to a stone keeping quiet!
> Will it not be able to teach?
> Behold, that thing is covered with gold and silver,
> and no breath at all is in its bowels.
> Yet, the Lord is in his holy temple;
> let all the earth be silent in his sight.
> (Hab 2:18–20)

As American biblical scholar John L. McKenzie, SJ, observes, "A fundamental presupposition of [Old Testament] revelation is that Yahweh is

49. According to Gerhard von Rad, the original story that the Deuteronomist received had merely indicated that the Israelites heard God at Horeb but did not see any form. The Deuteronomist, however, redacts his source to exhort his fellow Jews against idolatry: "From the standpoint of theology it is just this later stratum that is interesting. . . . The preacher takes up the statement contained in the tradition that at Horeb Israel merely heard Yahweh, but did not see him, in order to press its meaning theologically. For he has made the comparatively insignificant passage in the tradition the basis for a comprehensive attack on the worship of Yahweh in images" (Rad, *Deuteronomy*, 49). See also Weinfeld, *Deuteronomy 1–11*, 213.

a living God. . . . His vitality stands precisely in opposition to the confused identification of foreign gods with their images, which the Israelites scornfully point out can neither speak nor act. The vitality of Yahweh is perceived in His words and His actions, which are His self-manifestation, His revelation."[50] Indeed, for the biblical authors, the fact that the idols cannot speak is a telling proof of their falseness (see Pss 115 and 135, Jer 10:5, Wis 15:7). In the book of 1 Kings, the Deuteronomist historian recounts with mordant pleasure the famous contest between Elijah, the great prophet of Yahweh, and the false prophets of Baal. They are false because their god is false. And their god is false because he does not speak to them, has no voice, and cannot answer their prayers (see 1 Kgs 18:26–29). The Baalite prophets hop around an altar, slashing themselves bloody with knives, crying out to their "god." But, there is no answer. Perhaps, Elijah suggests mockingly, Baal does not hear them because he is taking a nap . . . ? Perhaps Baal is deep in thought . . . ? Perhaps he has left on a trip and is not there . . . ? Or perhaps Baal is using the restroom (v. 27) . . . ? Nevertheless, despite the Baalite prophets' sincerest endeavors, "a voice was not heard, neither did someone answer nor give heed to their praying" (v. 29). Yet, Yahweh's voice sets everything on fire (see vv. 37–38)![51]

Then, there is the New Testament.

When the Jerusalem authorities come to confront St. John the Baptist about his identity and his mission, "he says: 'I am *a voice calling out in the desert: "Make straight the way of the Lord,"* just as Isaiah the prophet said'" (John 1:23; italics in original). The Lord Jesus himself tells his followers not to keep silent, saying, "What I say to you in the shadows, say in the light; and what you hear in your ear, proclaim upon the housetops!" (Matt 10:27). Appearing in a vision to St. Paul, the glorious Christ

50. McKenzie, *Dictionary of the Bible*, 736.

51. As John L. McKenzie explains,

> The word of Yahweh made Yahweh Himself known, for the dialogue of the word is a personal encounter. In hearing His word, Israel knew Yahweh as the personal reality which His word expressed. . . . The word of Yahweh was creative, for He produced the world by His command. It was destructive, for at His word kingdoms fall. It was the hinge on which history turned, for it brought to pass each crisis which it announced. To Jeremiah it was a fire burning within him. The word of Yahweh never returns to Him without doing its work; the world passes but His word endures forever. (McKenzie, *Myths and Realities*, 243–44; see also 51–52)

commands him, "Do not fear, but speak, and you should not keep quiet!" (Acts 18:9).

What is more, the magisterium expressly challenges such a "quietistic" missiology. In *Evangelii Nuntiandi*, Pope St. Paul VI acknowledges the "wordless witness" of a Christian life.[52] But such a witness always remains insufficient. The pope writes in the very next section, "Even the finest witness will prove ineffective . . . if it is not explained, justified . . . and made explicit by a clear and unequivocal proclamation of the Lord Jesus. The Good News proclaimed by the witness of life . . . has to be proclaimed by the word of life. There is no true evangelization if the name, the teaching, the life, the promises, the kingdom and the mystery of Jesus of Nazareth, the Son of God are not proclaimed."[53]

It is worth noting that there certainly may be circumstances when, for prudential reasons, it is not possible for a Christian to communicate his or her faith. The witness of a Christian life might be the only kind of missionary activity open to the church, especially in places where the church's activities are restricted by law or culture. As Devadass mentions above, in Malaysia, *even insinuating* conversion to a Muslim is a criminal offense. So that might explain why in some contexts the private, unspoken witness of a Christian life has come to be relied upon as the appropriate methodology in lieu of actively seeking conversions. It is an understandable compromise within a menacing context. In the apostolic exhortation *Ecclesia in Asia*, Pope St. John Paul II notes that due to religious restrictions in many places, "*the silent witness of life*" may be the only way the church can proclaim God's kingdom.[54] Nevertheless, he describes this self-imposed "silent witness" as a form of *via crucis*, or "way of the cross"! It is to follow the path of suffering; it is not a normal state of affairs.

Reverend Edgar Javier's situation, however, is quite different, for he has no such contextual impediment. He comes from the Philippines, which is an overwhelmingly Catholic nation (79.6 percent of the population) with a long history in the faith.[55] Far from threatening, his context should be encouraging! Yet he seems to have made an ideological choice

52. Paul VI, *Evangelii Nuntiandi*, §21. The phrase used is "tacita testificatio" (see Paulus VI, "Episcopos, Sacerdotes et Christifideles," §21 [19]).

53. Paul VI, *Evangelii Nuntiandi*, §22 (see also §27).

54. John Paul II, *Ecclesia in Asia*, §23; italics in original.

55. See table 1.10, "Household Population by Religious Affiliation and by Sex: 2015," in Philippine Statistics Authority, *2021 Philippine Statistical Yearbook*, 1–21. Christianity first arrived in the Philippines in 1521 with the Spanish explorer Ferdinand Magellan. See Stearns, *Encyclopedia of World History*, 387.

to detach the church from the evangelizing mission and reject conversion as the object of that mission. Instead, he proposes the path of friendship and dialogue, which is oriented not towards conversion but to listening and learning, to reconciliation, and to silent mysticism. These are laudable intentions. But I fail to see how Javier's approach remains faithful to the Holy See's 1991 statement *Dialogue and Proclamation*, which while affirming the place and role of dialogue in the church's life, nevertheless states that the church's "sacred and major duty" is "to proclaim . . . Jesus and . . . invite people to become his disciples in the Church."[56] Furthermore, there are the words of Pope Francis, who Javier says is his favorite pope. In a moment of enthusiasm in the apostolic exhortation *Evangelii Gaudium*, Pope Francis exclaims, "How beautiful it is to see that young people are 'street preachers' (*callejeros de la fe*), joyfully bringing Jesus to every street, every town square and every corner of the earth!"[57] One presumes that those *callejeros* do not preach in silence! Finally, Javier's view even contradicts one of his fellow speakers, Agatha Ferei, who advocates for Catholics to expand their voice in the area of social communications. Indeed, she said they needed to *shout* their message from the digital rooftops! In this, Ferei has the support of Pope St. Paul VI, who asked Catholics "to leave no stone unturned in order that the means of social communication, in the midst of a world that seeks, as it were in darkness, the light that can save it, might proclaim from the roof-tops . . . the message of Christ, the Saviour, who is the Way, the Truth and the Life."[58]

56. Congregation for the Evangelization of Peoples and the Pontifical Council for Interreligious Dialogue, *Dialogue and Proclamation*, §76.

57. Francis, *Evangelii Gaudium*, §106.

58. Paul VI, "World Social Communications Day."

# Epilogue

## The Symposium on "Mission": Lights and Shadows

Was the symposium a success? Yes—in that it was held at all. Given the PNG church's sparse resources, the logistical difficulties of moving around the country, and the short time CTI had to prepare for it, it was an accomplishment. Catholic Theological Institute's President Joseph Vnuk, OP, Dean of Studies Brandon Zimmerman, and the many students who made it possible should be rightfully proud of their efforts. They are all to be commended highly and without reserve.

But asked another way, was the symposium a success *in what it set out to do*?

Did it offer participants a clear understanding of *mission* and what could be done to promote it?

Did it fill them with enthusiasm for bringing the message of Christ to others? For serving Christ in others?

Did it show them how church authorities were ready and willing to support laypeople in mission?

I hope so . . . but I worry.

### What Is *Mission*?

In my opinion, there was a certain vagueness and lack of focus among some of those who were called to speak on the church's evangelizing mission:

- Devadass describes *mission* as humankind's loving relationality among all its members, including the cosmos, since all have been created by God. For me, that begged the question, if everything stands in relation to everything else, then who is left for anyone to be sent to? *Mission* becomes a phantasmal category, a ghost. Or perhaps he meant that we are all sent to each other since we are all related. But then that would seem to dilute the unique character of Christian mission to the world since Christ charged us to go and proclaim the gospel to every creature (see Mark 16:15).

- Javier defines *mission* as everything that the church does—by which he probably means the complex reality of all the church's outreach to the world. Evangelization, then, would mean the active preaching of the gospel to nonbelievers. But he also says that only God does mission—and the church is not God. If one were to follow that through syllogistically, one might arrive at the complete obliteration of that "everything" which Javier says comprises the church's mission! For what is the church left to do? What is her God-given purpose?
- The participants in the panel discussion say the church's *mission* must now include all sorts of other concerns: "climate change" and the environment, migration, economic and gender equality. But is the church's mission to act as a "stand-in" for governmental or social agencies? Maybe. If the church could do it during parts of Europe's Middle Ages, then perhaps now. Yet the concern remains about the secular world overwhelming and usurping in some way the purely supernatural end of the church's mission . . . as, I think, many would agree did happen to the church during Europe's Middle Ages![1]
- Baleinakorodawa warned his listeners to not even ask him what mission meant! For him, *mission* meant activity. But if mission's theoretical base can be so easily disregarded, how does he or anyone else adjudge whether what he is doing is consonant or not with the church's "mission"? Yet Pope St. Paul VI writes with simple clarity in *Evangelii Nuntiandi* that *mission* is "nuntii evangelici propositio"—that is, "the setting forth of the gospel message," which is Jesus himself.[2] It is really that simple. Jesus is what Christians bring: first, in their personal witness to others, and second, in their words of proclamation of the hope that they have in Christ (see 1 Pet 3:15).

1. See e.g., Bokenkotter, *Concise History*, 110–96.

2. See Paul VI, *Evangelii Nuntiandi*, §5; Paulus VI, "Episcopos, Sacerdotes et Christifideles" §5 (8).

Perhaps all that could be hoped for was to instill in the participants an ardent desire to serve Christ in others. Or to get involved in the parish's life. I am thinking here of the talks by Paolo Baleinakorodawa and Andrew Moses. If so, then that would also surely deserve praise. And I do think the symposium was a success in highlighting those aspects. But in other ways, rather than stoking my missionary zeal, I felt deflated: for what could I, a believer in Jesus, bring to those nonbelievers who already had him in their midst? How could I rudely seek to teach others and lead them to baptism when that was God's work? (I am thinking here of Edgar Javier's talk.)

And so I was left with the question: "Baptized and sent" . . . but for *what*?

Surely, sent for witness.

And Christian witness was on display throughout the symposium: in Paolo Baleinakorodawa's several years spent ministering to convicts in a Filipino prison; in Paul Harricknen's efforts to make *Laudato Si'* more widely known in the secular realm; in John Glynn's establishment of a foundation, WeCARe, to help indigent women and children; in Bishop Rochus Tatamai's efforts to catechize his congregation—just to name a few.

I do not mean to discount in any way the real and concrete ways that Christian witness was being expressed in the life-situation of each person. But personally, I had hoped for more.

More to the point, I was perplexed by the lack of much discussion about actively bringing others to belief in Jesus Christ. And I was disturbed how that view, when it did come up, was usually treated with reticence. Of course, for some there were reasons for that. Reverend Devadass spoke frankly about the legal restrictions in Malaysia that prevented him and other Christians from openly and freely speaking of faith in Christ to Muslims. But other speakers—for example, Javier from the Philippines—seemed to have had no such restrictions. While saying the mandate remained, he seemed to put it on hold for quite theoretical reasons—namely, a commitment to religious pluralism. He saw any attempt to convert as a form of religious "exclusivism."

## A Problem Has Developed . . . and Is Worsening

Several speakers noted the general lack of knowledge of the faith as well as doctrinal confusion among Catholics. Two (Moses and Tatamai) were from different regions of PNG; the other (Baleinakorodawa), from Fiji.[3] I am from the USA. Having taught at several Catholic universities in America, I can attest to the lack of religious knowledge among my Catholic students. The faith seems as strange to them as a pterodactyl, were they to see one. In my own United States, for example, it is well documented that most Catholics are stunningly ignorant of Catholic belief as well as of religion in general. For example, according to the Pew Research Center study "What Americans Know About Religion," only 55 percent of the American Catholics surveyed were able to identify that Jesus Christ was the one who gave the Sermon on the Mount.[4] The study's judgment is curt but extremely worrying for anyone expecting a revitalization of mission among Catholics anytime soon: "Mainline Protestants, Catholics and Mormons closely resemble the general public [!] in their overall levels of religious knowledge."[5] This would, then, seem to be a global problem for the Catholic Church: it is not reserved to developing (so-called "third-world") regions of the planet.

Moreover, the "faith" is, correlatively, not being believed or lived.

Again, just from my own context of the USA, significant numbers of the American Catholic population do not accept the church's teaching—if they even know it—on God and the Eucharist, on sexual morality, and so on.

According to the Pew Research Center's most recent religious landscape study (2023–2024), 62 percent of Catholics say that they are "absolutely certain" of God's existence. Another 34 percent believe in God—but could not admit to being completely certain about it.[6] God's

3. Out of all the speakers, only Paul Harricknen, neither a cleric nor a specialist, advised his listeners to have both a Bible and a catechism—and to read them!

4. Pew Research Center, "What Americans Know," 31. The study's Jewish respondents came out as the most knowledgeable among the religious groups, being able to answer correctly half or more of the study's questions. They were followed by those who described themselves as "atheist" or "agnostic" ("What American Know," 28).

5. Pew Research Center, "What Americans Know," 28.

6. Pew Research Center, "Religious Landscape Study." *Nota bene*: In order to find the specific information for Catholics on the website, one must go to the section, "U.S. Religious Groups: Christians," and click on the hyperlink, "Catholic." Then, click on the tab "Beliefs and Practices" or "Social and Political Views." Finally, click the tab "Compare" for any subject.

existence is *dogma de fide divina et catholica definitum*, meaning that one cannot deny, or even doubt, it and still call himself a Catholic![7]

As for the Eucharist, a July 2019 study by the Pew Research Center found that only half (50 percent) of Catholic respondents knew that the Catholic Church teaches that the bread and wine used at Holy Mass are transformed by the celebrant into "the actual body and blood of Christ" (otherwise called "transubstantiation").[8] A follow-up study was later conducted by Pew researchers which focused more on Catholic respondents' personal belief in the church's teaching, rather than on their actual knowledge. Of the 50 percent of Catholics who could correctly identify Catholic teaching on the Eucharist, only 28 percent said that they believed it; 22 percent said they did not.[9] Out of *all* of the Catholic respondents, many (43 percent)—whether they knew the church's teaching or not—chose to believe that the bread and wine merely acted during Mass as "symbols" of Jesus' body and blood, and nothing more.[10] The transubstantiation of

7. See Ott, *Fundamentals of Catholic Dogma*, 17.

8. Pew Research Center, "What Americans Know," 22 (see also 26).

9. Smith, "Just One-Third."

10. Smith, "Just One-Third." Some challenged the Pew studies' findings based on (what they believed was) the confusing and ambiguous nature of the questions. For example, what does it mean to say that the bread and wine *actually* become Christ's body and blood? Or become Christ's *actual* body and blood? Would the results have been different if Pew had used the word *really* or *real* instead? And what about the distinction between *substance* and *accident*? Or of the essentially symbolic character of the sacramental system? (See e.g., Schlumpf, "Real Presence," 8, and Rausch, "What Do Catholics Mean." See also Gray, *Eucharist Beliefs*, 8–9.)

Yet, the Pew study was not directed at experts in Catholic theology but "non-experts," who would not have been expected to understand the intricacies of the church's eucharistic doctrine (like *res*, *sacramentum*, *substantia*, *species*). It was constructed, therefore, in language that (it was judged) those "non-experts" could for the most part understand. For most people (even trained theologians) to say that one thing "actually becomes" another is just about the same as saying that it "really becomes" the other. In other words, the one is changed into the other. So while the question in the Pew study is not a perfect statement of Catholic eucharistic doctrine, I am satisfied that the respondents probably understood it adequately enough—that is, what it meant to ask.

Others pointed to a previous study in 2011, which had indicated that in fact almost two-thirds of Catholic respondents (63 percent) did indeed believe that "during a Catholic Mass, the bread and wine really become the body and blood of Jesus Christ" (Gautier, "Knowledge and Belief"). The results of the study were published in D'Antonio et al., *American Catholics in Transition* (see esp. 107–22). The results appeared to be confirmed by a 2023 study conducted by the Center for Applied Research in the Apostolate (CARA). CARA's study found that the majority of Catholics—64 percent!—accepted Catholic teaching on the "real presence" of Christ in the Eucharist (see Gray, *Eucharist Beliefs*, 2, 32).

Yet, both studies (i.e., D'Antonio et al. and CARA) are problematic, not least because

the bread and wine at Mass into the body and blood of the Savior is also *de fide* Catholic teaching.[11]

On moral teachings, like abortion (which Vatican II called an unspeakable crime[12]), the majority of American Catholics—almost 60 percent—believe that abortion should be legally permissible in all or most cases![13] On homosexuality, the great majority of Catholics (74 percent) believe that it should be accepted—which admittedly can be interpreted in different ways since the term *homosexuality* could refer just to attraction and not activity. And "accepted" is a somewhat vague category. But on "gay marriage," the position is clear: 70 percent of Catholics are in favor of it—which probably should contextualize the previous percentage as meaning that the majority also accepts not just "same-sex" orientation but also homosexual acts themselves.[14] A large proportion of American Catholics (46 percent) thinks that there is no absolute standard for "right" or "wrong"; rather, each particular situation decides whether or not an act is good to do.[15]

In many cases, American Catholics' beliefs on all sorts of religious, political, and ethico-moral issues simply coincide with the general attitudes found in secular American society.[16] In *Gaudium et Spes* (the "Pastoral Constitution on the Church in the Modern World"), Vatican II's bishops called on Catholics to share the joys and hopes, the griefs and

---

the researchers for each seem to have been significantly confused over the concepts of "real presence" and "transubstantiation." For the terms are used interchangeably by each study, as if they mean the same thing. They most emphatically do not! "Real presence" refers to the thing or reality that starts to exist—in this case, the presence of the glorified Jesus himself—under the species of bread and wine; "transubstantiation" refers to the manner in which this thing or reality is brought about. The former refers to the mode or manner of Christ's presence effected in the Sacrament; the latter is the mode or manner *by which* it is effected. The ideas are not the same. See e.g., CCC, §§1374–77.

The fact that such a basic misunderstanding of Catholic eucharistic doctrine could have been allowed to slip past the designers of both studies—one of which (CARA) was done under the auspices of a major Catholic university, viz. Georgetown—calls into question, in my opinion, the validity of both the results and their interpretation. For if *the researchers themselves* could not correctly articulate Catholic doctrine on the Eucharist, does that not of itself reveal the problem?

11. See Ott, *Fundamentals of Catholic Dogma*, 373–83.

12. See Vatican II, *Gaudium et Spes*, §51.

13. Pew Research Center, "Religious Landscape Study."

14. Pew Research Center, "Religious Landscape Study."

15. Pew Research Center, "Religious Landscape Study."

16. See Pew Research Center, "Religious Landscape Study." See also Smith, "Decline of Christianity," 236–303.

anxieties, of human society.[17] They did not say to take over its beliefs and values in place of the gospel!

The faith is not being lived, either. According to a 2008 study by Georgetown University's Center for Applied Research in the Apostolate, one-third (33 percent) of American Catholics rarely or never goes to Sunday Mass. Only 20 percent go every week.[18]

According to the Pew Research Center's religious landscape study mentioned above, only 51 percent of Catholics surveyed said that they pray every day.[19] The great majority (67 percent) almost never reads the Bible.[20]

Vocations to the ordained ministry and religious life have plummeted since the 1970s and show no signs of increasing significantly in the foreseeable future.[21]

In the United States, the Catholic Church is hemorrhaging numbers badly: according to a 2015 study by the Pew Research Center, for every single person who converts to the Catholic Church, over six Catholics leave. Ex-Catholics make up thirty-one million people out of the US population. Their number could almost be regarded as a denomination all by itself: the "Recovering Catholic Church"! And the numbers have gotten worse since then: as of 2023–2024, the US Catholic Church now loses on average *8.4* Catholics for every one person who joins![22] Catholicism is no longer the predominant affiliation among Hispanics in the United States.[23] Even in Reverend Javier's overwhelmingly Catholic Philippines, less than *half* of Catholics practices Sunday Mass observance.[24]

If anything, the fiasco surrounding *Dominus Iesus* revealed that a profound fissure had developed—and has continued to develop—in bedrock aspects of the church's faith.

17. Vatican II, *Gaudium et Spes*, §1.

18. See Gray and Perl, *Sacraments Today*, 20. That was in 2008. In the 2023 CARA study mentioned above, the number had dropped to 17 percent (see Gray, *Eucharist Beliefs*, 1, 15).

19. Pew Research Center, "Religious Landscape Study."

20. Pew Research Center, "Religious Landscape Study."

21. See e.g., Center for Applied Research in the Apostolate, "Frequently Requested Church Statistics."

22. See Smith, "Decline of Christianity," 53, 103.

23. See Pew Research Center, "Changing Religious Landscape."

24. Social Weather Stations, "First Quarter 2017."

In 2008, the Pew Research Center, which conducts sociological research, did a survey in which it questioned various groups of Americans regarding their views of their own professed religion as well as that of others. For my purposes, I will focus here on the responses of "White Catholics" since they still constitute a plurality of members in the USA church.

According to the survey, the great majority (84 percent) of Catholic respondents believed that multiple religions could lead a person to salvation. In other words, while Catholicism itself was also salvifically effective, it was not the only faith by which one could be saved. Indeed, when asked if Catholicism were the "one, true faith" that led to eternal life, only 11 percent of Catholics were willing to say so.[25]

When asked how eternal life was achieved or determined, many Catholics (47 percent) ascribed it solely to a person's moral activity, apart from any sort of actual belief in anything.[26]

For those who advocate and emphasize "orthopraxis" over "orthodoxy," that result might seem encouraging—that is, until one looks at the survey's "breakdown" of which actions in particular were important for the respondents. Mostly, moral action was understood as "being a good person" or something just as vague and generic. Moral action is considered, then, in the abstract. *In the abstract*, if one wanted to be saved, it was better to be a "good person" (whatever that might mean).

Perhaps, at the very base level of an appropriate morality, one might have suggested (at least) following the "Golden Rule" . . . except only 5 percent of the Catholics surveyed thought that even the "Golden Rule" ought to apply specifically to one's salvation.[27]

But what about acting or behaving like the Lord Jesus? Or, maybe, adhering to biblical teaching, like the Ten Commandments of God? Each of these options garnered only 1 percent of approval among "White Catholics."[28]

A minority of Catholics—13 percent—was of the opinion that religious belief itself—that is, believing the right thing (I guess?)—was determinative for gaining eternal life. Again, this might encourage those who worry that the Catholic Church, especially in her leadership, has been too concerned with "litmus tests" for orthodoxy. Also, again—even for this

25. Pew Research Center, "Eternal Life."

26. Pew Research Center, "Eternal Life."

27. Pew Research Center, "Eternal Life."

28. Pew Research Center, "Eternal Life."

group, which placed the accent solely on one's proper belief—only a minority (3 percent) thought that *believing specifically in Jesus* would affect whether one achieved eternal life or not. The same number (3 percent) thought that one's belief in God was important to achieve that goal. Most of the respondents (7 percent) thought, on the contrary, that one needed to believe in his or her "own truth"! Maybe, I guess, that could include Jesus or God in some way, but also maybe not necessarily.[29]

This study came out in 2008—several years after *Dominus Iesus*. I am not sure that the results would have been significantly different had it been conducted eight years earlier than *Dominus Iesus*.

How, then, are people who are so poorly instructed in the faith and who are so poorly practicing it supposed to be missionary disciples? What faith can they share with others?

As I was reading the words above, while editing this book, my principal thought was this: the word *malaise* does not do justice to this situation. Nor does *crisis* suffice. I cannot find a word that is strong enough to convey my feelings of fear and concern for Christ's body, the church. Moreover, there is no word to express my sadness that my Lord Jesus is not loved or respected as he should be even among those who (might still) call themselves his disciples. Then, there is anger . . . that such disbelief and indolence has been allowed to get this far. For it did not happen overnight; and I do not believe that it has happened by chance.

Do I think that the bishops of the church, including the popes, recognize that there is a critically dangerous crack in the church's faith throughout the Catholic "world"? To some extent, yes—there is a feeling.

Of course, around the time when *Dominus Iesus* came out, there erupted with full force the controversy over certain alarming sexual scandals in the life of the church's clergy. (I know from my own personal experience that these episodes had already been going on for several decades in the church but were not being dealt with by the authorities—or were being covered up.) So I believe that many church leaders became overwhelmed by the magnitude of that terrible situation and could not bear to carry the extra burden of having to address the catastrophic collapse of faith and practice among so many Catholics. Much easier to just announce another "World Youth Day" (hoping that might move the needle a bit)! Or have the pope canonize another round of saints from

29. Pew Research Center, "Eternal Life."

"under-represented" groups. Other bishops, I think, were just happy to accept denial and move on to other things.

*Ecco, si muove.*

## "Good" People Don't Need Jesus . . . ?

At their 2007 meeting in Aparecida, Brazil, the Latin American and Caribbean bishops declared that a person's life in Christ grows by being given away to others.[30] But as the Latin expression runs, "Nemo dat quod non habet," or "No one gives what he or she does not have."

Something is happening—and none of it good—when there is such a collapse in both the knowledge and living of the faith in such disparate locales of the church. I do not know where the source lies: in the pastors, who are possibly not teaching, or in the parents, who are not exercising spiritual oversight over themselves or their children. I cannot judge this; nor do I judge anyone. Instead, I just observe the consequences.

In an article on Catholic mission, the American theologian Paul Knitter tells the story of an encounter that he had with a priest, an assistant to a Mexican bishop, during one of the meetings of an interreligious "peace council" that he sat on.

Knitter and the priest were sitting at a meal on the last day of the group's meeting. Referring to one of the Buddhist participants in the meeting—named Maha Ghosananda—the priest volunteered the following to Knitter:

> You know, after these three years of knowing Maha and coming to feel his deep holiness, peace, and persistent commitment to justice, I could never, never try, or even think of trying, to convert him to Christianity. That would make no sense. It would be wrong. Knowing him, working with him, I am convinced that he should remain what he is, a holy Buddhist.[31]

The priest continued, "I'm certain of what I just said. And yet, it contradicts what I'm supposed to believe as a Christian."[32]

According to Vatican II's solemn doctrine found in the Dogmatic Constitution on the Church, even those who have not yet received the "good news" about Christ are nonetheless related and ordered to the

30. Consejo Episcopal Latinoamericano, *Documento Conclusivo*, §360.

31. Knitter, "Catholics and Other Religions," 319.

32. Knitter, "Catholics and Other Religions," 320.

body of Christ, the church. In other words, all people are directed toward belief in Christ and adherence to his community. The council's bishops continue that whatever goodness or truth is found either within non-Christians or in their presence (*apud illos*) serves as a preparation for the church's proclamation to them of the message about Jesus and, ultimately, their entry into his body, the church, through baptism.[33] In other words, the moral goodness of someone who does not believe in God or in Christ, his or her acceptance of the truth as he or she can find it—these are not ends *in and of themselves*. They are leading somewhere; they have a purpose; they tend towards fulfillment and completion.

Now, let us retrace the sentiments expressed by Knitter's priest-friend, the assistant to a Catholic bishop.

The priest said that he would never try—would not even think of trying (which seems a weird statement, since he already mentions it)—to offer salvation in Christ to his Buddhist interlocutor. This was so to him because he felt that Ghosananda was already a morally good man according to his own religious belief and practice.

Yet, this raises some questions:

The priest himself was (presumably) also committed to the pursuit of holiness, peace, and justice. And he pursued those things as a disciple of Jesus Christ. It begs the question: What, in fact, made his own religious commitment to Jesus qualitatively different from Maha's? The implication of his comment seems to be that both Ghosananda's Buddhist beliefs and the priest's Christian beliefs ultimately have the same *terminus*. They each result in ethico-spiritual fulfillment, albeit in different ways—which is (of course) indifferentism writ large.

The priest's comment seems to betray the (now much-assailed) reductionism of the Enlightenment, whose thinkers had categorized all religion, especially Christianity, as simply an ethical concern. No religion was either revelatory or inspired; rather, religion was merely a repository of moral precepts. Given this, it would have perforce made no sense to the priest for him to have sought to offer to his Buddhist interlocutor—or to any other non-Christian at the meeting—faith in Jesus. For religion's effectiveness lay not in *theologoumena* or doctrines but in ethico-moral praxis. And Maha had, in his judgment, already reached that.

Knitter's priest follows the logical lines of his indifferent Modernism—namely, to have offered Jesus to his Buddhist friend as the decisive

33. See Vatican II, *Lumen Gentium*, §§14 and 16. See Tanner, *Decrees*, 2:861.

fulfillment of his righteous endeavors made absolutely no sense to him; it had no meaning for someone who was (in that priest's judgment) already a good person.[34] But the priest, who was an assistant to a Catholic bishop, added more ominously that it would even have been *wrong* to have tried to convert his Buddhist interlocutor to Christianity. In other words, he thought that it would have been an evil thing to do—a disbenefit—to Ghosananda if the priest were to have suggested that he cap off his acknowledged goodness with the acceptance of Jesus in faith.

Moreover, if Maha could already achieve ethico-spiritual values by adhering to the Buddha's *dharma*—and had apparently done so—then what did the priest, as a professed Christian, have to offer him? What could Maha learn from him? Well, the priest answers that himself: nothing.

His attitude, then, is the death of dialogue.[35]

If the priest truly felt that he had nothing of his own Christian faith to offer to his Buddhist interlocutor, then what did he think that he had to offer to their dialogue together? In order for it to be a true and authentic exchange, interreligious dialogue (we are told) demands that each partner engage in it from the integrity of his or her own beliefs or faith. This is the only way to have a truly enriching encounter among different views. The authenticity of dialogue rests on the foundation of each member's actual belief in the religious system that he or she claims to follow.[36] That is not to say that each believer might not have questions about or even disagreements with his or her own religious tradition. But if dialogue partners can on their own dismiss so cavalierly what seem to be essential aspects of their religion's self-understanding, then we may be able to say that we have a dialogue of *religious people* and their own opinions. But can we still say that we truly have a dialogue of *religions* anymore?

34. Consider the priest's statement, "I am convinced that he should remain what he is, a holy Buddhist." This was meant (I imagine) to have sounded irenic, but it rings like a *tour de force* of hubris. It is he, the priest, who will decide what his Buddhist interlocutor should be allowed to be.

35. If a righteous Buddhist following Buddhism does not warrant conversion to Christ, then what about a holy atheist following the natural law?

The priest's comment also, in my opinion, reveals the extent to which the malodorous heresy of Pelagianism wafts its way through much of interreligious encounter. For the assumption is that men and women can by their own efforts achieve supernatural goals, whereas the necessity of God's grace is hardly, if ever, mentioned.

36. See e.g., Dupuis, "Church's Evangelizing Mission," 27–28.

So this is where we are six decades after the Second Vatican Council: the pendulum of Catholic thinking has swung from "outside the church, no one at all is saved" to "it would be wrong to try to convert someone to Jesus."[37]

As summarized above, Vatican II's bishops reaffirmed at the highest level of their teaching authority that the church had a binding mission to proclaim to all peoples the "good news" that God had brought union with him and salvation through his Son, Jesus Christ.

But the "bones" of this doctrine have no flesh, if not put into practice.

And even the bones will rot away if they become diseased.

The priest talking with Knitter must have realized the "disease" in his comments since he adds uneasily, "I'm certain of what I just said. And yet, it contradicts what I'm supposed to believe as a Christian."[38] Yet if the priest were to follow his own logic, there is no Christianity that is necessary *for anyone* to believe in.

Yet as Bishop Rochus Tatamai relates encouragingly, there are people—perhaps even many (I hope)—who hunger to know the faith. "Some more!" was the response that his PNG congregation gave him after he had finished teaching them. The truth is attractive. As Lady Wisdom says in Sirach's hymn,

> Come over to me, everyone, who desires me,
> and with my products be filled.
> For my teaching is sweet above honey,
> and my inheritance is above honey and the honeycomb. . . .
> They who eat me, they shall still hunger;
> and they who drink me, they shall still thirst.
> The one who hears me, he shall not be confused;
> and the ones who work by me, they shall not sin:
> they who explain me, they shall have eternal life.
> (Sir 24:26–27, 29–31)

But if pastors are uninterested in meeting the desire of their flock—or worse, criticize their zeal for spreading the faith as "proselytism" or their commitment to the truth of the faith as "exclusivism"—then how is it any wonder people's interest in mission withers on the branch?

37. Although, discord on the matter of the church's evangelizing mission was already on display as early as the 1974 Synod of Bishops, whose participants could not even agree on producing a statement on the topic. See Dupuis, "Synod of Bishops."

38. Knitter, "Catholics and Other Religions," 320.

## Matthew 28:19–20 and the Missionary Mandate

We were told at the symposium that the missionary mandate remains.

But where should one look for its essential paradigm?

I have argued that the pericope of Matt 28:16–20, particularly verses 19–20, ought to still function as the basic model or archetype for Christian mission.

First and foremost, it functions as such for the Gospel According to Matthew. Matthew 28:19–20 defines the gospel as a missionary document and Matthew's community as a missionary community. By *missionary*, Matthew means exactly what Jesus says—namely, to make disciples of all nations, to make nonbelievers into believers. Matthew's missionary enterprise includes baptism and catechesis as necessary consequences, not as disjunctive choices that one could choose to do or not.

Second, by acting as a recapitulation of Matthew's Gospel, Matt 28:19–20 brings us back to the person of Christ himself, whose teaching is clearly a focus of the evangelist. Thus, a stronger—not a lessened—Christocentrism is called for. One needs to look first at Matthew's Gospel and the teachings of Jesus to understand what discipleship looks like. Only then will one understand how the evangelist expects mission to the nations to be conducted. The Christian missionary must take Jesus Christ himself as his or her model for mission and the Sermon on the Mount as his or her "battle plan" for bringing the gospel to nonbelievers. Such Christocentrism will hedge against certain self-interested or distorted interpretations, as could be found when the Scripture became entangled with Western colonialism and imperialism. On the contrary, Jesus' disciples should beware of becoming wolves in sheep's clothing (see Matt 7:15), instead of reflecting the Good Shepherd who lays down his life for the sheep (see John 10:11, 14).

It is true that for much of the first fifteen hundred years of Christianity's existence, Matt 28:19–20 was not seen as the "go-to" text for mission. Yet the need for missionary work seems to have always been understood and carried out, with the gospel being brought to all corners of the Mediterranean world and, later, to Asia, Africa, and the "New World." It seems to have been a deeply ingrained instinct of the church to spread the gospel message.

The Anabaptists recovered the universal appeal of Christ's mandate in Matt 28:19–20, highlighting that it applied to all Christians. The Baptist William Carey brought the Scripture to the fore of the Protestant imagination, propelling its status as the "Great Commission"—as the biblical text *par excellence* for defining Christian mission to the world. What the Anabaptists did was recover the essentially egalitarian nature of the Great Commission. True, it was addressed to the apostles after the resurrection—"the eleven" (Matt 28:16a)—but the apostles were intended to represent all followers of Christ. It follows that those who have been baptized and taught according to the mandate of Christ then themselves stand under the call of the risen Christ in Matt 28 to make disciples. The mandate, then, applies to all Catholics as part of their baptism. They are, as the symposium declared, "baptized and sent"!

Granted, Matthew's is not the only Gospel with a missionary commissioning. Missionary zeal can be found in Mark's Gospel, where Jesus instructs the apostles to preach the gospel to every creature in the whole world (see 16:15). It is found in John's Gospel where the risen Christ sends out the apostles just as he was sent by the Father (see 20:21). And in Luke's Gospel, the Lord tells the apostles that they will be his witnesses to the ends of the earth (see 24:47; see also Acts 1:8). What sets Matthew apart, perhaps, is that the mission given by Jesus in Matt 28 is so clearly the focus of the whole Gospel. The end defines the whole; it defines how God is "with us" from the Gospel's very first chapter. How will Jesus be Emmanuel, "God-with-us"? By his followers' making disciples of others, baptizing them in his name, and teaching them the commandments he gave to his community of followers.

So to understand even the end of Matthew's Gospel one must understand it from the beginning. And to understand the gospel's entirety one must look to its conclusion.

## Proclamation and Witness

I am skeptical of any view of mission which would advocate silence as its primary and (even) preferred mode. This perspective tends to interiorize mission to the point that proclamation hardly ever seems to happen at all. A humble, quiet witness certainly has its place in Christian life. As Jesus the son of Sirach teaches in his book,

> There is one silent, who is found wise,
> and there is one hateful, because he is brazen in speaking.
> There is one silent not having a response,
> and there is one silent knowing the proper time.

> A wise person will be silent for the time being,
> yet one quarrelsome and inconsiderate, they will not observe the time. (Sir 20:5–7)

There is wisdom in silence, in quietly living out the gospel while one waits for the appropriate occasion to speak the word of Christ. Jesus describes his disciples as lights for the world, whose good works should be seen by all people, who will then be led to give glory to God (see Matt 5:14–16). As St. Francis of Assisi directed his friars above, they should always be preaching the gospel—at the very least, by their example![39] But nowhere in the Gospels does Jesus advocate a purely silent witness. On the contrary, he declares, "Nothing is hidden, which shall not be revealed, and secret, which shall not be known. What I say to you in the shadows, say in the light; and what you hear in your ear, proclaim upon the housetops!" (Matt 10:26–27; see also Luke 12:3).[40]

Clearly, it is not always possible to proclaim Christ to non-Christians. To know when to do so requires prudence as well as respect for a person's interlocutor. Further, as mentioned already above, there may be legal strictures or even persecutory forces at work in a person's country that limit his or her ability to speak about Jesus to others. None of these, however, should be used to justify a "missiology of silence" that would seem to justify eliminating proclamation altogether.

Granted, Reverend Javier is right that the work of conversion is *God's* work. It is brought about in the souls of nonbelievers through the gracious activity of his most holy and life-giving Spirit. Thus, Pope St. John Paul II writes that God the Holy Spirit is the principal agent of mission.[41] That having been said, conversion does not happen in a vacuum. It also involves some human effort: a word of hope in Christ, the giving of a Bible or catechism, the invitation to Mass, simply asking someone if he or she had ever considered becoming Catholic. How could proclaiming

39. In its 1984 document *Dialogue and Mission*, the Secretariat for Non-Christians proffered the example of St. Charles de Foucauld "who carried out mission in a humble and silent attitude of union with God, in communion with the poor, and in universal brotherhood" (*Dialogue and Mission*, §17). According to Pope Francis's 2022 apostolic constitution *Praedicate Evangelium*, this Vatican office is now known as the Dicastery for Interreligious Dialogue.

40. There were times when Jesus did choose to remain (mostly) silent, for example, in the Synoptic Gospels, during his trials (see e.g., Mark 14:53–65 and parallels and Mark 15:1–5 and parallels). Or in John's Gospel when he was first asked by the crowd whether or not the adulterous woman ought to be stoned to death (John 7:53—8:11).

41. See John Paul II, *Redemptoris Missio*, §21.

Jesus Christ to those who do not yet know or accept him, or calling them into his body, the church, be seen as in any way antagonistic to the will of God, "who wills every human being to be saved and to come to an acknowledgement of truth" (1 Tim 2:4)?[42]

Reverend Devadass confirms the missionary mandate while noting that its emphasis has been lessened. Personal witness is now emphasized, for as Pope St. Paul VI said, people believe more in authentic witnesses than in teachers, and they believe in teachers on account of their witness.[43] This is very true. It is important to—indeed, the *sine qua non* of—Christian proclamation that people be seen to be living the words that they preach. The Christian message must be seen to be liberating and life-giving to those who call themselves followers of Christ. If people are not living it, then why follow it? Why listen to the words that come out of a nonpractitioner's mouth?

Yet Pope St. Paul VI also states clearly that witness in and of itself is not enough; it is incomplete without a clear and unequivocal explanation of the reason for it, which is belief in Jesus.[44] Both witness and proclamation are integral elements of Christian mission. They ought not to be placed at loggerheads as if one were of necessary value and the other not, or less so. The message of Christ is poisoned at its root by lack of witness or poor witness of life, but the witness is unfinished and withered without proclamation of one's following of the Lord Jesus. In the apostolic letter *Ubicumque et Semper*, by which he established the Pontifical Council for Promoting the New Evangelization, Pope Benedict XVI stated,

> It is the duty of the Church to proclaim always and everywhere the Gospel of Jesus Christ. He, the first and supreme evangelizer, commanded the Apostles on the day of his Ascension to the Father: "Go therefore and make disciples of all nations, baptizing them in the name of the Father and of the Son and of the Holy Spirit, teaching them to observe all that I have commanded

42. Note well, please, that I am not assuming here my own form of Pelagianism, as if Christians' efforts were absolutely and necessarily needed by God to effect the conversion of any person's soul. The followers of Christ, solely through their own efforts, do not make conversions happen. But I am resisting a sort of heretical tendency, derived from John Calvin (AD 1509–1564), which sees God's grace as irresistible to those whom he chooses to save. There is, then, little or no room for human freedom and cooperation either in the acceptance of grace by the nonbeliever or in its offer through the church. See e.g., *CCC*, §§1987–2029 (see also §1742).

43. See Paul VI, *Evangelii Nuntiandi*, §41.

44. See Paul VI, *Evangelii Nuntiandi*, §22.

> you" (Matt 28:19–20). Faithful to this mandate, the Church . . . ever since she received the gift of the Holy Spirit on the day of Pentecost (cf. Acts 2:14), has never tired of making known to the whole world the beauty of the Gospel as she preaches Jesus Christ . . . who, by his death and Resurrection, brought us salvation and fulfilled the promise made of old. Hence the mission of evangelization, a continuation of the work desired by the Lord Jesus, is necessary for the Church: it cannot be overlooked; it is an expression of her very nature.[45]

While addressing the bishops of Nicaragua during their *ad limina* visit to Rome, Pope St. John Paul II explicated, "The Church feels constantly challenged by Jesus' mandate to proclaim the Gospel to every creature [see Mark 16:15], a mandate which entrusts itself to the authentic strengths [*las fuerzas vivas*] of every particular Church in order that this proclamation might reach every sphere of human life. To that effect, the message must be clear and precise: an explicit and prophetic proclamation of the Resurrected Lord . . . so that with luck the word of life is transformed into a personal commitment to Jesus, Savior of mankind and of the world."[46]

## A World That Hates Christ

Christ's mandate to proclaim is a challenge not just to Christians but also to the non-Christian world, which does not always want to hear it and which can oppose it. Reverend Devadass knows about this opposition to the gospel message in his native Malaysia. Still, I worried that he tended to ignore the presence of opposition to and (even) hatred of Christ in the Scriptures that he proposed for mission. For example, Devadass proposed as the prime text for mission John 20:21: "As the Father has sent me, I also send you." Yet he forgot the context of the scene—namely, the disciples were hiding behind locked doors for fear of the authorities (v. 19)![47] Yes,

45. Benedict XVI, *Ubicumque et Semper*.

As per Pope Francis's 2022 apostolic constitution, *Praedicate Evangelium*, the council has been merged into the Dicastery for Evangelization.

46. John Paul II, "To the Bishops of Nicaragua," §2. See also Juan Pablo II, "Conferencia Episcopal del Nicaragua."

47. Devadass also overlooks negative details in his other examples: for instance, in Mark's Gospel, Jesus' first formal attempt to proclaim the "good news" is interrupted by a demoniac's shriek: "What is there between us and you, Jesus Nazarene? Have you come to destroy us?" (Mark 1:24a-b). As for Devadass's example from Luke's Gospel, I need only point out how the people become so enraged at Jesus' message that they try

Jesus was sent, and he sends his disciples out into the world . . . but not to a world that will welcome them. On the contrary, he sends them to a world that will hate them as it has hated him: "If the world hates you, know that it has had hatred for me prior to you" (John 15:18).[48] Yes, Jesus had a mission for which he was sent. It ultimately led to his "hour" upon the cross (see John 12:27).[49] I do not believe that Bl. John-Baptist Mazzucconi was martyred because he lacked anthropological skill, as someone at the symposium claimed. He was killed by some indigenes because he challenged their evil practices.[50] As Pope St. John Paul II declared at his beatification, "The Christian message, that Mazzucconi proclaimed to the natives of Woodlark, was an open condemnation of their conduct. . . . And notwithstanding the immense charity and untiring dedication of the Blessed, his own preaching provoked irritation and hatred."[51] Like Jesus, Mazzucconi brought a strange message (see John 6:60) and an alien Spirit (14:17) to the "world" of Woodlark Island, PNG. That message is still opposed and hated today.

As Christ's body, the church, like her Master, wrestles "against the principalities, against the powers, against the world's rulers of these shadows, against the spirits of wickedness in the heavens" (Eph 6:12). Vatican II's *Ad Gentes* avers to this spiritual contest: by her missionary activity, the church reclaims from the devil's influence (*imperium*) whatever truth, goodness, and grace is found among men, restoring them to Christ, their Author. In that way, "whatever good is found to be sown in the hearts and minds of men, or in [their] rites and cultures . . . not only is not lost, but is healed, uplifted, and perfected for the glory of God, the shame of the demon, and the bliss of men."[52] When asked above about the presence of the Evil One in the missions, Paolo Baleinakorodawa was evasive: he was not sure what was meant by *devil*. He was sure, however, that there was "social injustice," in other words, the evil that men and women do to each other. This troubled me, not least because Jesus tells his followers to pray that they may be freed "from *the evil one*" (Matt 6:13, emphasis

to throw him over a cliff (see Luke 4:29)!

48. John's Gospel is clear about the world's hatred of Jesus: see 3:20; 15:19, 23–24; 17:14.

49. It is through the "hour" of his humiliation and exaltation that Jesus will make his return to the Father. See Brown, *Gospel According to John (I–XII)*, 517–18.

50. See e.g., Wiltgen, *Founding*, 179–80.

51. Ioannes Paulus II, "Andegavensibus Martyribus," §2b (560); my translation.

52. Vatican II, *Ad Gentes*, §9. See Tanner, *Decrees*, 2:1019.

added; see similarly John 17:15)! Quite separate from man's proverbial inhumanity to man, the church is clear that there exists a being whose constant will and effort is to oppose God.[53] In a general audience, given in 1972, Pope St. Paul VI spoke plainly, "We find sin, which is the perversion of human freedom and ultimate cause of death, because it is separation from God the source of life . . . and then, in its turn, we find the occasion and effect of a working in us and in our world of a hidden and adversarial agent, the Evil Spirit [*il Demonio*]. Evil is not even above all a deficiency, but an efficiency, a living being, spiritual, perverted and perverting."[54] He continued, "He departs from the bounds of the teaching of the Bible and of the church who refuses to recognize this reality as existing; or rather who makes of it a standalone principle, not even having the reality, as every creature has whose origin is from God; or who explains it as a pseudo-reality, a conceptual and fanciful personification of the unknown causes of our misfortunes."[55]

The devil is real. He is a person. He has powers that he can—and does—choose to exercise against God's holy will. Jesus encountered this diabolical being and his "anti-kingdom" even before his ministry started: "And [the devil] bore [Jesus] up and showed him all the kingdoms of the region of the earth in a moment of time. And the Devil said to him: 'To you I will give this whole power and their glory, because to me it is handed over, and to whom I will, I give it'" (Luke 4:5–6). On the contrary, the prayer of Jesus is that his Father's reign should be triumphant: "Let your kingdom come!" (Luke 11:2d; see also Matt 6:10). And the response of the church after she has recited Jesus' prayer in the Sacred Liturgy is to acclaim, "For the kingdom, the power and the glory are yours now and forever."[56] The kingdom of God, therefore, is at war with the "kingdom" of Satan.[57] In baptism, the church exorcizes the candidates, taking them away from the devil and claiming them for God's kingdom:

> Almighty ever-living God,
> who sent your Son into the world
> to drive out from us the power of Satan, the spirit of evil,

53. See *CCC*, §§391–95, 2850–54.

54. Paolo VI, "Udienza generale"; my translation. *Nota bene*: I am grateful to those in the forums of WordReference.com for helping me translate the text.

55. Paolo VI, "Udienza generale"; my translation.

56. "The Order of Mass," in Catholic Church, *Roman Missal*, 665 (§125).

57. The conflict between God's kingdom and the devil's "anti-kingdom" is outlined, for example, in Luke 11:18 and Rev 2:13, 11:15, 16:10.

> and bring the human race, rescued from darkness,
> into the marvelous Kingdom of your light:
> we humbly beseech you
> to free these [people] from Original Sin,
> to make them the temple of your glory,
> and to grant that your Holy Spirit may dwell in them.[58]

Christians are initiated into Christ's army, into his military campaign, against the powers of evil that seek to sow injustice.[59] We ignore the world's opposition and the devil's hostile presence at our own peril . . . and at that of the church's evangelizing mission!

## An Evangelizing Mission That Is Everything . . . Except Proclamation

Pope St. John Paul II says in *Ecclesia in Oceania* that the church's mission is "to speak a word of hope to the world."[60] This hopeful word is encapsulated in the paschal troparion of the Eastern churches:

> Christ is risen from the dead, trampling death by Death, and to those in the tombs giving life![61]

The proclamation of the message that Jesus, God's Son and the messiah of Israel, is not dead, that he is alive and brings salvation to the world, is the church's evangelizing mission.

The panel discussion raised several issues that could constitute parts of the new evangelizing mission for the church—namely, environmental issues, poverty, migration, and gender equality.

Certainly, these are undeniable concerns. I do not deny that they deserve the church's attention.

But what are they in the light of Jesus Christ: his precious teaching, his salvific death and resurrection, his return in glory?

Overall, the panel's speakers seemed focused on what could be done practically: Nahak spoke about the PNG bishops' partnering with the Seventh-day Adventists to produce Bible studies on climate change. Both Donatus Nahak and Paul Harricknen encouraged participants to make

58. Catholic Church, *Baptism of Children*, 22 (§49).

59. For St. Paul's use of militaristic, warlike imagery in Christian life, see Punt, "Paul."

60. John Paul II, *Ecclesia in Oceania*, §26.

61. Galadza et al., *Divine Liturgy*, 501–4.

Pope Francis's encyclical *Laudato Si'* known and appreciated. Harricknen encouraged everyone to have a Bible and catechism. But other aspects showed a less religious focus: Catherine Nongkas, for example, tried to impart the importance of care for the earth to her students at Port Moresby's Don Bosco Tech. But the same insight could also be found at a secular school. Archbishop John Ribat is certainly a religious figure, but I am not convinced experimental seabed mining comes under the purview of his magisterial office.

We really need to be cautious in this regard. The church now fulfills her evangelizing mission in a secularized world. But that is no reason to secularize her mission. In *Ecclesia in Oceania*, Pope St. John Paul II writes, "[The church's] mission is simple and clear: to propose . . . to human society the entire Gospel of salvation in Jesus Christ."[62] The world is concerned with environmental damage, with poverty and migration, with inequality between boys and girls. Indeed, it should be! It is, however, not so concerned to hear a message about God's unconditional love, of sin and redemption, of salvation in Jesus Christ. To the extent that the church is a human *as well as* a divine reality, I can understand why her members feel the need to share the concerns of the world.[63] I think, though, that it must be said: *no matter how important or how urgent are the problems of the secular world, they do not pertain essentially to the church's evangelizing mission.*

Rather, the church's essential mission is supernatural; it is not natural. In a 1956 address in French to experts in archaeology, history, and art, Pope Ven. Pius XII explained,

> [The Church's] divine founder, Jesus Christ, has not given her such a mandate or fixed a goal in the cultural order. The aim that Christ assigns her is strictly religious; it is even the synthesis of all which includes the idea of religion, the unique and absolutely authentic [*véritable*] religion: The church must lead men and women to God, in order that they might surrender themselves to him without reserve and also find in him inner, perfect peace. You see why Christ has confided to the church all his truth and all his grace.

62. John Paul II, *Ecclesia in Oceania*, §18.

63. See *CCC*, §771.

> The church can never lose sight of this strictly religious, supernatural aim. The purpose [*Le sens*] of all her activities . . . cannot do anything but contribute to it.[64]

In *Ecclesia in Oceania*, Pope St. John Paul II explains that in the social services the church provides—which are many—"their *overarching concern* is to play their part in the Church's mission to tell the truth of Jesus Christ, to walk his way and to live his life."[65] Thus, any social benefits a society may derive from the church's efforts come ultimately from her following of Christ. As Vatican II's *Gaudium et Spes* tells us at its very beginning, "the joys and the hopes, the griefs and the anxieties" of the world are also shared by the church.[66] But she exists to tell the "story" about God's ultimate fulfillment of these joys and hopes and his answer to the world's griefs and anxieties, which is the "good news" of his son, Jesus Christ. If she does not—if she forgets this—then she becomes no more than any other social service organization, which is her death. After having been elected, Pope Francis celebrated Mass with the cardinal-electors. During his homily for that liturgy, he warned,

> We can journey as much we want, we can build many things, but if we do not confess Jesus Christ, nothing will come of it. We will become a charitable NGO, but not the church, the Bride of Christ. . . . When one does not build on stone . . . what follows is what happens to children on the beach when they make sandcastles: It all falls down; it is without consistency. . . . When Jesus Christ is not confessed, the worldliness of the devil is confessed, the worldliness of the demon.[67]

Without a doubt, the church participates in not just the sufferings but also the jubilations of the world. How could she not bind the wounds of the injured (see Matt 25:31–46) or laugh with those who rejoice (see Rom 12:15)? But her purpose is always for her divine Master: doing his will, increasing

64. Pius XII, "Allocutio Cultoribus," 212; my translation. See also Vatican II, *Gaudium et Spes*, §§42 and 76.

65. John Paul II, *Ecclesia in Oceania*, §35; emphasis added. In the same document, he states that through the social apostolate, "Catholic institutions allow the light of the Gospel to penetrate cultures and societies, evangelizing them from within, as it were" (John Paul II, *Ecclesia in Oceania*, §32; see also §26).

66. Vatican II, *Gaudium et Spes*, §1.

67. Francesco, "Santa Messa"; my translation. Pope Francis actually said the church would become "a pitiful [*pietosa*] NGO"—not a "charitable [*assistenziale*]" one. Apparently, someone at the Vatican thought a change in wording was necessary. Video of the homily can be seen at *Telegraph*, "Pope Francis' First Mass."

his kingdom. As His Holiness Pope Bl. John Paul I stated during his general audience given on September 20, 1978, while the joys of this world are "good and encouraging, [they] must not be absolutized."[68] He continued, "They are something, not everything; they serve as a means, they are not the supreme purpose; they do not last for ever, but only for a short time. 'Christians,' St. Paul wrote, 'deal with the world as though they had no dealings with it. For the form of this world is passing away' (cf. 1 Cor 7:31). Christ had already said: 'Seek first of all the kingdom of God' (Mt 6:33)."[69] On the one hand, the blessed pope was sure that the church, both in her hierarchy and in her laypeople, can never insist enough on "the great problems of freedom, justice, peace, development" as well as on their solution. However, he warned, "It is wrong, on the other hand, to state that political, economic and social liberation coincides with salvation in Jesus Christ, that the *Regnum Dei* is identified with the *Regnum hominis*, that *Ubi Lenin ibi Jerusalem*."[70] To forget these words means the distortion—even the death—of the church's evangelizing mission, for it would lose its true purpose.

I mention the above because a comfortable *modus vivendi* seems to have developed between the church and the world. Church authorities choose to maintain a social presence (one might say *relevance*) through institutions, like schools, hospitals, and so forth. But they also choose not to disturb a society otherwise by actively proclaiming to it God's salvation in Jesus Christ. The Federation of Asian Bishops' Conferences is a case in point: although accepting proclamation *in principle*, the FABC nevertheless deems it to be too confrontational. Instead, the bishops of FABC state their preference for following other avenues, like the practice of interreligious dialogue.[71] Some propose a "compromise vision" in which the church's evangelizing mission is not limited so rigidly and specifically to proclamation but necessarily includes the promotion of the "values" of the "kingdom" that was proclaimed by Christ himself. In that way, the church's social aspect may yet remain as the expression—even the most prominent one—of her mission. Thus, they believe, the church might still fulfill her evangelizing mission through indirect means, like running hospitals, setting up schools and orphanages, and so forth.

This is understandable in places where the gospel's proclamation is restricted (for example, in Malaysia) or the church is persecuted (for

68. John Paul I, "General Audience."
69. John Paul I, "General Audience."
70. John Paul I, "General Audience."
71. See e.g., Tan, "*Missio Inter Gentes*."

example, in China). But what about places where the exercise and propagation of the faith is free and protected by law (for example, in PNG, Australia, the USA)?

And what happens when the church's social institutions are less needed and the church's social apostolate becomes less relevant? What is left to offer . . . except proclamation?

And if the commitment to proclamation is unclear or has been left aside, why do any of the church's social programs exist?

Indo-Spanish theologian Raymond Panikkar noted the problem inherent in this situation presciently in an article written many years ago: "Indirect Methods in the Missionary Apostolate." Some had argued that the church had to use "indirect methods" (schools, hospitals, orphanages, etc.) in order to fulfill her mission on earth. Panikkar, however, rejected this argument as a form of Pelagianism. Moreover, "it would require a policy of strategy and scheming in direct opposition and plain contradiction to the spirit and the letter of the Gospel."[72] He wrote, "History proves that the Church, as such, never purposely introduced 'indirect methods'; though what was started as a direct method may be considered indirect in the opinion of a following generation, and as such may continue only by virtue of historical inertia. The works of mercy, for instance, which were the crown of glory of the 'missions' and are now becoming the crown of thorns, were started as direct and not indirect means of apostolate."[73] Panikkar recommended turning over such social activities to secular authority.

Where I would disagree with Panikkar is in considering the "works of mercy" necessarily indirect methods. They can be considered "direct" methods insofar as their carrying out is based on the explicit command of Christ to feed the hungry, clothe the naked, visit the sick and the imprisoned, and so forth (see Matt 25:31–46). It also includes championing the values of God's kingdom (for example, justice, equality, peacemaking, solidarity, and so forth), whose reign Jesus came to preach and inaugurate. Granting that social and historical circumstances may have modified the focus somewhat, these activities are still indispensably linked to the following of Jesus Christ and are still required by his gospel.[74] Where

72. Panikkar, "Indirect Methods," 112.

73. Panikkar, "Indirect Methods," 112.

74. It is certainly the case in PNG, for example, that the church and missionaries provide an *ersatz* "social welfare system" that the PNG government itself is not capable of providing yet. Reverend Glynn's group, WeCARe, is just one of innumerable

these methods become indirect and (perhaps) otiose from Panikkar's point of view is when the rationale for them, which is serving Christ and making him known, is gone or taken away. If any Catholic social institution loses sight of its divine calling, then it is like salt which has lost its flavor. It is good for nothing except to be thrown out into the street (see Matt 5:13). Then it becomes for the church, as Panikkar says above, "a crown of thorns." One should note in this regard the comments offered by Guinean cardinal Archbishop Robert Sarah. In an article that he authored, Sarah warned against attempts to abolish civilization's "sacred foundation," for in trying to do so humanity risked losing civilization's "protective and insuperable boundaries."[75] An "entirely profane world," he writes, would be like "a vast expanse of quicksand": everything would be open to "the winds of arbitrariness"; every relationship would become "fragile and fickle."[76] He continues,

> Some ask the Catholic Church to play this solid foundation role [of the sacred in society]. They would like to see her assume a social function, namely to be a coherent system of values, a cultural and aesthetic matrix. But the Church has no other sacred reality to offer than her faith in Jesus, God made man. Her sole goal is to make possible the encounter of men with the person of Jesus.[77]

This encounter with Christ, Sarah continued, is offered through the church's doctrines as well as her life of worship and prayer. Her response to the world must always be that of the blessed apostle Paul, who chose to know nothing, except the Crucified Jesus (see 1 Cor 2:2).[78] Sarah cautioned, "[The church] must stop thinking of herself as a substitute for humanism or ecology. These realities, although good and just, are for her but consequences of her unique treasure: faith in Jesus Christ."[79] These are sobering comments, directed perhaps against both sides of the spectrum: on the one hand, those who would want the church to remain within the sphere of "social forces"—that is, running schools and hospitals but not challenging society with the demands of the gospel; on the other hand,

---

examples of this reality.

75. Sarah, "Credibility of the Catholic Church."

76. Sarah, "Credibility of the Catholic Church."

77. Sarah, "Credibility of the Catholic Church."

78. Sarah, "Credibility of the Catholic Church."

79. Sarah, "Credibility of the Catholic Church."

those who might want a return to an antiquated "Christendom"—the church usurping to some extent the legitimate autonomy of societal institutions. On the contrary, the church is not an earthly kingdom in either sense—that is, in the way of running social institutions or in deposing princes and kings. Previously, due to historical realities, the church may have acted as a substitute for societal and governmental structures, thus creating through sheer force of presence a Christian civilization among people (because the church was everywhere and had a hand in everything). Such is not the case anymore. Rather, a Christian civilization will be created through bringing people, both the evangelized and not, into a meeting with the Savior, Jesus Christ. Any benefits to society must overflow from that meeting-place of persons. It cannot be forced on others . . . but it cannot be forgotten, either.

Much has been said above, and much more could still be said. But I will end here with Pope St. John Paul II's homily at the beatification of John-Baptist Mazzucconi. Mazzucconi was one of the founding members of PIME, the Pontifical Institute of Foreign Missions. He was sent to Oceania, specifically Woodlark Island, PNG, in 1852, where he worked for two years. The mission was not a success, and he returned to Australia to recuperate. He later returned to the mission, not knowing that it had actually already been abandoned. He was murdered when the ship on which he was travelling was attacked by natives. The church determined that his death was the result of *odium fidei*, or "hatred of the faith." So the process of his canonization was moved along, and he was beatified in 1984 by Pope St. John Paul II. In his homily at the Mass of Beatification, Pope St. John Paul II said the following about Mazzucconi, who died so that others might know and accept Christ:

> We must demand of ourselves the courage of the Faith, of unfailing faithfulness to Jesus Christ, to His Church, in times of trial as in daily life. Our world, which is much too often indifferent or ignorant, expects a witness from Christ's disciples that is without equivocation, which, one might say, evokes that given by the martyrs celebrated today: Jesus Christ is alive; prayer and the Eucharist are essential for us to live His life, devotion to Mary sustains us as His disciples; our attachment to the Church makes us one with our faith; our unity as brothers and sisters is the sign *par excellence* of Christians; true justice, purity, love, forgiveness, and peace are the fruits of the Spirit of Jesus; missionary passion is part of this witness; we cannot keep our burning lamp hidden.[80]

80. Ioannes Paulus II, "Andegavensibus Martyribus," §6 (562–63); my translation.

# Appendix

## Message of His Eminence Archbishop Fernando Cardinal Filoni, Prefect of the Congregation for the Evangelization of Peoples, to Participants in the Missiological Symposium "Baptized and Sent," Held September 24–25, 2019, at Catholic Theological Institute, Bomana, Papua New Guinea[1]

*Author's Note: What is given below is a reproduction of Cardinal Filoni's letter to the symposium. As such, any idiosyncrasies of spelling, capitalization, or format have been retained.*

Dear brothers and sisters of the Catholic Church in Papua New Guinea and the Solomon Islands, peace to you all in Our Lord Jesus Christ!

I am delighted to extend my cordial greeting to all of you who have generously accepted the invitation to gather and celebrate this important ecclesial event in preparation of the Extraordinary Missionary Month of October 2019, which was called by Our Holy Father, Pope Francis, with the theme "Baptized and sent: the Church of Christ on mission in the world" (www.october2019.va).

One hundred years have passed since the Apostolic Letter *Maximum Illud* was issued by Pope Benedict XV. That document and the ensuing fruitful evangelical renewal of the Church's mission, which was defined at the Second Vatican Council and in the Magisterium of the post-conciliar

1. I am grateful to Reverend Agostino Divittorio of the Holy See's Dicastery for Evangelization for providing me with a copy of Cardinal Filoni's message. I am also grateful to His Excellency Archbishop Maurizio Bravi, the Apostolic Nuncio to PNG and the Solomon Islands, for his kind permission in allowing me to reproduce the message here.

*Nota bene*: italics in original.

Popes, are an occasion for us all to give sincere thanks to God and to all the Christians who have generously given their lives for the sake of the Gospel and the building of the Church throughout the world, especially in Papua New Guinea and the Solomon Islands, lands so richly filled with natural goodness and the missionary spirit of Jesus Christ.

Pope Francis recently wrote: "On 30 November 2019, we will celebrate the hundredth anniversary of the promulgation of the Apostolic Letter *Maximum Illud*, with which Pope Benedict XV sought to give new impetus to the missionary task of proclaiming the Gospel. In 1919, [...] Pope [Benedict XV] recognized the need for a more evangelical approach to missionary work in the world, [and] laid special emphasis on the *missio ad gentes*, employing the concepts and language of the time, in an effort to revive, particularly among the clergy, a sense of duty towards the missions" (Letter of the Holy Father Francis for the centenary of the promulgation of the Apostolic Letter "Maximum Illud" on the activity of missionaries in the world, 22 October 2017).

When originating from an encounter with Christ, mission establishes relationships which are in constant movement, forever capable of faithfulness and conversion to God for the salvation of humanity. Thus, Pope Benedict XV hoped to purify the Church's work, placing due emphasis on the authentic mission of Jesus Christ.

In celebrating this centenary, our current Pope likewise invites us to renew the missionary call of all the baptized, not simply leaving this fundamental dimension of our faith to missionary Institutes alone. The work of evangelization must become a paradigm of the Church's daily life, orienting our activities and engagements toward the salvation of the entire world (see {*Evangelii Gaudium*} 15). All we are and all we do as dioceses, parishes, ecclesial movements and Church groups should reveal that our missionary work is a permanent part of our lives and not simply reduced to certain moments, but is rather a constant desire for the transformation of the world in Christ.

As Pope Francis stated in his Apostolic Exhortation *Evangelii Gaudium*, "Let us learn from the saints who have gone before us, those who confronted the difficulties of their own day, [...] and pause to rediscover some of the reasons which can help us to imitate them today. The primary reason for evangelizing is the love of Jesus which we have received, the experience of salvation which urges us to ever greater love of him. What kind of love would not feel the need to speak of the beloved, to point him out, to make him known? If we do not feel an intense desire to share this love, we need to pray insistently that he will once more touch our hearts" (EG 263–264). This experience of love is what motivates the saints, from whom we draw strength as we seek the unique mission Jesus grants to each one of us at this time, based on our specific vocation and the environment in which we currently find ourselves. Aiding us on this missionary journey are the multitude of saints, such as Blessed John Mazzucconi, an Italian priest from the Pontifical Institute for Foreign Missions who was martyred while spreading the Gospel in this very land, and Blessed Peter To Rot, one of your own, who was beatified as a Martyr in 1995. As we draw near to the Extraordinary Missionary Month of October 2019, Pope Francis invites us to reflect and pray about our personal call to be missionary disciples.

In conclusion, I thank each and every one of you, your local Churches and your pastors, the National Direction [read: Director] of the Pontifical Mission Societies in Papua New Guinea and the Solomon Islands and all its diocesan missionary collaborators for organizing this Symposium and for all that you are doing to make Pope Francis' missionary initiative fruitful. In the coming month of October, the celebration of the Extraordinary Missionary Month will fill us with joy and gratitude for the gift of faith and for the mission of Jesus Christ and his Church. I pray for all of you and for all the people of Papua New Guinea and the Solomon Islands, that your baptismal witness to the Christian faith may be fruitful in the Holy Spirit, may build up the Holy Church of God among you, and may bring peace and prosperity, justice and fraternity to all.

United in prayer and in mission, I assure you of my prayers for a joy-filled Symposium, a blessed Extraordinary Missionary Month, and a lifetime of missionary service.

*Fernando Cardinal Filoni*
Prefect

# Bibliography


Abbott, Walter, and Joseph Gallagher, eds. *The Documents of Vatican II*. Introduction by Lawrence Shehan. Piscataway, NJ: New Century, 1966.

Accattoli, Luigi. "Religioni, inopportuno il documento Ratzinger." *La Corriere della Sera*, Sept. 26, 2000, 18.

Allen, John L., Jr. "Cardinal Kasper Balances Values with Reality." *National Catholic Reporter*, May 11, 2001, 13.

———. "Exclusive Claim." *National Catholic Reporter*, Sept. 15, 2000, 3, 5, 7.

———. "Gap Between Theory, Reality." *National Catholic Reporter*. Sept. 22, 2000, 6–7.

———. "Oceans of Peace." *National Catholic Reporter*, Oct. 6, 2000, 14–15.

Anderson, Floyd, ed. *Council Daybook: Vatican II, Session 4—Sept. 14, 1965 to Dec. 8, 1965*. Washington, DC: National Catholic Welfare Conference, 1966.

Andrews, E. A., ed. *A New Latin Dictionary Founded on the Translation of Freund's Latin-German Lexicon*. Revised and enlarged by Charlton T. Lewis and Charles Short. Harper's Latin Dictionary. New York: Harper & Bros., 1891.

Anwyl, Edward. *Celtic Religion in Pre-Christian Times*. London: Archibald Constable, 1906.

Asia South Pacific Association for Basic and Adult Education (ASPBAE) and Papua New Guinea Education Advocacy Network. *PNG Education Experience Survey and Literacy Assessment—A Report on 5 Provinces: New Ireland, NCD, Chimbu, Sandaun and Gulf Provinces*. Canberra: ASPBAE, 2011. https://dokumen.tips/documents/education-language-and-literacy-education-experiencevii-executive-summary.html?page=1.

Atterbury, Anson P. "The Many-Sided Christ." *Biblical World* 25 (1905) 450–56.

Benedict XV. *Maximum Illud*. Encyclical letter. Holy See, Nov. 30, 1919. http://www.vatican.va/content/benedict-xv/en/apost_letters/documents/hf_ben-xv_apl_19191130_maximum-illud.html.

Benedict XVI. "Homily at the Mass of the Imposition of the Pallium and Conferral of the Fisherman's Ring for the Beginning of the Petrine Ministry of the Bishop of Rome." Holy See, Apr. 24, 2005. https://www.vatican.va/content/benedict-xvi/en/homilies/2005/documents/hf_ben-xvi_hom_20050424_inizio-pontificato.html.

———. "Homily During the Apostolic Journey to München, Altötting and Regensburg." Holy See, Sept. 10, 2006. http://www.vatican.va/content/benedict-xvi/en/homilies/2006/documents/hf_ben-xvi_hom_20060910_neue-messe-munich.html.

———. "It Became Increasingly Clear to Me That John Paul II Was a Saint." Interview by Wlodzimierz Redzioch. In *Stories About Saint John Paul II, Told by His Close Friends and Co-Workers*, edited by Wlodzimierz Redzioch, 15–23. Translated by Michael J. Miller. San Francisco: Ignatius, 2015.

———. "Meeting with Muslim Religious Leaders, Members of the Diplomatic Corps, and Rectors of the Universities in Jordan." Address. Holy See, May 9, 2009. https://www.vatican.va/content/benedict-xvi/en/speeches/2009/may/documents/hf_ben-xvi_spe_20090509_capi-musulmani.html.

———. "Message for the 41st World Communications Day." Holy See, May 20, 2007. http://www.vatican.va/content/benedict-xvi/en/messages/communications/documents/hf_ben-xvi_mes_20070124_41st-world-communications-day.html.

———. "To Participants in the General Assembly of the Pontifical Mission Societies." Address. Holy See, May 14, 2011. http://www.vatican.va/content/benedict-xvi/en/speeches/2011/may/documents/hf_ben-xvi_spe_20110514_pom.html.

———. *Ubicumque et Semper*. Apostolic letter. Holy See, Sept. 21, 2010. https://www.vatican.va/content/benedict-xvi/en/apost_letters/documents/hf_ben-xvi_apl_20100921_ubicumque-et-semper.html.

———. "Visit to the Grotto of St. Paul." Address. Holy See, Apr. 17, 2010. http://www.vatican.va/content/benedict-xvi/en/speeches/2010/april/documents/hf_ben-xvi_spe_20100417_grotta-malta.html.

Boadt, Lawrence. *Reading the Old Testament: An Introduction*. Mahwah, NJ: Paulist, 1984.

Boer, Harry R. *Pentecost and Missions*. London: Lutterworth, 1961.

Bokenkotter, Thomas. *A Concise History of the Catholic Church*. Rev. and exp. ed. New York: Doubleday, 2005.

Bosch, David J. "The Scope of Mission." *International Review of Mission* 73 (1984) 19–32.

———. "The Structure of Mission: An Exposition of Matthew 28:16–20." In *Exploring Church Growth*, edited by Wilbert R. Shenk, 218–48. Grand Rapids: Eerdmans, 1983.

———. *Transforming Mission: Paradigm Shifts in Theology of Mission*. American Society of Missiology 16. Maryknoll, NY: Orbis, 1991.

Bradshaw, Paul F., et al. *The Apostolic Tradition: A Commentary*. Edited by Harold W. Attridge. Hermeneia: A Critical and Historical Commentary on the Bible. Minneapolis: Fortress, 2002.

Brown, Raymond E. *The Gospel According to John (I–XII)*. Anchor Bible 29. Garden City, NY: Doubleday, 1966.

———. *The Gospel According to John (XIII–XXI)*. Anchor Bible 29A. Garden City, NY: Doubleday, 1970.

Brown, Raymond E., and Robert North. "Biblical Geography." In *NJBC*, art. 73, §§1–115.

Brown, Raymond E., et al., eds. *The New Jerome Biblical Commentary*. With a foreword by Carlo Maria Martini. Englewood Cliffs, NJ: Prentice Hall, 1990.

Bultmann, Rudolf. *Theology of the New Testament*. Vol. 1. Translated by Kendrick Grobel. New York: Scribner's Sons, 1951.

Carey, William. *An Enquiry into the Obligations of Christians, to Use Means for the Conversion of the Heathens*. Leicester: Ann Ireland, 1792. http://www.gutenberg.org/ebooks/11449.

Carmignac, Jean. *Le Mirage de l'eschatologie: Royauté, règne, et royaume de Dieu . . . sans eschatologie*. Paris: Letouzey et Ané, 1979.

Catholic Church. *Catechism of the Catholic Church: With Modifications from the Editio Typica*. 2nd ed. New York: Doubleday, 1997.

———. *Code of Canon Law*. Holy See. https://www.vatican.va/archive/cod-iuris-canonici/cic_index_en.html.

———. *Nova Vulgata Bibliorum Sacrorum Editio*. 2nd ed. Revised by order of Pope Paul VI and promulgated under the authority of Pope John Paul II. Rome: Libreria Editrice Vaticana, 1986. https://www.vatican.va/archive/bible/nova_vulgata/documents/nova-vulgata_index_lt.html.

———. *The Order of Baptism of Children: English Translation According to the Second Typical Edition*. 2nd ed. Promulgated by authority of Pope Paul VI. Collegeville, MN: Liturgical, 2020. https://www.scribd.com/document/502563108/the-order-of-baptism-of-children.

———. *Ordinary Time: Weeks 18–34*. Vol. 4 of *The Liturgy of the Hours, According to the Roman Rite*. Prepared by the International Commission on English in the Liturgy. Published by authority of Pope Paul VI. New York: Catholic Book, 1975.

———. *Rite of Christian Initiation of Adults: Study Edition*. Prepared by the International Commission on English in the Liturgy and the Bishops' Committee on the Liturgy. Published by authority of Pope Paul VI. Chicago: Liturgy Training, 1988.

———. *The Roman Missal*. Promulgated by authority of Pope Paul VI, revised at the direction of Pope John Paul II. 3rd ed. N.p.: n.p., 2011. Internet Archive. https://archive.org/details/roman-missal-third-edition_202411/mode/2up.

Center for Applied Research in the Apostolate (CARA). "Frequently Requested Church Statistics." http://cara.georgetown.edu/frequently-requested-church-statistics.

Central Intelligence Agency. "Malaysia." The World Factbook. https://www.cia.gov/the-world-factbook/countries/malaysia/#people-and-society.

———. "Papua New Guinea." The World Factbook. https://www.cia.gov/the-world-factbook/countries/papua-new-guinea/#people-and-society.

Chia, Edmund. "*Dominus Iesus* and Asian Theologies." *Horizons* 29 (2002) 277–89.

———. "Mission As Inter-Religious Dialogue." In *A Century of Catholic Mission: Roman Catholic Missiology 1910 to the Present*, edited by Stephen B. Bevans, 216–23. Regnum Edinburgh Centenary Series 15. Oxford: Regnum, 2013.

———. "Mongolia: Youngest Church on Earth Turns 25." *National Catholic Reporter*, Sept. 14, 2017. https://www.ncronline.org/news/guest-voices/mongolia-youngest-church-earth-turns-25.

Chilton, Bruce, ed. *The Kingdom of God in the Teaching of Jesus*. Issues in Religion and Theology 5. Philadelphia: Fortress, 1984.

Clooney, Francis X. "*Dominus Iesus* and the New Millennium." *America*, Oct. 28, 2000, 16–18.

Congregation for the Doctrine of the Faith. *Dominus Iesus*. Holy See. https://www.vatican.va/roman_curia/congregations/cfaith/documents/rc_con_cfaith_doc_20000806_dominus-iesus_en.html.

Congregation for the Evangelization of Peoples and Pontifical Commission for Interreligious Dialogue. *Dialogue and Proclamation*. Holy See. http://www.vatican.va/roman_curia/pontifical_councils/interelg/documents/rc_pc_interelg_doc_19051991_dialogue-and-proclamatio_en.html.

Congregation for the Evangelization of Peoples and Pontifical Mission Societies. *Baptized and Sent: The Church of Christ on Mission in the World; Extraordinary Missionary Month, October 2019*. Milan: Edizioni San Paolo, 2019. http://www.october2019.va/content/dam/october2019/documenti/la-guida-mmsott2019/DEF%20WEB_Interno_Mese%20Missionario%20-%20ING_v6-1.pdf.

———. *Extraordinary Missionary Month, October 2019: Final Report*. Edited by Fabrizio Meroni. Vatican City: n.p., 2020. http://www.october2019.va/content/dam/october2019/documenti/BOOK%20EMM%20OCT%202019%20CON%20COPERTINA.pdf.

Consejo Episcopal Latinoamericano. *Documento Conclusivo: Discípulos y misioneros de Jesucristo para que nuestros pueblos en Él tengan vida "Yo soy el Camino, la Verdad y la Vida" (Jn 16,4)*. 3rd ed. Proceedings of the Fifth General Conference of the Bishops of Latin America and the Caribbean, Aparecida, Brazil, May 13–31, 2007. Bogotá: CELAM, 2008. https://www.celam.org/aparecida/Espanol.pdf.

Coser, Lewis A. "Society." In *Dictionary of Anthropology*, edited by Thomas Barfield, 436–37. Malden, MA: Blackwell, 1997. Repr., 2002.

Council of Trent. "Decree Concerning Original Sin." Papal Encyclicals Online. https://www.papalencyclicals.net/councils/trent/fifth-session.htm.

Cunliffe, Barry. *The Ancient Celts*. New York: Penguin, 1997.

D'Antonio, William V., et al. *American Catholics in Transition*. New York: Rowman & Littlefield, 2013.

D'Costa, Gavin. "The Impossibility of a Pluralist View of Religions." *Religious Studies* 32 (1996) 223–32.

DiNoia, J. Augustine. "'Dominus Iesus' Presented by Fr. Augustine Di Noia [*sic*], O.P." Lecture given at St. Mary's Church, New Haven, CT, 2001. Internet Archive, 1:24:02. https://archive.org/details/Dhspriory-DomineIesusPresentedByFrAugustineDiNoiaOP798.

Dulles, Avery. "The Church and the Kingdom." In *A Church for All Peoples: Missionary Issues in a World Church*, edited by Eugene LaVerdiere, 13–27. Collegeville, MN: Liturgical, 1993.

———. *Magisterium: Teacher and Guardian of the Faith*. Introductions to Catholic Doctrine. Naples, FL: Sapientia Press of Ave Maria University, 2007.

———. *The Resilient Church: The Necessity and Limits of Adaptation*. Garden City, NY: Doubleday, 1977.

———. "Vatican II: Substantive Teaching." *America*, Mar. 31, 2003, 14–17.

Dunn, Matthew W. I. "The CDF's Declaration *Dominus Iesus* and Pope John Paul II." *Louvain Studies* 36 (2012) 46–75.

———. "CTI Symposium: 'Baptized & Sent.'" YouTube, playlist. https://www.youtube.com/playlist?list=PL6IpobGrsLNK1PPeG_EHIUX5R-k9ojxum.

———. "Dr. Matty Attends 'Baptized & Sent' Symposium at CTI . . . in PNG!—Apostolic Nuncio." Posted Oct. 1, 2019. YouTube video, 16:30. https://www.youtube.com/watch?v=ePBpBDkFwIs.

———. "Dr. Matty Attends 'Baptized & Sent' Symposium at CTI . . . in PNG!—Bp. Rochus Tatamai." Posted Oct. 7, 2019. YouTube video, 16:12. https://www.youtube.com/watch?v=t9U597FGuIU.

———. "Dr. Matty Attends 'Baptized & Sent' Symposium at CTI . . . in PNG!—Fr. Andrew Moses." Posted Oct. 6, 2019. YouTube video, 1:24:48. https://www.youtube.com/watch?v=QbsP14olrjQ.

———. "Dr. Matty Attends 'Baptized & Sent' Symposium at CTI . . . in PNG!—Fr. Clarence Devadass." Posted Mar. 16, 2023. YouTube video, 1:16:13. https://www.youtube.com/watch?v=uXDaZ9oqsOo.

———. "Dr. Matty Attends 'Baptized & Sent' Symposium at CTI . . . in PNG!—Fr. Edgar Javier, SVD." Posted Oct. 2, 2019. YouTube video, 1:07:50. https://www.youtube.com/watch?v=G6IaL5liQWU&t=3126s.

———. "Dr. Matty Attends 'Baptized & Sent' Symposium at CTI . . . in PNG!—Fr. Joseph Vnuk, OP." Posted Oct. 1, 2019. YouTube video, 6:39. https://www.youtube.com/watch?v=ksy2mKdhuE4.

———. "Dr. Matty Attends 'Baptized & Sent' Symposium at CTI . . . in PNG!—Mr. Paolo Baleinakorodawa." Posted Oct. 2, 2019. YouTube video, 1:10:16. https://www.youtube.com/watch?v=dteWuiqgvaQ.

———. "Dr. Matty Attends 'Baptized & Sent' Symposium at CTI . . . in PNG!—Mrs. Agatha Ferei." Posted Oct. 7, 2019. YouTube video, 55:54. https://www.youtube.com/watch?v=E9Qc4jAExb4&t=2525s.

———. "Dr. Matty Attends 'Baptized & Sent' Symposium at CTI . . . in PNG—Panel Discussion." Posted Mar. 16, 2023. YouTube video, 1:17:38. https://www.youtube.com/watch?v=fXTz31OeS-g.

———. "Fr. Augustine DiNoia, O.P., Lecture—'Dominus Iesus.'" Posted May 23, 2025. YouTube video, 1:24:09. https://www.youtube.com/watch?v=Cd2Ktpc3Huc&t=39s.

———. Review of *Interreligious Dialogue: The Official Teaching of the Catholic Church from the Second Vatican Council to John Paul II (1963–2005)*, by the Pontifical Council for Interreligious Dialogue, edited by Francesco Gioia. *Irish Theological Quarterly* 73 (2008) 410–12. https://doi.org/10.1177/0021140008073003 1017.

———. "Still on Christ's Mountain: Matthew 28:19–20 as a Continuing Paradigm for Mission." *Fellowship of Catholic Scholars Quarterly* 45 (2024/2025) 354–71.

Dupuis, Jacques. "Apostolic Exhortation *Evangelii Nuntiandi* of Pope Paul VI (8th December 1975)." *Vidyajyoti* 40 (1976) 218–30.

———. *Christianity and the Religions: From Confrontation to Dialogue*. Translated by Phillip Berryman. Maryknoll, NY: Orbis, 2002.

———. "The Church's Evangelizing Mission in the Context of Religious Pluralism." *Pastoral Review* 1 (2005) 20–31.

———. "Synod of Bishops, 1974." *Doctrine and Life* 25 (1974) 323–48.

———. *Toward a Christian Theology of Religious Pluralism*. With the notification of the Congregation for the Doctrine of the Faith. Maryknoll, NY: Orbis, 2001.

Elliger, K., and W. Rudolph, eds. *Biblia Hebraica Stuttgartensia*. 5th ed. Stuttgart: Deutsche Bibelgesellschaft, 1997.

The Fathers of the Church: A New Translation. 147 vols. Washington, DC: Catholic University of America Press, 1947–.

Federation of Asian Bishops' Conferences. "Conclusions of the Asian Colloquium on Ministries in the Church." In *Federation of Asian Bishops' Conferences, Documents from 1970 to 1991*, edited by Gaudencio B. Rosales and C. G. Arevalo, 67–92. Vol. 1 of *For All The Peoples of Asia*. Quezon City, Philippines: Claretian, 1997.

———. "A Renewed Church in Asia: A Mission of Love and Service." In *Federation of Asian Bishops' Conferences, Documents from 1997 to 2001*, edited by Franz-Josef Eilers, 1–16. Vol. 3 of *For All The Peoples of Asia*. Quezon City, Philippines: Claretian, 2002.

France, R. T. *The Gospel of Matthew.* The New International Commentary on the New Testament. Cambridge: Eerdmans, 2007.

Francesco. "Omelia per la Santa Messa con i cardinali." Holy See, Mar. 14, 2013. http://www.vatican.va/content/francesco/it/homilies/2013/documents/papa-francesco_20130314_omelia-cardinali.html.

Francis. *Amoris Laetitia.* Apostolic exhortation. Holy See, Mar. 19, 2016. https://www.vatican.va/content/francesco/en/apost_exhortations/documents/papa-francesco_esortazione-ap_20160319_amoris-laetitia.html.

———. *Christus Vivit.* Apostolic exhortation. Holy See, Mar. 25, 2019. https://www.vatican.va/content/francesco/en/apost_exhortations/documents/papa-francesco_esortazione-ap_20190325_christus-vivit.html.

———. *Evangelii Gaudium.* Apostolic exhortation. Holy See, Nov. 24, 2013. http://www.vatican.va/content/francesco/en/apost_exhortations/documents/papa-francesco_esortazione-ap_20131124_evangelii-gaudium.html.

———. *Gaudete et Exsultate.* Apostolic exhortation. Holy See, Mar. 19, 2018. https://www.vatican.va/content/francesco/en/apost_exhortations/documents/papa-francesco_esortazione-ap_20180319_gaudete-et-exsultate.html.

———. *Laudate Deum.* Apostolic exhortation. Holy See, Oct. 4, 2023. https://www.vatican.va/content/francesco/en/apost_exhortations/documents/20231004-laudate-deum.html.

———. *Laudato Si'.* Encyclical letter. Holy See, May 24, 2015. http://www.vatican.va/content/francesco/en/encyclicals/documents/papa-francesco_20150524_enciclica-laudato-si.html.

———. "Letter to Fernando Cardinal Filoni for the Centenary of the Promulgation of the Apostolic Letter '*Maximum Illud*' on the Activity of Missionaries in the World." Holy See, Oct. 22, 2017. https://www.vatican.va/content/francesco/en/letters/2017/documents/papa-francesco_20171022_lettera-filoni-mese-missionario.html.

———. "Message for World Mission Day 2019." Holy See, June 9, 2019. http://www.vatican.va/content/francesco/en/messages/missions/documents/papa-francesco_20190609_giornata-missionaria2019.html.

———. *Praedicate Evangelium.* Apostolic constitution. Holy See, Mar. 19, 2022. https://www.vatican.va/content/francesco/en/apost_constitutions/documents/20220319-costituzione-ap-praedicate-evangelium.html#Dicastery_for_Evangelization.

Fredericks, James. "The Catholic Church and the Other Religious Paths: Rejecting Nothing That Is True and Holy." *Theological Studies* 64 (2003) 225–54.

Freeman, Hal. "The Great Commission and the New Testament: An Exegesis of Matthew 28:16–20." *Southern Baptist Journal of Theology* 1 (1997) 14–23.

Galadza, Peter, et al., eds. *The Divine Liturgy: An Anthology for Worship.* Ottawa: Metropolitan Andrey Sheptytsky Institute of Eastern Christian Studies, 2004.

Gautier, Mary. "Knowledge and Belief About the Real Presence." *National Catholic Reporter*, Oct. 28–Nov. 10, 2011, 27a.

Gioia, Francesco, ed. *Interreligious Dialogue: The Official Teaching of the Catholic Church from the Second Vatican Council to John Paul II (1963–2005).* Boston: Pauline Books and Media, 2006.

Gray, Mark M. *Eucharist Beliefs: A National Survey of Adult Catholics.* Washington, DC: Center for Applied Research in the Apostolate, 2023. https://static1.

squarespace.com/static/629c7d00b33f845b6435b6ab/t/6513358329f868492a786ea6/1695757700925/EucharistPollSeptember23.pdf.

Gray, Mark M., and Paul M. Perl, eds. *Sacraments Today: Belief and Practice Among U.S. Catholics*. Center for Applied Research in the Apostolate. Washington, DC: Georgetown University, 2008. https://web.archive.org/web/20221127192406/cara.georgetown.edu/sacramentsreport.pdf.

Habig, Marion A., ed. *St. Francis of Assisi, Writings and Early Biographies: English Omnibus of the Sources for the Life of St. Francis*. Translated by Raphael Brown et al. 4th rev. ed. Chicago: Franciscan Herald, 1983. Repr., Bangalore: Asian Trading Corporation, n.d.

Hare, Douglas R. A. *Matthew*. Interpretation: A Bible Commentary for Teaching and Preaching, edited by James Luther Mays. Louisville: John Knox, 1993.

Harrington, Daniel J. "The Gospel According to Mark." In *NJBC*, art. 41, §§1–109.

Harris, W. T., and F. Sturges Allen, eds. *Webster's New International Dictionary of the English Language*. Rev. ed. Springfield, MA: G. & C. Merriam, 1923.

Holmes, Michael W., ed. *The Apostolic Fathers*. Translated by J. B. Lightfoot and J. R. Hanner. 2nd ed. Leicester, UK: Apollos, 1989.

Ignacio de Loyola. *Ejercicios espirituales de S. Ignacio de Loyola, fundador de la Compañía de Jesús*. Phototypical reproduction of original. Rome: Stabilimento Danesi, 1908.

Ignatius of Loyola. *The Spiritual Exercises of Saint Ignatius of Loyola Translated from the Spanish with a Commentary and a Translation of the "Directorium in Exercitia."* Translated by W. H. Longridge. 2nd ed. London: Robert Scott, 1922.

Ioannes Paulus II. "In Petriana Basilica Habita ob Decretos Ven. Guillelmo Repin et XCVIII Sociis Eius Andegavensibus Martyribus, et Ven. Ioanni Mazzucconi, Beatorum Caelitum Honores." *Acta Apostolicae Sedis* 76 (1984) 558–63. https://www.vatican.va/archive/aas/documents/AAS-76-1984-ocr.pdf.

———. "Litterae Encyclicae de Perenni Vi Mandati Missionalis." *Acta Apostolicae Sedis* 83 (1991) 249–340. https://www.vatican.va/content/john-paul-ii/la/encyclicals/documents/hf_jp-ii_enc_07121990_redemptoris-missio.html.

John XXIII. *Humanae Salutis*. Apostolic constitution. Holy See, Dec. 25, 1961. http://www.vatican.va/content/john-xxiii/la/apost_constitutions/1961/documents/hf_j-xxiii_apc_19611225_humanae-salutis.html.

———. *Princeps Pastorem*. Encyclical letter. Holy See. https://www.vatican.va/content/john-xxiii/en/encyclicals/documents/hf_j-xxiii_enc_28111959_princeps.html.

John Paul I. "General Audience." Holy See, Sept. 20, 1978. https://www.vatican.va/content/john-paul-i/en/audiences/documents/hf_jp-i_aud_20091978.html.

John Paul II. *Angelus*. Address. Holy See, Oct. 1, 2000. https://www.vatican.va/content/john-paul-ii/en/angelus/2000/documents/hf_jp-ii_ang_20001001.html.

———. *Christifideles Laici*. Apostolic exhortation. Holy See, Dec. 30, 1988. https://www.vatican.va/content/john-paul-ii/en/apost_exhortations/documents/hf_jp-ii_exh_30121988_christifideles-laici.html.

———. *Ecclesia in America*. Apostolic exhortation. Holy See, Jan. 22, 1999. http://www.vatican.va/content/john-paul-ii/en/apost_exhortations/documents/hf_jp-ii_exh_22011999_ecclesia-in-america.html.

———. *Ecclesia in Asia*. Apostolic exhortation. Holy See, Nov. 6, 1999. https://www.vatican.va/content/john-paul-ii/en/apost_exhortations/documents/hf_jp-ii_exh_06111999_ecclesia-in-asia.html.

———. *Ecclesia in Oceania*. Apostolic exhortation. Holy See, Nov. 22, 2001. http://www.vatican.va/content/john-paul-ii/en/apost_exhortations/documents/hf_jp-ii_exh_20011122_ecclesia-in-oceania.html.

———. "Message for the 24th World Communications Day." Holy See, May 27, 1990. http://www.vatican.va/content/john-paul-ii/en/messages/communications/documents/hf_jp-ii_mes_24011990_world-communications-day.html.

———. "Message for the 26th World Communications Day." Holy See, May 31, 1992. http://www.vatican.va/content/john-paul-ii/en/messages/communications/documents/hf_jp-ii_mes_24011992_world-communications-day.html.

———. *Novo Millennio Ineunte*. Apostolic letter. Holy See, Jan. 6, 2001. https://www.vatican.va/content/john-paul-ii/en/apost_letters/2001/documents/hf_jp-ii_apl_20010106_novo-millennio-ineunte.html.

———. "Opening Address at the Puebla Conference." In *Puebla and Beyond: Documentation and Commentary*, edited by John Eagleson and Philip Scharper, 57–71. Translated by John Drury. Maryknoll, NY: Orbis, 1979.

———. *Redemptoris Missio*. Encyclical letter. Holy See, Dec. 7, 1990. https://www.vatican.va/content/john-paul-ii/en/encyclicals/documents/hf_jp-ii_enc_07121990_redemptoris-missio.html.

———. "To the Bishops of India on their '*Ad Limina*' Visit." Address. Holy See, Apr. 6, 1989. https://www.vatican.va/content/john-paul-ii/en/speeches/1989/april/documents/hf_jp-ii_spe_19890406_india-ad-limina.html.

———. "To the Bishops of Nicaragua on their '*Ad Limina*' Visit." Address. Holy See, Sept. 21, 2001. https://www.vatican.va/content/john-paul-ii/en/speeches/2001/september/documents/hf_jp-ii_spe_20010921_nicaragua-ad-limina.html.

———. "To the Bishops of Papua New Guinea and the Solomon Islands." Address. Holy See, May 8, 1984. https://www.vatican.va/content/john-paul-ii/en/speeches/1984/may/documents/hf_jp-ii_spe_19840508_vescovi-papua-nuova-guinea.html.

———. "To the Third General Conference of the Latin American Episcopate." Address. Holy See, Jan. 28, 1979. https://www.vatican.va/content/john-paul-ii/en/speeches/1979/january/documents/hf_jp-ii_spe_19790128_messico-puebla-episc-latam.html.

———. *Ut Unum Sint*. Encyclical letter. Holy See, May 25, 1995. https://www.vatican.va/content/john-paul-ii/en/encyclicals/documents/hf_jp-ii_enc_25051995_ut-unum-sint.html.

———. *Veritatis Splendor*. Encyclical letter. Holy See, Aug. 6, 1993. https://www.vatican.va/content/john-paul-ii/en/encyclicals/documents/hf_jp-ii_enc_06081993_veritatis-splendor.html.

———. "Welcome Ceremony upon Arrival in Papua New Guinea." Address. Holy See, May 7, 1984. https://www.vatican.va/content/john-paul-ii/en/speeches/1984/may/documents/hf_jp-ii_spe_19840507_arrivo-papua-nuova-guinea.html.

Jones, E. Stanley. *The Christ of the Indian Road*. Repr., London: Hodder and Stoughton, 1927.

Juan Pablo II. "A los miembros de la Conferencia Episcopal del Nicaragua en visita '*ad limina*.'" Address. Holy See, Sept. 21, 2001. https://www.vatican.va/content/john-paul-ii/es/speeches/2001/september/documents/hf_jp-ii_spe_20010921_nicaragua-ad-limina.html.

———. "En la inauguración de la III Conferencia General del Episcopado Latinoamericano." Address. Holy See, Jan. 28, 1979. https://www.vatican.

va/content/john-paul-ii/es/speeches/1979/january/documents/hf_jp-ii_spe_19790128_messico-puebla-episc-latam.html.

Just, Felix. "New Testament Statistics." Electronic New Testament Educational Resources. https://catholic-resources.org/Bible/NT-Statistics-Greek.htm.

Karris, Robert J. "The Gospel According to Luke." In *NJBC*, art. 43, §§1–198.

Kasper, Walter. "Keine Änderung der Ökumene-Politik Roms." Interview. *Die Furche*, Feb. 1, 2001, 9.

Kavunkal, Jacob. "Mission or Evangelization?" *Mission Studies* 21 (2004) 55–64.

Keener, Craig S. "Matthew's Missiology: Making Disciples of the Nations (Matthew 28:19–20)." *Asian Journal of Pentecostal Studies* 12 (2009) 3–20.

Kloppenborg, John S. *Q, the Earliest Gospel: An Introduction to the Original Stories and Sayings of Jesus*. Louisville: Westminster John Knox, 2008.

Knitter, Paul E. "Catholics and Other Religions: Bridging the Gap Between Dialogue and Theology." *Louvain Studies* 24 (1999) 319–54.

Koehler, Ludwig, and Walter Baumgartner, eds. *Lexicon in Veteris Testamenti Libros*. With supplement. Grand Rapids: Eerdmans, 1951.

Lackie, John, ed. *Chambers Dictionary of Science and Technology*. Edinburgh: Chambers Harrap, 2007.

Latourette, Kenneth Scott. *A History of the Expansion of Christianity*. 7 vols. New York: Harper & Bros., 1937–1945.

Lewis, C. S. *Mere Christianity*. Rev. and enlarged ed. New York: Macmillan, 1952.

Lohmeyer, Ernst. *Das Evangelium des Matthäus: Nachgelassene Ausarbeitungen und Entwürfe zur Übersetzung und Erklärung*. Edited by Werner Schmauch. Kritisch-exegetischer Kommentar über das Neue Testament. Göttingen: Vandenhoeck and Ruprecht, 1962.

Loisy, Alfred. *The Gospel and the Church*. Translated by Christopher Home. With an introduction by Newman Smyth. New York: Scribner's Sons, 1912.

Lumko Institute. "SACBC: Southern African Catholic Bishops' Conference." http://sacbcoldsite.org.za/about-us/associate-bodies/lumko-institute.

Lutheran World Information. "Cardinal Kasper: The Ecumenical Problem Is a Heartfelt Concern." Lutheran World Federation, Mar. 2, 2001. https://web.archive.org/web/20010427193246/http://lutheranworld.org:80/News/LWI/EN/000276.EN.html.

Luz, Ulrich. *Matthew 21–28: A Commentary*. Edited by Helmut Koester. Translated by James E. Crouch. Hermeneia: A Critical and Historical Commentary on the Bible. Minneapolis: Fortress, 2005.

Marty, Martin, et al. "Rome and Relativism: 'Dominus Iesus' and the CDF." *Commonweal*, Oct. 20, 2000, 12–15.

Masuda, Masashi. "*Dominus Iesus*: A Plea for Vatican III." *Japan Mission Journal* 54 (2000) 274–83.

McBrien, Richard P. *The Church: The Evolution of Catholicism*. New York: HarperCollins, 2008.

McCloskey, Pat. "Great Saying but Tough to Trace." *St. Anthony Messenger*, Oct. 2001, 50.

McDonnell, Kilian. "Imperial Claims?" *Christian Century*, Oct. 18, 2000, 1038–42.

McKenzie, John L. *Dictionary of the Bible*. New York: Macmillan, 1965. Repr., New York: Simon & Schuster, 1995.

———. "The Gospel According to Matthew." In *The Jerome Biblical Commentary*, edited by Raymond E. Brown et al., art. 43, §§1–206. Englewood Cliffs, NJ: Prentice Hall, 1968.

———. *Myths and Realities: Studies in Biblical Theology*. Milwaukee, WI: Bruce, 1963.

Meier, John P. "Jesus." In *NJBC*, art. 78, §§1–57.

———. *Mentor, Message, and Miracles*. Vol. 2 of *A Marginal Jew: Rethinking the Historical Jesus*. Anchor Bible Reference Library. New York: Doubleday, 1994.

———. *The Roots of the Problem and the Person*. Vol. 1 of *A Marginal Jew: Rethinking the Historical Jesus*. Anchor Bible Reference Library. New York: Doubleday, 1991.

———. "Two Disputed Questions in Matt 28:16–20." *Journal of Biblical Literature* 96 (1977) 407–24.

———. *The Vision of Matthew: Christ, Church, and Morality in the First Gospel*. Theological Inquiries: Studies in Contemporary Biblical and Theological Problems, edited by Lawrence Boadt. Ramsey, NJ: Paulist, 1979.

Melloni, Alberto. "Expunged and Forgotten Texts and Messages of Vatican II." In *The Oxford Handbook of Vatican II*, edited by Catherine E. Clifford and Massimo Faggioli, 133–47. Oxford: Oxford University Press, 2023.

Michel, Otto. "Der Abschluß des Matthäusevangeliums: Ein Beitrag zur Geschichte der Osterbotschaft." In *Das Matthäus-Evangelium*, edited by Joachim Lange, 119–33. Darmstadt: Wissenschaftliche Buchgesellschaft, 1980.

Mineral Policy Institute. "DSM in PNG." Solwaramining: Deep Sea Mining in the Pacific. https://web.archive.org/web/20191211190924/https://www.solwaramining.org/.

Morrisey, Francis G. "Papal and Curial Pronouncements: Their Canonical Significance in Light of the 1983 Code of Canon Law." *Jurist* 50 (1990) 102–25.

Nestle, Eberhard, and Erwin Nestle. *Novum Testamentum Graece*. Edited by Barbara Aland et al. 28th ed. Stuttgart: Deutsche Bibelgesellschaft, 2012.

*New York Times*. "Text of Final Report Adopted by Synod of Bishops in Rome." Dec. 8, 1985, 34.

1985 Extraordinary Synod. *The Final Report of the 1985 Extraordinary Synod*. Eternal Word Television Network. https://www.ewtn.com/catholicism/library/final-report-of-the-1985-extraordinary-synod-2561.

Office of International Religious Freedom. "2019 Report on International Religious Freedom: Malaysia." US Department of State. https://www.state.gov/reports/2019-report-on-international-religious-freedom/malaysia.

Office of Laity and Family (OLF). "Seven Steps Method of Gospel Sharing." Federation of Asian Bishops' Conferences. https://web.archive.org/web/20150214115742/www.fabc.org/offices/olaity/asipa.html.

O'Malley, John W. "Vatican II: Did Anything Happen?" *Theological Studies* 67 (2006) 3–33.

Ott, Ludwig. *Fundamentals of Catholic Dogma*. Edited in English by James Bastible. Translated by Patrick Lynch. 4th ed. Cork: Mercier, 1955. Repr., Rockford, IL: TAN, 1974.

Panikkar, Raymond. "Indirect Methods in the Missionary Apostolate: Some Theological Reflections." *Indian Journal of Theology* 19 (1970) 111–13.

Paolo VI. "Messaggio per la Giornata Missionaria Mondiale 1972." Holy See, May 19, 1972. https://www.vatican.va/content/paul-vi/it/messages/missions/documents/hf_p-vi_mes_19720519_world-day-for-missions-1972.html.

———. "Udienza generale." Holy See, Nov. 15, 1972. http://www.vatican.va/content/paul-vi/it/audiences/1972/documents/hf_p-vi_aud_19721115.html.

Pathrapankal, Joseph. "Christian Evangelization in the Context of Religious Pluralism." *Third Millennium: Indian Journal of Evangelization* 10 (2007) 27–50.

Paul VI. "Audience Générale de Paul VI." Holy See, Oct. 2, 1974. http://www.vatican.va/content/paul-vi/fr/audiences/1974/documents/hf_p-vi_aud_19741002.html.

Paul VI. *Evangelii Nuntiandi.* Apostolic exhortation. Holy See, Dec. 8, 1975. https://www.vatican.va/content/paul-vi/en/apost_exhortations/documents/hf_p-vi_exh_19751208_evangelii-nuntiandi.html.

———. "Homily at the Ordination of the First Bishop Born in New Guinea." Holy See, Dec. 3, 1970. http://www.vatican.va/content/paul-vi/en/homilies/1970/documents/hf_p-vi_hom_19701203_sidney.html.

———. "Message for the World Social Communications Day." Holy See, Mar. 26, 1968. http://www.vatican.va/content/paul-vi/en/messages/communications/documents/hf_p-vi_mes_19680326_ii-com-day.html.

Paulus VI. "Adhortatio Apostolica ad Episcopos, Sacerdotes et Christifideles Totius Catholicae Ecclesiae: De Evangelizatione in Mundo Huius Temporis." *Acta Apostolicae Sedis* 68 (1976) 5–76. https://www.vatican.va/archive/aas/documents/AAS-68-1976-ocr.pdf.

———. "Solenne Inizio della Seconda Sessione del Concilio Ecumenico Vaticano II." Holy See, Sept. 29, 1963. https://www.vatican.va/content/paul-vi/la/speeches/1963/documents/hf_p-vi_spe_19630929_concilio-vaticano-ii.html. *Nota bene*: the title is given in Italian, but the text is indeed in Latin.

Pawlikowski, John T., et al. "*Dominus Iesus*: A Panel Discussion." *Catholic Theological Society of America Proceedings* 56 (2001) 97–116. https://ejournals.bc.edu/index.php/ctsa/article/view/4464/3978.

Perkins, Pheme. "The Gospel According to John." In *NJBC*, art. 61, §§1–244.

Perrin, Norman. *Jesus and the Language of the Kingdom: Symbol and Metaphor in New Testament Interpretation*. Philadelphia: Fortress, 1976.

———. *The Kingdom of God in the Teaching of Jesus.* New Testament Library. Philadelphia: Westminster, 1963.

———. *Rediscovering the Teaching of Jesus.* New York: Harper & Row, 1976.

Pew Research Center. "America's Changing Religious Landscape." May 12, 2015. https://www.pewresearch.org/religion/2015/05/12/americas-changing-religious-landscape.

———. "Catholicism." https://www.pewresearch.org/topic/religion/religions/christianity/Catholicism.

———. "Many Americans Say Other Faiths Can Lead to Eternal Life." Dec. 18, 2008. https://www.pewresearch.org/religion/2008/12/18/many-americans-say-other-faiths-can-lead-to-eternal-life.

———. "Religious Landscape Study: Catholics." https://www.pewresearch.org/religion/religious-landscape-study/religious-tradition/catholic.

———. "What Americans Know About Religion." July 23, 2019. https://www.pewresearch.org/wp-content/uploads/sites/20/2019/07/Religious-Knowledge-full-draft-FOR-WEB-2.pdf.

Philippine Statistics Authority. *2021 Philippine Statistical Yearbook.* https://psa.gov.ph/system/files/psy/2021%20PSY_final_compressed.pdf.

Pius XI. *Rerum Ecclesiae*. Encyclical letter. Holy See, Feb. 28, 1926. https://www.vatican.va/content/pius-xi/en/encyclicals/documents/hf_p-xi_enc_28021926_rerum-ecclesiae.html.

Pius XII. "Allocutio Cultoribus, Docentibus et Dirigentibus Unionis Internationalis et Magnis Institutis atque Lyceis de Archeologia, de Historia ac de Artis Historia in Urbe Decem Abhinc Annos Conditae." *Acta Apostolicae Sedis* 48 (1956) 210–16. https://www.vatican.va/archive/aas/documents/AAS-48-1956-ocr.pdf.

Pius XII. *Evangelii Praecones*. Encyclical letter. Holy See, June 2, 1951. http://www.vatican.va/content/pius-xii/en/encyclicals/documents/hf_p-xii_enc_02061951_evangelii-praecones.html.

———. *Fidei Donum*. Encyclical letter. Holy See, Apr. 21, 1957. https://www.vatican.va/content/pius-xii/en/encyclicals/documents/hf_p-xii_enc_21041957_fidei-donum.html.

Pontifical Council for Culture. "The *Via Pulchritudinis*, Privileged Pathway for Evangelisation and Dialogue." Holy See. https://www.vatican.va/roman_curia/pontifical_councils/cultr/documents/rc_pc_cultr_doc_20060327_plenary-assembly_final-document_en.html.

Punt, J. "Paul, Military Imagery, and Social Disadvantage." *Acta Theologica* S23 (2016) 201–24.

Rabenstein, K. I. "Mazzucconi, Giovanni Battista, Bl." In *New Catholic Encyclopedia*, edited by Thomas Carson et al., 2nd ed., 9:390. Detroit: Gale; Washington, DC: Catholic University of America, 2003.

Rad, Gerhard von. *Deuteronomy: A Commentary*. Old Testament Library, edited by Peter Ackroyd et al. Philadelphia: Westminster, 1966.

Rahlfs, Alfred, ed. *Septuaginta, Id Est Vetus Testamentum Graece iuxta LXX Interpretes*. 2 vols. 4th ed. Stuttgart: Württembergische Bibelanstalt, 1935.

Ratzinger, Joseph. "Answers to Main Objections Against *Dominus Iesus*." Interview with *Frankfurter Allgemeine Zeitung*, Sept. 22, 2000. Eternal Word Television Network. https://web.archive.org/web/20010214225612/www.ewtn.com/library/Theology/OBDOMIHS.HTM.

Rausch, Thomas P. "What Do Catholics Mean When We Say the Eucharist Is 'the True Body and Blood' of Christ?" *America*, Nov. 12, 2021. https://www.americamagazine.org/faith/2021/11/12/eucharist-real-presence-241625.

Robert, A., and A. Feuillet. *Introduction to the New Testament*. Translated by Patrick W. Skehan et al. New York: Desclee, 1965.

Roberts, Alexander, and James Donaldson, eds. *The Ante-Nicene Fathers: Translations of the Writings of the Fathers Down to A.D. 325*. 10 vols. 1885–1887.

Robinson, J. Armitage, trans. *St Irenæus: The Demonstration of the Apostolic Preaching*. Translations of Christian Literature, ser. 4: Oriental Texts. New York: Macmillan, 1920. https://archive.org/details/demonstrationofaooiren/mode/2up.

Ross, Anne. *The Pagan Celts*. Updated ed. London: Batsford, 1986.

Roy-Lysencourt, Philippe. "The Reception of the Second Vatican Council by Traditionalist Catholics." In *The Oxford Handbook of Vatican II*, edited by Catherine E. Clifford and Massimo Faggioli, 360–78. Oxford: Oxford University Press, 2023.

Saint Tikhon's Monastery, trans. *The Holy Mysteries*. Vol. 1 of *The Great Book of Needs*. Exp. and supplemented. South Canaan, PA: St. Tikhon's Seminary Press, 1998.

Sarah, Robert. "On the Credibility of the Catholic Church." *National Catholic Register*, Aug. 14, 2021. https://www.ncregister.com/commentaries/on-the-credibility-of-the-catholic-church.

Schaff, Philip, and Henry Wace, eds. *A Select Library of the Nicene and Post-Nicene Fathers of the Christian Church.* 2nd series. 14 vols. 1890–1900.

Schlumpf, Heidi. "Real Presence: Do Catholics 'Actually' Believe." *National Catholic Reporter*, Sept. 6–19, 2019, 1, 8.

Schnackenburg, Rudolf. *God's Rule and Kingdom.* Translated by John Murray. 2nd enlarged ed. New York: Herder and Herder, 1968.

Schweitzer, Albert. *The Quest of the Historical Jesus: A Critical Study of Its Progress from Reimarus to Wrede.* Translated by W. Montgomery. With a preface by F. C. Burkitt. 2nd English ed. London: A & C Black, 1911.

Secretariat for Non-Christians. *Dialogue and Mission.* Dicastery for Interreligious Dialogue. https://www.dicasteryinterreligious.va/dialogue-and-mission-1984.

Senior, Donald, and Carroll Stuhlmueller. *The Biblical Foundations for Mission.* Maryknoll, NY: Orbis, 1983.

Smith, Gregory A. "Just One-Third of U.S. Catholics Agree with Their Church That Eucharist Is Body, Blood of Christ." Pew Research Center, Aug. 5, 2019. https://www.pewresearch.org/short-reads/2019/08/05/transubstantiation-eucharist-u-s-catholics.

Smith, Gregory A., et al. "Decline of Christianity in the U.S. Has Slowed, May Have Leveled Off: Findings from the 2023–24 Religious Landscape Study." Pew Research Center, Feb. 26, 2025. https://www.pewresearch.org/wp-content/uploads/sites/20/2025/02/PR_2025.02.26_religious-landscape-study_report.pdf.

Soares-Prabhu, George M. "Two Mission Commands: An Interpretation of Matthew 28:16–20 in the Light of a Buddhist Text." *Biblical Interpretation* 2 (1994) 264–82.

Social Weather Stations. "First Quarter 2017 Social Weather Survey: 48% of Filipino Adults Attend Religious Services Weekly; 85% Said Religion Is Important." Apr. 13, 2017. http://www.sws.org.ph/swsmain/artcldisppage/?artcsyscode=ART-20170413105521.

Stanley, David M., and Raymond E. Brown. "Aspects of New Testament Thought." In *The Jerome Biblical Commentary*, edited by Raymond E. Brown et al., art. 78, §§1–182. Englewood Cliffs, NJ: Prentice Hall, 1968.

Stearns, Peter N., ed. *The Encyclopedia of World History: Ancient, Medieval, and Modern Chronologically Arranged.* 6th ed. New York: Houghton Mifflin, 2001.

*St. Louis Review.* "Bishop Helmsing's Statement 'Condemning' National Newspaper." Oct. 18, 1968, 6.

Streeter, Burnett Hillman. *The Four Gospels: A Study of Origins, Treating of the Manuscript Tradition, Sources, Authorship, and Dates.* New York: Macmillan, 1925.

Stutt, Amanda. "Nautilus Minerals Officially Sinks, Shares Still Trading." Mining.com, Nov. 26, 2019. http://www.mining.com/nautilus-minerals-officially-sinks-shares-still-trading.

Sullivan, Francis A. *Creative Fidelity: Weighing and Interpreting Documents of the Magisterium.* Mahwah, NJ: Paulist, 1996.

Suthanthiraraj, Kavitha. *Unseen, Unsafe: The Underinvestment in Ending Violence Against Children in the Pacific and Timor-Leste.* N.p.: Save the Children Australia, ChildFund Australia, Plan International, World Vision International, 2019.

https://resourcecentre.savethechildren.net/pdf/stc01615_unseen-unsafe-report_web-1.pdf.

Tan, Jonathan Y. "*Missio Inter Gentes*: Towards a New Paradigm in the Mission Theology of the Federation of Asian Bishops' Conferences (FABC)." *Mission Studies* 21 (2004) 65–95.

Tanner, Norman P., ed. *Decrees of the Ecumenical Councils.* 2 vols. Washington, DC: Georgetown University Press, 1990.

*Telegraph.* "Pope Francis' First Mass as Pontiff—In Full." Posted Mar. 14, 2013. YouTube video, 1:24:50. https://www.youtube.com/watch?v=sdWZWDqhCdA.

Thomas Aquinas. *Commentary on the Sentences.* Translated by Christopher Decaen. The Aquinas Institute. https://aquinas.cc/la/en/~Sent.I.

———. *Summa Contra Gentiles.* Translated by Laurence Shapcote. The Aquinas Institute. https://aquinas.cc/la/en/~SCG1.

———. *Summa Theologiae.* Translated by Laurence Shapcote. The Aquinas Institute. https://aquinas.cc/la/en/~ST.I.

UCA News. "Final Statement of Seventh FABC Plenary Assembly." Last updated Apr. 10, 2000. https://www.ucanews.com/story-archive/?post_name=/2000/04/11/final-statement-of-seventh-fabc-plenary-assembly&post_id=1116.

Vatican II. *Ad Gentes.* Decree. Holy See, Dec. 7, 1965. https://www.vatican.va/archive/hist_councils/ii_vatican_council/documents/vat-ii_decree_19651207_ad-gentes_en.html.

———. *Dei Verbum.* Dogmatic constitution. Holy See, Nov. 18, 1965. https://www.vatican.va/archive/hist_councils/ii_vatican_council/documents/vat-ii_const_19651118_dei-verbum_en.html.

———. *Dignitatis Humanae.* Declaration. Holy See, Dec. 7, 1965. https://www.vatican.va/archive/hist_councils/ii_vatican_council/documents/vat-ii_decl_19651207_dignitatis-humanae_en.html.

———. *Gaudium et Spes.* Pastoral constitution. Holy See, Dec. 7, 1965. https://www.vatican.va/archive/hist_councils/ii_vatican_council/documents/vat-ii_const_19651207_gaudium-et-spes_en.html.

———. *Lumen Gentium.* Dogmatic constitution. Holy See, Nov. 21, 1964. https://www.vatican.va/archive/hist_councils/ii_vatican_council/documents/vat-ii_const_19641121_lumen-gentium_en.html.

———. *Nostra Aetate.* Declaration. Holy See, Oct. 28, 1965. https://www.vatican.va/archive/hist_councils/ii_vatican_council/documents/vat-ii_decl_19651028_nostra-aetate_en.html.

———. *Sacrosanctum Concilium.* Constitution. Holy See, Dec. 4, 1963. https://www.vatican.va/archive/hist_councils/ii_vatican_council/documents/vat-ii_const_19631204_sacrosanctum-concilium_en.html.

———. *Unitatis Redintegratio.* Decree. Holy See, Nov. 21, 1964. https://www.vatican.va/archive/hist_councils/ii_vatican_council/documents/vat-ii_decree_19641121_unitatis-redintegratio_en.html.

Viviano, Benedict T. "The Gospel According to Matthew." In *NJBC*, art. 42, §§1–168.

Washburn, Christian D. "The Theological Priority of *Lumen Gentium* and *Dei Verbum* for the Interpretation of the Second Vatican Council." *Thomist* 78 (2014) 107–34.

Weinfeld, Moshe. *Deuteronomy 1–11.* Anchor Bible 5. New York: Doubleday, 1991.

Weller, Philip T., ed. and trans. *The Sacraments and Processions*. Vol. 1 of *The Roman Ritual in Latin and English with Rubrics and Plainchant Notation*. Milwaukee, WI: Bruce, 1950. Repr., Boonville, NY: Preserving Christian Publications, 2022.

Wheelwright, Philip. *Metaphor and Reality*. Bloomington: Indiana University Press, 1962.

Wilhelm, Joseph, and Thomas B. Scannell. *The Sources of Theological Knowledge, God, Creation and the Supernatural Order*. With a preface by Henry Cardinal Manning. 3rd ed. Vol. 1 of *A Manual of Catholic Theology Based on Scheeben's "Dogmatik."* New York: Benziger, 1906.

Willis, Wendell, ed. *The Kingdom of God in 20th-Century Interpretation*. Peabody, MA: Hendrickson, 1987.

Wiltgen, Ralph M. *The Founding of the Roman Catholic Church in Melanesia and Micronesia, 1850–1875*. Princeton Theological Monograph Series 84. Eugene, OR: Pickwick, 2008.

Wright, Addison G. "Wisdom." In *NJBC*, art. 33, §§1–59.

Wright, Addison G., et al. "A History of Israel." In *NJBC*, art. 75, §§1–193.

Wright, David F. "The Great Commission and the Ministry of the Word: Reflections Historical and Contemporary on Relations and Priorities (Finlayson Memorial Lecture, 2007)." *Scottish Bulletin of Evangelical Theology* 25 (2007) 132–57.

www.ingramcontent.com/pod-product-compliance
Lightning Source LLC
LaVergne TN
LVHW050624100826
845148LV00011B/1728

*9781666775068*